MANAGEMENT RESEARCH

Second Edition

Mark Easterby-Smith
Richard Thorpe
Andy Lowe

SAGE Publications
London • Thousand Oaks • New Delhi

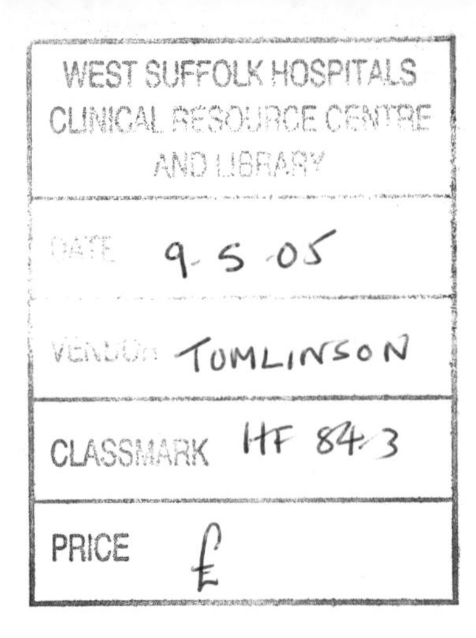

First Published 2002
Reprinted 2002, 2003, 2004

SAGE Publications Ltd
1 Olivers Yard, 55 City Road
London EC1Y 1SP

SAGE Publications Inc
2455 Teller Road
Thousand Oaks, California 91320

SAGE Publications India Pvt Ltd
B-42 Panchsheel Enclave
PO Box 4109
New Dehli 110 017

British Library Cataloguing in Publication data

A catalogue record for this book is available from the British Library

ISBN 0 7619 7284 6
ISBN 0 7619 7285 4 (pbk)

Typeset By M Rules
Printed and bound in Great Britain by
The Cromwell Press Ltd, Trowbridge, Wiltshire

Contents

About the Authors

Mark Easterby-Smith is Post-graduate Dean at the Lancaster University School of Management and Professor in the Department of Management Learning. He has a first degree in Engineering Science and a PhD in Organizational Behaviour. During the 1970s, he was involved in evaluation of management development programmes and systems at Durham University Business School. Subsequent research has covered international management development, organizational learning and knowledge transfer within international organizations. He has carried out fieldwork in the UK, India and China. This, and continuing research, has led to a number of books including: *Management Development in the Organisation*, Macmillan, 1978; *Auditing Management Development*, Gower, 1980; *Evaluation of Management Education, Training and Development*, Gower, 1986/94; *The Challenge to Western Management Development*, Routledge, 1989; and *Organisational Learning and the Learning Organizaton*, Sage, 1998.

While at Lancaster he has been director of the post-graduate research programme in the Department of Management Learning, Head of Department and director of the School's Doctoral Programme. Externally he spent several years as a visiting faculty member on the International Teachers' Programme, acting as director when it was held at the London Business School in 1984. During the early 1990s he was national co-ordinator of the Management Teaching Fellowship Scheme funded by the UK's Economic and Social Research Council (ESRC) which was responsible for training 180 new faculty members across UK management schools. He is currently a Council Member of the British Academy of Management, and the Academy for Social Sciences, and is also a member of the ESRC Post-graduate Training Board.

Richard Thorpe is Director of the Graduate School of Business at Manchester Metropolitan University Business School and Professor in Management in the Department of Management. He is responsible for co-ordinating research within the Business School. After spending a number of years in industry, culminating in managing a manufacturing company in the Highlands of Scotland, he joined Strathclyde University. There, as a research fellow he undertook a national study of incentive payment schemes in Britain. This work led to collaboration in two publications: *Incentive Schemes in Britain 1978–1980* (Department of Employment) and *Payment Schemes and Productivity*

(Macmillan). In 1980 he joined Glasgow University where he continued to widen his research experience making regular contributions to the Scottish Business School's Doctoral Programme. In 1983 he attended the International Teachers' Programme in Sweden where he met Mark and embarked on a PhD under Mark's supervision. The research related to aspects of small- and medium-sized company growth and development. It was in grappling with issues of methodology that he met Andy Lowe and this was how the link between the writers was forged.

In the 1990s Richard contributed as a tutor to the ESRC Teaching Fellowship Scheme, he has been Secretary and Vice-Chair of the British Academy of Management and currently has responsibility for membership issues. His recent publications include: *Organisational Strategy and Technological Adaptation to Global Change*, Macmillan, 1998; *Remuneration Systems*, Financial Times/Prentice Hall, 2000; *Global Change: The Impact from the Far East*, Palgrave, 2000; *Creating Organizational Realities: The Manager as Practical Author*, Sage, 2002.

Andy Lowe holds an MBA degree from Aston University and a PhD from Glasgow University. He is Director of Studies of the Business Faculty Post-graduate Programme at the University of Strathclyde in Glasgow. He is also a Lecturer and subject leader in International Marketing Research on the MSc in International Business in the Department of Marketing, and is Director of Studies for the MSc in International Marketing delivered by open learning in SE Asia. In the 1990s he was involved in three major grounded theory research studies. In 1996 he was awarded the EU Postdoctoral Research Fellowship at the Swedish School of Economics in Helsinki, Finland. In 1997 he was invited by the European Institute for Advanced Studies in Management to co-ordinate an international seminar on grounded theory with one of its co-founders, Dr B. G. Glaser. Dr Lowe is the co-ordinator of the Grounded Theory Research Institute in Mill Valley, California and can be accessed at www.groundedtheory.com

Details of his recent publications are to be found at www.strath/marketing/staff/index.html

Acknowledgements

This book is based on the personal research experience of the authors. However thanks should also go to a number of colleagues who have contributed to the text through both their encouragement and their ideas, which have to varying degrees been reflected in the text.

Worthy of retaining special mention in this second edition is Ardha Danielli. Steve Baron has helped at the drafting stage of our quantitative chapter and both Jean Blanquet and Diana Massam have helped us substantially with the appendix on searching the literature. Jean-Claude Usunier provided a valuable critique of the first edition of the book from a European perspective, and then led development of a French translation which is now in its second edition. Thanks should also go to Andrew Lock for his insights on the preparation of research proposals, and to Colin Eden for his views on the process aspects of interviewing. We have learnt a great deal from our own students including several who have explicitly helped with parts of the text. Scott Taylor, Joep Cornelissen, Sophie Hogg, Janet Ilieva and Tony Beasley deserve particular mention.

Our editor at Sage for the first edition of the book was Sue Jones. She provided us with the initial inspiration, and since then Rosemary Nixon and Kiren Shoman have encouraged, and occasionally hectored us, with this second edition. Since the first edition has been disseminated very widely within the academic community we have been fortunate to receive a good measure of suggestions from readers over the years, and we are grateful to these people for taking the trouble of letting us know how they thought it might be improved. Naturally we have incorporated their ideas whenever they fit into the wider framework.

Finally, we would like to thank our families for their tolerance whilst this book was being written, and re-written – we hope they will consider the outcome to be worth the effort.

Acknowledgements

Preface to the First Edition

Most people write books for two main reasons: to acquire fame (or notoriety) and to make money. We are no exception to this general principle; but in case we are not outrageously successful on either score we can offer some other reasons.

First of all we have written the book for the research community in management; for anyone who is actually doing some research, whether it be a student project, a doctoral thesis, or a company-based investigation. Even experienced researchers still find the existing methodology literature to be of limited value in practice, and our message to the research community is that management research is both more complex and more simple than is normally implied by the text books. It is more complex in that when conducting research into managing/managers/management, a number of factors beyond the technicalities of research design, or the use of particular methods assume considerable importance. These start with the philosophical issues underlying management research, because the worldview of the researcher can influence both the selection of methods and judgements about the quality and value of outcomes. Political issues are also important here because of the frequent need to gain access to organizations and to handle the dynamics of power within and between organizations.

On the other hand research should be more simple because it needs to be appropriate to the limited task in hand, and not designed just to follow elaborate rules and procedures. It is largely about being able to compromise, to pose the right questions, and to answer them in a way that satisfies the majority of interested parties. It should also be concerned with developing deeper insights into the processes and techniques of management, but this often has to be conducted in parallel with the more pragmatic interests of researchers and those who help them.

Second, we have written for those on the receiving end of management research. They may be the clients of formal research projects, and the people who might benefit from, or be harmed by, the process and results of the research. For these people we hope to provide insights both into what management research is, and into what it can be. We also hope that the book will provide them with a basis for evaluating the quality of research designs in case they are in the business of commissioning projects that will be carried out by others.

Third, we have written the book for ourselves. Writing provides an excellent discipline for clarifying one's ideas, and a stimulus for exploring new areas. We have also found it a considerable challenge to work together on the production of the book. We have brought to the venture some very different experiences, frameworks and personal styles. Indeed, the only things that we may genuinely have in common are an interest in climbing and a commitment to collaborative work. We suspect that the diversity represented by the three authors will be seen both as the strength and the weakness of the book. The task of knitting together these different styles into a reasonably coherent whole has, at times, not been easy. But we have also found that the challenges we have posed and the deadlines we have placed upon each other have been extremely stimulating. The opportunity to compare and exchange ideas, through meetings and writing has, we believe, enabled us to develop our ideas considerably beyond their starting points. And in a way that is how we regard the book as a whole: not as a final statement on management research methods, but as one point reached in a journey of discovery. We hope that readers will use it in the same way.

Preface to the Second Edition

Much water has flown under the bridge since the first edition of this book was published. It has now sold over 30,000 copies and appears to have become established as a key text book both in the UK and to some extent overseas. This modest success has been gratifying to our egos and has led a little to our notoriety although, publishing being what it is, it has not contributed greatly to pockets. One of the reasons for the success of the first edition is that it is still one of the very few books which provides a holistic treatment of management research. In other terms, its coverage ranges from highbrow philosophical issues to practical tips and advice on politics and other practical issues. We have also tried to be even-handed between positivist and interpretative methods, even though one does not have to rub hard to spot our personal biases. So, in this second edition we intend to continue in the holistic tradition.

Substantial developments in research methodology have taken place over the last decade, especially in relation to qualitative methods. These include a sharpening of ideas around ontology and epistemology, the development of the notion of reflexivity, continuing debate around postmodernity, growing awareness of the problems of international research, further debate on the merits and substance of 'grounded theory', and refinements in methods of qualitative data collection and analysis. It is also evident that the research agenda is being taken more seriously in educational settings. Ten years ago, a knowledge of methodology was only crucial at the Doctoral level; nowadays, a good knowledge of methodology is also expected at Masters' levels, and a number of institutions are incorporating significant amounts of methodology into undergraduate and Batchelors' courses.

The spread of methodology across management courses provides a new challenge if we are to continue the coverage of major issues and concepts in a way which is still accessible to most readers. Insofar as there are generic issues and problems which cut across research at all levels we believe that this is still possible, although occasionally we indicate where a specific point is more relevant to one level or another. But we also recognize that the increasing specialization of the field of management research has created a need for deeper treatment of some topics, and accordingly Richard and Mark have agreed with Sage to edit a series of books which provide deeper treatment of many of the issues discussed in this volume.

The Sage Series on Management Research now has four volumes in print, and further titles are in the pipeline. Given that the problems addressed in management research are particularly interesting and tricky, it is hoped that the series will both facilitate the development of advanced methodologies in management research, but will also be recognized as making a significant contribution elsewhere in the social science community. In this new edition we will indicate when deeper treatment of a particular topic is available, or is likely to become available in the new series.

This leads to our aims for the new edition of this book. The first aim is obvious: we intend to update the book with research ideas and methods that have come into currency over the last decade. Second, we will incorporate ideas and suggestions that have been made by students and colleagues who have not only read the book, but also been good enough to give us feedback on what they liked/disliked about it, and how it might be strengthened. We are very grateful to colleagues and others for the help we have received in this respect. Third, we include a number of additional examples to illustrate key points based both on our further experiences as researchers and on the trials and tribulations of others whose work we have supervised or assisted over the last ten years. Fourth, we intend to put something back into the 'pot', as it were. Not only do we hope that this edition will be seen as a contemporary statement of the state of management research, but also the launch of the new series with Sage should enable further development of the field of management research in its own right.

PART ONE

STARTING MANAGEMENT RESEARCH

1 Introduction to Management Research

This book is written for people who are doing research into management, possibly for the first time, where their research involves collecting and interpreting information and deciding what to do with it. It is also intended for experienced people who wish to tackle new kinds of research problems or methods, and who are aware of the limited literature which provides both theoretical and practical guidance.

Our aim is to draw together the main threads of management research and to provide a bridge between theoretical and practical issues. This inevitably involves much selectivity, and we feel it is only fair to start by sharing some of our assumptions about management and research. First, we do not see management research as being the exclusive preserve of 'experts'. Most people spend a lot of time trying to make sense of everyday experiences, whether in their personal lives or at work. Managers are in some respect paid to determine actions in uncertain circumstances; to create order out of chaos. In this context research can be seen as a way of accelerating the process of understanding, and hence it should lead not only to a better understanding of management, but also better understanding for managers about how best to go about their work.

This leads directly to our second point. In the past, much attention has been given to describing, coding and counting events, often at the expense of understanding why things are happening. This has led to a predominance of quantitative research methods which are geared, for example, to finding out how many people hold particular views, or how corporate performance can be measured. By contrast, qualitative methods might concentrate on exploring in much greater depth the nature and origins of people's viewpoints, or the reasons for, and consequences of, the choice of corporate performance criteria. In this book, therefore, we intend to redress this balance a little, by giving more prominence to the use of *qualitative* methods, without totally abandoning consideration of the design and application of *quantitative* methods.

Our third point is that it is unwise to conduct research without an awareness of the philosophical and political issues that lie in the background. The decision to study a topic in a particular way always involves some kind of philosophical choice about what is important. A study that examined variations in corporate performance for a range of companies in France during the decade following the 1973 oil crisis would need to assume that the performance of any company was tangible, and ultimately reduceable to a single number for any period of time. The alternative would be to see the idea of 'performance' as unique to each company and the creation of endless discussion and negotiation between individuals and coalitions who are involved with that company. In the former case it is the numbers, and in the latter case it is the perceptions, that are important; and it is for the researcher to decide where the emphasis should lie.

While philosophical issues may seem hidden in research methods, it is hard to escape political factors in management research. Access to companies can be obstructed by managers if they see a piece of research being harmful to their, or their company's, interests; and there is always the danger of research data and results being used out of context to strengthen the case of one group against another. The researcher should therefore be prepared to confront ethical issues, and to be aware of his or her own values in this process.

These are some of the main assumptions, or prejudices, that have given rise to this book. They influence both the overall structure and our choice of content, particularly in the second and third parts. In this first part we consider a number of preliminary aspects of management research, and this chapter begins by considering the nature of management and the different forms that research may take in this context.

WHAT IS MANAGEMENT?

There are many views about what constitutes 'management', and clearly the notion of management as an activity is not new: the Egyptians built their pyramids, the Chinese built the Great Wall and the Mesopatamians learned to irrigate their land and wall their cities. All these feats required a high degree of co-ordination and although many had a captive labour force there must have been some organization of work, even if rudimentary. Formal records of production management techniques can be traced back to Mencius (372–289 BC). This Chinese philosopher dealt with models and systems, and pointed to the advantages of the division of labour, putting the concepts rediscovered over 2000 years later into perspective.

There is a distinction that can be made between management as a 'cadre' of people, and management as an activity. Management as a cadre are those members of an organization who carry the title of manager and who commonly share similar beliefs about their status and right to manage. Usually the title manager is given to people in the organization hierarchy who are at one or more levels above 'first-line' supervision. This definition can be applied most easily in a traditional manufacturing company. However, with the growth of the service sector, the move from hierarchical structures to lean empowered organizations, the development of virtual teams and global corporations, the traditional means of defining a manager is becoming increasingly problematic (Castells, 2000). Handy (1989, 1996) has noted this change, when he says that in new organizations, everyone must have management skills. It is not just the traditional resources such as people, capital and technology which need to be managed nowadays; an increasing emphasis is being placed on the management of intangibles such as quality and knowledge, and many authors (e.g. Pralahad and Hamel, 1990; Nonaka and Takeuchi, 1995; Moingeon and Edmondson, 1997) now believe that these factors hold the secret to competitive advantage.

The modern use of the term 'management' derives from the USA, with the requirement for business and entrepreneurial skills at the turn of the century when American industries and railroads were developing very rapidly (Lawrence, 1986). From these beginnings management was put forward as an important subject that could, and should, be taught in schools of management.

The creation of management schools in the first half of the twentieth century led to greater systematization of techniques and knowledge. Much of this was based on the principles that managers had distilled from their own experiences. Two of the dominant figures during this period were Taylor (1947), and Fayol (1916/50) who classified the main functions that managers should perform, such as: planning, organizing, co-ordinating and controlling. Although this *classical* view of management has much face validity, later researchers were to show that these functions had little resemblance to what managers, whether good or bad, actually did in their work (Mintzberg, 1973).

A further impetus was given to management after 1945 by the widespread development of business schools outside the US, and by the attempts of US schools to seek greater academic respectability for their disciplines. In their influential report sponsored by the Ford Foundation, Gordon and Howell (1959) stressed the importance of analytic approaches to management and the need to select students and faculty on their academic credentials rather than their managerial calibre. This led to the strengthening of academic disciplines, such as Finance, Marketing, Operations Research and Organizational Behaviour.

During the 1960s the view developed that the key to effective management was the ability to take decisions, particularly under conditions of uncertainty (Simon, 1959; Cyert and March, 1963). This *decision theory* approach therefore emphasized the importance of techniques that could be used to analyse the environment within which decisions must be made, and ways of reaching decisions which will work as well as possible, even if they are not completely ideal. Quantitative methods of analysis and model-building still dominate the curricula of many business schools, especially in the USA and France.

With both the classical and decision theory approaches there is some confusion between what management is, and what it ought to be; because of this confusion they are often described as 'normative' theories of management. Each theory also has implications about the questions that are worth researching, and the methods that should be used to do this. However during the last three decades these theories have come under considerable attack from two separate, but related quarters.

The classical view has been attacked by researchers such as Stewart (1967), Mintzberg (1973), Kotter (1982) and Hales (1986) who, as we have indicated above, found almost no evidence of managers behaving as they are supposed to do. Instead of standing back and directing enterprises strategically, most managers, even top ones, spend most of their time talking to people; they work long hours at an unrelenting pace; their work patterns are varied, fragmented and reactive; and there is rarely any time for planning ahead and anticipating crises. Consequently, those who follow the *work activity* view argue there is little point in trying to get them to behave according to the classical text books. Rather, managers should be helped to deal with the realities of their jobs through managing their own time and becoming more skilled at working and negotiating with others.

The second line of attack has come from employers, and has been readily assisted by a number of academics (Livingston, 1971; Hayes and Abernethy, 1980; Peters and Waterman, 1982). The main argument is that the emphasis on analytic techniques is of limited value, and may even be harmful to companies. It is more important for managers to exhibit leadership, to provide collective visions, and to mould the culture and values of the organization in appropriate directions. This line has given rise to a view of management as a set of *competencies* which represent the skills that need to be demonstrated in the course of effective managerial work (Boyatzis, 1982; Silver, 1991; Evers and Rush, 1996).

Even the academic establishment in the USA has begun to accept that the content and process of management courses may not be fully appropriate to the needs of the modern manager. Following the publication of a mildly critical report about how the system should adapt to meet the challenges of the future (Porter and McKibbin, 1988), there was a rapid growth in courses and research into topics such as leadership, entrepreneurship and international management. There has also been a relaxation in the strict accreditation criteria of US business schools, and they are now allowed more freedom to determine the content of their MBA courses provided they are able to justify it against their own objectives. But there may well be too much inertia in a system that produces around 80,000 MBAs and 250,000 undergraduates per annum. Academics complain that research into topics such as international management is still seen as less prestigious than research into mainstream disciplines (Boyacigiller and Adler, 1991; Steers et al., 1992) and moreover, the changes to curricula still treat 'management' as a subject that can define clear answers to problems which can then be taught to students who will subsequently apply them in their management work. Changes have been incremental rather than radical.

The last decade has seen the rise of much literature which takes a *critical* view of management. This has come from various sources, including postmodernism which rejects the rationality that is so strongly embedded in the idea of management (Hassard and Parker, 1993); social constructionism which emphasizes that the most important part of management involves making sense of ambiguous and complex situations through conversations and dialogue (Shotter, 1993; Pye, 1995; Weick, 1995) and critical theory which tends to see management as an agent in maintaining wider power differences in society (Alvesson and Wilmott, 1992). To date there have been few attempts to articulate appropriate methodologies for conducting empirical research into management from a critical perspective. Although we attempt to summarize the main implications later in this book, we are pleased to say that one of the first books in the new Sage Series on Management Research provides methodological treatment of critical management research (Alvesson and Deetz, 2000).

Views of management	*Key features*
Classical	Functional activities
Decision theory	Optimizing decisions
Work activity	Actual managerial behaviour
Competencies	Skills required for effective performance
Critical	Social construction and political role

FIGURE 1.1 Five views of management

The five views summarized in Figure 1.1 are by no means the only views about what management is, or should be; but they are important historically. In the context of the present book, the implications should be self-evident: the procedures for management research are likely to vary considerably according to the view that you take of the nature of management. If you are interested, for example, in the work activity view of management, then you will be interested in observational methods that provide a structured description of managerial activities and roles within real organizations; if you are interested in management as a socially constructed activity, then you are more likely to be interested in gathering stories, narratives and conversations about management.

WHY IS MANAGEMENT RESEARCH DISTINCTIVE?

Despite the maturation of management as an area of study, the majority of books on research methods still derive from cognate disciplines such as sociology, education and psychology. External critics might regard this as further proof of the intellectual shallowness of management as a discipline; we prefer to see it as an indication that the richness of substantive research problems in the management field has not left enough time for deep methodological reflections. Whatever the reasons, it is evident that some of the methodology books coming out of the social sciences are very good indeed, and we make full use of both recent and classic texts in this volume. However, we also believe that management research poses some unusual problems which are not often encountered in the broader social sciences. There is therefore a need to rethink some of the traditional techniques and methods; there is also an opportunity for those in the management field to use the challenges of their field setting to develop new research methods and traditions which might eventually be seen to have validity outside the field of management. How, then, is management research different? In our view there are three main factors that make management research distinctive.

First, despite the progress towards creating distinct disciplines within management, the practice of management is largely *eclectic*: managers need to be able to work across technical, cultural and functional boundaries; they need to be able to draw on knowledge developed by other disciplines such as sociology, anthropology, economics, statistics and mathematics. The dilemma for the researcher, then, is whether to examine management from the perspective of one discipline, or whether to adopt a transdisciplinary approach (Tranfield and Starkey, 1998). The former is often seen to be the safer course for those who wish to gain respectability from academic peers; but the latter is more likely to produce results that are of use to practising managers.

Second, managers tend to be *powerful* and busy people. They are unlikely to allow research access to their organizations unless they can see some commercial or personal advantage to be derived from it. This means, as we shall see in Chapter 4, that access for fieldwork can be very difficult and may be hedged with many conditions about confidentiality and publication rights; feasible research questions may be determined more by access possibilities than by theoretical considerations. Nowadays, managers have to count very carefully the cost of their time and therefore short interviews, fitted into busy schedules, are likely to be much more feasible than unstructured observations and discussion which can take a lot of time.

Third, management requires both thought and *action*. Not only do most managers feel that research should lead to practical consequences, they are also quite capable of taking action themselves in the light of research results. Thus research methods either need to incorporate within them the potential for taking actions, or they need to take account of the practical consequences that may ensue with or without the guidance of the researcher. The distinction between theory and practical action has been neatly encapsulated in the work of Michael Gibbons who describes two forms of research: Mode 1 which concentrates on the production of knowledge by 'scientists'; and Mode 2 which is characterized by the production of knowledge from application. Some management scholars argue that management research should follow the latter approach with an emphasis on practical application – others suggest that both theoretical and practical work is required, and Ann Huff when President of the US Academy of Management argued for a compromise 'Mode 1½' position (Huff, 2000).

Admittedly each of these factors is not unique to management research. The problem of multiple disciplines exists in educational research, and the access problem is very evident in organizational sociology. But the possible combination of all three suggests to us that some of the traditional assumptions and practices in social research may well need rethinking. This is what we do in this book, and it is something that is being taken further in the new Series.

TYPES OF RESEARCH AND THEIR OUTCOMES

However, for the time being we need to start with some of the existing concepts and ideas, and consider how they relate to management research. In this section, therefore, we look at some of the main classifications of research: pure, applied and action research. These are distinguished primarily by the outcomes that are assumed to emerge – although, as ever, the distinctions do not hold clearly in practice.

Pure Research

The key feature of pure research is that it is intended to lead to theoretical development – there may, or may not, be any practical implications. There are at least three forms that theoretical developments may take. First, there is the popular view that scientific research is about *discovery*. This is when a totally new idea or explanation emerges from empirical research, which may revolutionize thinking on that particular topic. A well-known example in management is the Hawthorne Study (Roethlisberger and Dickson, 1939) where research into the effect of physical conditions at work led to the discovery that social conditions, including the act of carrying out research, have a major impact on productivity and work behaviour.

Discoveries are rare and unpredictable, and we will discuss the reasons for this further in the next chapter. A more common outcome from research is what we call an *invention*, where a new technique, method or idea is created to deal with a particular kind of problem. Examples would include Scientific Management (Taylor, 1947), Total Quality Management (Walton, 1989), or Business Process Engineering (Hammer and Champy, 1993). Each of these are based on direct experiences of their inventors, rather than exhaustive fieldwork; they all have considerable commercial potential, but were produced to deal with a general kind of problem.

We call the third type of outcome from pure research, *reflection*. This is where an existing theory, technique or group of ideas is re-examined, possibly in a different organizational or social context. For example, one could examine to what extent Herzberg's theory of motivation (Herzberg et al., 1959), which was developed in the USA, could be applied in UK or German companies. Results from the comparison could lead to revision and modification of the theory or to further ideas about cultural differences. This form of research is less spectacular than discovery or invention, but is very widely used, especially for doctoral theses.

One of the key features of pure research is that its results are openly disseminated through books, articles, conference papers or theses, addressed mainly at an academic audience. Dissemination is seen as a major responsibility for the researcher, and career progress for academics depends on getting the fruits of their work placed in the most prestigious journals, which is seen as proof of the quality of the work.

Applied Research

Applied research is intended to lead to the solution of specific problems, and usually involves working with clients who identify the problems and who may pay for their solution. Although theory may have a part to play in applied research, it is the application of theory that is important in this case. Applied research projects frequently form the foundation of dissertations for MBA and other Masters students, although to gain academic approval it is still important to *explain* the rationale behind any proposals that are made and to provide a critical review of the research process which led to them. Phillips and Pugh (1987) make a similar point when they introduce the distinction between 'what' and 'why' questions. The former must be answered for the client's benefit, but the latter must be covered for academic purposes. One common form of applied research is the evaluation of the process and results of a particular course of action – such as the introduction of a new Knowledge Management system into a company.

The results of applied research always need to be reported to the client, who is likely to evaluate the quality of the research in terms of its usability. This starts to raise issues around the motivations of individual clients, the politics of the settings in which they work and the ethics of passing information from informants on to clients. There is always the potential to publish the results of applied research in practitioner or professional journals provided the results can be shown to have wider significance, although this possibility often raises questions of commercial confidentiality and the need to maintain good relationships with the initial client. In Chapter 4 we will discuss in more detail issues such as ethics, confidentiality and the control of information.

Action Research

A number of research approaches have developed in management which do not fit neatly into either of the above categories, and we have grouped these under the heading of action research. A common feature of these approaches is that the research no longer tries to maintain a distance and separation from the thing that is being researched. Indeed, the aim of the research may well be to have a direct and immediate impact; and hence it is accepted that change should be incorporated into the research process itself. Perhaps the most elegant definition comes from Rappoport (1970: 499): 'Action research aims to contribute both to the practical concerns of people in an immediate problematic situation and to the goals of social science by joint collaboration within a mutually accepted ethical framework'.

Classical action research starts from the idea that if you want to understand something well you should try changing it, and this was most frequently adopted in Organization Development where practitioners worked with groups in order to improve their effectiveness (French and Bell, 1978; Homan, 1979). New paradigm research stresses the importance of establishing collaboration between researcher and researched, leading to the development of shared understandings (Reason and Rowan, 1981; Reason and Bradley, 2000). This is most easily done when working with individuals or small groups. Finally, Action Learning is not so much a research approach, but an educational process that makes extensive use of action research methods (Pedler, 1998). Students are expected to learn from tackling real problems in their own, or others', organizations, and these projects are reviewed regularly within a 'set' of 5–8 students, each of whom are tackling their own projects at the same time. Revans (1980) stresses that projects should be open-ended problems, rather than 'puzzles' with identifiable solutions, and for this reason a focus on change is often chosen.

Because of the collaborative features of action research, participants (the researcher and the researched) are likely to learn a lot from the process itself, and their interest may be on what happens next rather than on any formal account of research findings. But it may still be worth writing up action research as a narrative, so that a record is maintained of how understanding changes and develops over time.

Choosing Types of Research

As we shall see in Chapters 3 and 4 there are many factors, both political and philosophical, which can influence the way research is designed and conducted in practice. But it is also possible to effect the subsequent outcomes by a careful choice of initial style and strategy.

At undergraduate levels, research is likely to be specific and bounded, either as an assignment for tutors or as a question posed by a client. Common tasks include small market research studies, or interview-based studies of employee attitudes. In most cases a single method will be used and this may also be specified in advance. The opportunities for choice are mainly around how a method is used and how results are interpreted and communicated. As will be seen in the second part of the book there is plenty of scope in these areas.

When research is being conducted as part of a Masters degree there is more autonomy. It is usually best to adopt a flexible strategy, because within any learning process there will be mistakes and false starts. If a project is to last for 3–4 months then evaluation research is often the easiest option. This involves looking at some system or practice that already exists and making recommendations for how it might be changed and improved. The greater the attempt to encourage change, the nearer it will come to pure action research. Involvement in change can lead to rich and interesting results, and it may be a valuable experience for people seeking work in consultancy. The drawbacks are about timing and communications. First, it may take a long time to get anything to happen and it will then be hard to make a clear endpoint to the research; second, it may not be easy to draw out the full significance of complex experiences when writing them up for academic purposes.

More is possible with longer project periods, but even with PhDs the time never seems sufficient for what is being attempted. Doctoral work needs to produce theoretical contributions with some degree of originality, and the easiest ways of doing this are either to replicate known studies with one or two of the variables, such as country or industrial sector, being changed, or by looking at a practical problem from two different theoretical perspectives. It is through contrasts that new ideas and insights are most easily created. It is quite unrealistic to expect great discoveries from every doctoral project, but it seems that the chances will be improved if both pure and applied elements are incorporated into the research.

The examples above have all assumed that research will involve the collection of empirical data. This certainly makes sense for those who are wishing to use their research experiences as a basis for subsequent careers in management or consultancy practice, and it is normally expected that dissertations at Batchelors, Masters and Doctoral levels will include some original data. But it is also important to demonstrate that research builds on ideas developed by others, and a good grasp of the field in question is a prerequisite for good empirical research. This is known as scholarship, or as 'armchair theorizing' to its detractors. Scholarship is an essential part of the academic role; it may also have an important part to play as research where it involves organizing and reinterpreting the work of others to produce new ideas and perspectives.

In conclusion, although we give a lot of advice about research methods in this book it should not be seen as definitive. The researcher must be prepared to continually use his or her own judgement – and this, as Buchanan (1980) suggests, is one of the most important outcomes from the use of research projects in management development programmes. Research is always hedged about with uncertainty and risk. Those who learn to work effectively, and independently with this uncertainty will find they possess a skill that can be transferred very easily into roles outside the academic world.

2 The Ingredients of Successful Research

There is no simple way of ensuring that research will be successful. The types and contexts of research vary so widely that 'ideal' strategies will differ from situation to situation. And if the research is worth doing, then one is likely to be dealing with a problem which is not fully understood, and for which the ideal course of investigation cannot be charted in advance with any certainty. Nevertheless there are a number of factors which seem to increase the chances of research being successful – all things being equal. Four such factors are discussed in this chapter: motivation, support, style and personal qualities. The chapter concludes with some thoughts about one of the biggest problems of all: getting started.

MOTIVATION

Phillips and Pugh (1987: 29) offer seven pieces of advice on how *not* to get a PhD, the first one being, 'not to *want* a PhD'. We can express the point in a positive way by saying that much determination and single-mindedness are essential to completing any significant piece of research. There is so much uncertainty about the processes and outcomes of any project, and the work invariably expands beyond anything considered reasonable at the outset, so it is not an activity for the faint-hearted. Here we distinguish between three apparent motives for researchers: as a vehicle for learning; as a basis for personal growth and advancement; and as a means of enhancing managerial skills.

It is now very common for management courses, particularly if they lead to qualifications, to contain an element of research. Many taught courses use the project or dissertation as a kind of 'capstone', as a way of integrating the different functional disciplines such as accounting and marketing which are often taught separately in business schools. Projects are also a popular way of enabling students to *learn* from direct engagement with the outside world. They can provide them with greater confidence in their own opinions as well as an opportunity to test out the validity of the theories offered by the text books. Students react differently to projects. Some will treat them instrumentally, as a way of achieving a pass on the course; some may use them to obtain contacts, experience and credibility which will help with job-hunting; and others find themselves getting absorbed by their projects, and excited at the novel possibility of studying something in depth.

This links to the second main source of motivation, *personal growth and career development*. There are many possibilities here. People may register for research degrees because they want to be given an external discipline for examining something in which they have long held a passionate interest; they may want to prove to themselves that they can do research; or they may simply want to belong to a research 'community' for a few years. For those wishing to develop careers as academics a research 'identity' is essential. This means that a consistent thread to an individual's research interests is sought when assessing candidates for appointments, and it is easiest to achieve this consistency when one is driven by strong personal interest.

The third source comes from a recognition that research experiences may lead to the *enhancement of managerial skills* and the solution of problems at work. As we suggested in the first chapter, research may help to develop judgement; this includes the skills of judging what information is important, how and when to obtain it, and how best to communicate results. It is also likely to strengthen independence, because of the lack of prior rules and the need to initiate, structure and monitor progress on one's own for most of the time. But most of all it develops an individual's critical facilities in relation to judging the quality of evidence used to support particular courses of action. These skills are likely to become more important for managers as the business environment becomes more complex and unpredictable.

Some people may well have all three of the above reasons for doing research. At the very least it helps if one has a combination of 'internal' and 'external' pressures, such as a strong interest in a particular topic and clear expectations and deadlines from a sponsor, or one's family. And when embarking on research, especially where it involves a long term commitment, it is worth considering one's motives carefully.

SUPPORT AND SUPERVISION

Research work can be very demanding on the individual. There are many uncertainties, doubts and crises that enter into most research projects. From her interviews with students, Phillips (1984) identified seven main stages in the process of conducting a PhD. These were: enthusiasm; isolation; increased interest; increasing independence; boredom; frustration; and a job to be finished. Not every research project necessarily goes through precisely the same seven stages, but ups and downs are inevitable. The emotional cost of these crises can be quite high, and hence it is important to consider the support, both technical and emotional, that can be obtained.

When the research is part of an academic degree the most obvious source of support is the supervisor or tutor. But not all supervisors are ideal. The following points are based on a combination of our, and others', experiences about the behaviour of supervisors who seem most successful at the task of supervising doctoral degrees. These points might be taken into account by those who are able to influence their choice of supervisor. First, he or she must possess some technical expertise, although some would argue that a general knowledge of the research area and of relevant methodologies is perhaps more useful than a very deep knowledge of the subject to be investigated. But as the field of management develops, then specialist knowledge of debates and recent literature in the chosen area is increasingly important. Moreover, the supervisor who is personally active as a researcher is also likely to belong to the international networks which control the leading journals and conferences. These networks provide a source of external examiners for doctoral candidates and also act as gateways into academic careers.

With regard to the practical aspects of the relationship, Phillips (1984) found that the better supervisors tend to set regular, and realistic, deadlines, although they do not interfere too much with the detail of the work. A 'responsive' style seems most appropriate if the researcher is to be encouraged to become autonomous and independent; and it also helps if the supervisor is prepared and willing to respond quite rapidly to any problems or written work. Ideally the supervisor should be prepared to 'turn round' draft chapters and reviews within a week or two, despite the growing pressures on academics. Availability is very important, and for this reason the guru with a string of brilliant publications, but who is never available for consultations, may not necessarily be the best supervisor.

The relationship between supervisor and student is also important because it must be strong enough to cope with the different stages of the research process (Deem and Brehony, 1997). Ideally there should be mutual commitment between the two parties, and this should, if possible, result from the initial choice and negotiation process. It should also be recognized that the role of the supervisor can be difficult at times. From our own experiences as supervisors there is often a nagging doubt that the advice one is giving may be wrong, and in most cases students will move beyond the existing knowledge of the supervisor during the course of the project. In the case of a doctoral thesis this is almost an inevitable consequence of the requirement for originality in a PhD thesis. But also in Masters and undergraduate dissertations which involve tackling broad-based problems the work is likely to fall outside the specialist area of the supervisor who therefore has to rely on 'generic' supervisory skills such as asking challenging questions or pointing the student(s) to alternative sources of expertise. There is also a delicate balance required between providing feedback, which highlights weakness in a piece of work, and providing praise and encouragement to try harder. The way out of this dilemma is to put across the message: 'this is fine in the following respects . . . but it could be made even better in these areas . . . and the way I'd go about it is . . .!'

Not everyone is lucky enough to have a supervisor, and even when one has one there may be elements of ambiguity in the relationship. Hence it is always worth considering alternative sources of support. One of the best forms of support can come from colleagues, either through naturally occurring friendships, or through constructing a 'support set' – a group of four or five researchers committed to meeting regularly every few weeks to discuss their research progress and problems. It helps if the members of this set are working in related fields, but they should not be too close because this can sometimes generate conflict and competition. This set may have a tutor (or set advisor) who can help it to organize itself, and possibly, provide specialist advice and support. The members of the set should be able to use it to 'bounce' ideas off each other, and, particularly for those who are researching part-time, to provide contact with others who may be going through similar experiences of doubt, confusion and disillusionment as themselves.

It is also important to recognize the potential for support outside one's immediate institution. Those wishing to develop academic careers will need to develop links within the broader community working in a particular area, and, as we have pointed out above, this should be regarded as a crucial responsibility for the supervisor. But many of the better academic conferences will also organize doctoral days where doctoral students get the chance to present their ideas informally with leading figures in their field. By the second year of a doctoral thesis one should be submitting papers to conferences, possibly in conjunction with the supervisor initially (how else can overworked supervisors maintain their research outputs?!). It is through presenting papers at such conferences that one can develop contacts with other collaborators and potential sponsors; and it forms an induction into the academic community which can be both reassuring and motivating for one's own research.

We have concentrated above on support for doctoral students since the long timescales mean that the relationship is very important. Those carrying out research as part of taught courses work under different time pressures and may be supervised both by an academic and a client/practitioner. In this case group supervision may be the norm, as with action learning sets or group-based projects. Though there is an important distinction here in that within an action learning set the members will be looking at different topics, while members of a group project team will be focusing on the same issue. The downside of group projects is, of course, that they now have to work as a team and this provides the added complication of having to work effectively in a group situation.

For those planning careers as practitioners it can also be important to attend professional conferences. The opportunities for instant visibility and fame are less, simply because platforms are normally reserved for people who already have established reputations. Nevertheless, such conferences can put one in touch with what are considered to be the hot issues and fashionable ideas, and they may also lead to the establishment of personal contacts which have direct career implications. In addition, the rise of the Internet has created considerable networking opportunities for people on a global scale both via public conferences and through private e-mail exchanges.

STYLE AND CREATIVITY

In the previous section we explained why emotional support was a key factor in the successful completion of research work. Here we focus more on ways of ensuring that the research will be of good quality and will contain some originality. We argue that this is determined largely by the personal style and approach adopted by the researcher.

A fascinating study into the personal factors that contribute to discoveries in medicine is provided by Austin (1978), an American neurosurgeon who had become dissatisfied by the trite explanations provided by scientists about how great discoveries come about. He differentiated between four factors, or forms of 'chance', which seem to underlie many of these discoveries.

- Chance 1 is simply *blind luck*. Although this may often be important, it is unlikely to be the only reason for a breakthrough. Relying on blind luck can take a long time. Austin reminds us that in bridge if you wait for 13 spades to turn up in a hand of cards, the odds are 635 million to one against.
- Chance 2 derives from the researcher being *in motion*. Nobody, it has been said, trips over anything whilst sitting down. The greater the curiosity, resilience and persistence of the researcher, the more likely he or she is to find something of significance.
- Chance 3 comes from having a *prepared mind* and being ready to see new relationships and solutions. This means being aware of past research that has been conducted through searching the literature and talking to other researchers, whilst at the same time being prepared to think outside existing frameworks and knowledge.
- Chance 4 is a product *of individualized action*. This means encouraging distinctive, even eccentric, hobbies and lifestyles. In particular, the researcher should try to take a broad interest in people and other disciplines. Creativity is often born from associations and links made across traditional boundaries.

There are many examples of scientific research where the above elements of 'chance' are demonstrated. But the illustration that Austin himself uses is Fleming's discovery of penicillin in 1928. In an interview after world war II, Fleming commented that the discovery of penicillin was almost entirely a matter of luck: 'like winning the Irish Sweepstake'. But Austin shows that this was not only a matter of blind luck. Fleming, by all accounts, was a tireless researcher; his great aim being to discover a new antiseptic, and even after the penicillin discovery he was extremely busy making and selling antibacterial vaccines. Thus he was a man who was continuously *in motion*.

It was his *prepared mind* which enabled him to note the effect on colonies of bacteria when a stray spore of a rare mould fell by accident onto his culture dish. Nine years earlier he had discovered the bacterial enzyme Lysozyme when . . . 'whilst suffering from a cold, his own nasal drippings had found their way into a culture dish. He noted that the bacteria round the mucus were killed and astutely followed up the lead' (Austin, 1978: 74). The parallels between these, and other experiences would be easy to perceive. *Individualized action* enters into the story because Fleming was a keen swimmer and water polo player. He had not chosen to train and work at the old St Mary's hospital because of the excellence of its scientific facilities, but because it had a good swimming pool. The laboratories were basic, badly equipped, cold and 'contaminated by organisms swirling in and out of the London fog' (Austin, 1978: 92). This made them a particularly good breeding ground for bacteria and stray spores! In this example it is possible to see all four forms of chance at work, and Austin suggested that major discoveries are most likely to take place when several forms coincide. This is what he calls the 'unifying observation' of the Fleming effect.

Unfortunately not all researchers are destined to make major discoveries. Indeed it is wise to content oneself with, what we have termed, invention or reflection; discovery is but a bonus, which may be made more likely if one follows Austin's prescriptions. The bulk of research is much more humdrum. This is true both for the social and natural sciences. Many sociologists have carried out detailed studies of the way that the natural sciences progress, and the consensus is that it is a gradual process, with much hard graft and very few genuine breakthroughs. Latour and Woolgar (1979) demonstrated in a classic study of a biological laboratory how scientific 'facts' emerged through a process of debate which was linked to the career strategies and progress of individual researchers. More recently, the study by Law (1994) into the management and organization of a particle physics research laboratory shows the impact of factors such as funding, politics and status hierarchies on the way scientific knowedge is produced and recognized. He also commented self-reflexively on his debates with colleagues and various changes of heart in the course of doing his own research study. These issues will be considered in more depth in the following two chapters.

Phillips and Pugh (1994) identify three characteristics of good research, whether it be grand or humble, and which distinguish it from activities such as decision-making or consultancy. First, it is based on an *open system of thought*. This requires continual testing, review and criticism of others' ideas, and a willingness to hazard new ideas, even if one can't find half a dozen references to support one's view. Second, one must always be prepared *to examine data critically*, and to request the evidence behind conclusions drawn by others. Third, one should always try to *generalize the research*, but within stated limits. This means attempting to extract understanding from one situation and to apply it to as many other situations as possible.

The first two of these characteristics may require researchers to be aware of their own preconceived views (or self-reflexive, as Law, 1994 describes it), and to be willing to look for information that will disconfirm what they already believe to be the case. This willingness to have current beliefs disproven is important if new ideas are to be developed, and it also has a strong philosophical justification. The requirement for generalization may be either descriptive, where one wishes to demonstrate that the characteristics of one setting are similar to those in other settings, or it can be theoretical, where one demonstrates that the ideas developed within one context are relevant and useful in very different contexts. Both of these issues will be developed further in Chapter 3.

PERSONAL QUALITIES

The qualities required by researchers are not easy to define. Turner (1988) compares the researcher to an expert cook, who finds it difficult to explain what he does but claims that the end result is evidence of his proficiency. There are many tacit skills involved in research. Although it is possible to develop formal skills and knowledge through training, these tacit skills can only be fully acquired through experience, and this necessarily implies working with others who are able to pass on the tacit skills that they have previously acquired. This is where the relationship with the supervisor is very important, and if one gets the chance to work on a project with experienced researchers, this can be very valuable.

In this section we have listed what we believe to be the important qualities of researchers. These are based partly on our own experiences and partly on external sources such as the ESRC Guidelines for Management Research Training (ESRC, 2001). The resulting qualities we have classified according to whether they comprise knowledge, skills or personal attributes. This classification is based substantially on Burgoyne and Stuart's (1976) work into the attributes of effective managers, and it is here that we think the greatest transferability lies between managing and researching. The skills and knowledge areas are progressively more specific to the conduct of research. These are 'core' qualities, which are important in any form of research, and are listed in Figure 2.1. Those interested in a rough diagnosis of their strengths and weaknesses as researchers can rate themselves on each quality using the following 1 to 4 scale:

4 Possess to a high degree
3 Possess to a moderate degree
2 Possess to a limited extent
1 Have virtually none of these

If you have managed to rate yourself on the above qualities, then any ratings below 3 may be cause for concern (with the possible exception of item 5). What to do about any apparent deficiencies is, of course, a different matter. As a generalization: 'knowledge' can be acquired by reading and talking, or by attending courses; 'skills' can be acquired through practising them, either in a simulated or a real environment; and 'personal qualities' can be acquired, with much difficulty, through life or educational experiences. This book certainly cannot offer everything. It provides a reasonable coverage of items 1, 2, 3, 8, 9 and 10; and it touches on 6, 7, 12, 13 and 18. As for the rest, they may be acquired most easily by working with other researchers, in the form of apprenticeship suggested above by Turner (1988).

We believe that management researchers do need a broad training in skills and knowledge because of the diversity and complexity of problems in the management domain. Hence we refer to the following list as 'core' attributes. Beyond a certain point, however, specialization begins to creep in. One form of

Knowledge/awareness of		Skills and abilities		Personal qualities	
1 Different assumptions about the world	☐	7 Planning, organizing and managing one's own time	☐	13 Self awareness	☐
2 Qualitative and quantitative research methods	☐	8 Searching libraries and on-line data sources	☐	14 Clarity of thought	☐
3 Range of research designs	☐	9 Interviewing and observation	☐	15 Sensitivity to events and feelings	☐
4 Immediate subject of study	☐	10 Structuring and arguing a case in writing	☐	16 Emotional resilience	☐
5 Related subjects and disciplines	☐	11 Defending and arguing views orally	☐	17 Creativity	☐
6 Key networks and contacts in chosen research area	☐	12 Gaining support and cooperation from others	☐	18 Learning from experience	☐
Total	☐	*Total*	☐	*Total*	☐

FIGURE 2.1 Core attributes of competent researchers

specialization depends upon whether the researcher is following a primarily quantitative or qualitative path. Thus if someone is carrying out analytic research into financial markets, they may not need to use any qualitative data in their research, and training in qualitative methods may seem a great irrelevance. But we still feel that it is important that they are able to appreciate and evaluate the qualitative work of others because it could still have some bearing on their own research. In addition, there is a trend towards more mixing of subjects and methodologies. Thus quantitative subjects may be tackled with qualitative methods, as in behavioural accounting; and qualitative subjects can be tackled with quantitative methods, such as frequency counts in textual analysis.

Irrespective of the position taken on the qualitative/quantitative divide, researchers will need to be skilled in the use of different methods for such things as seeking information, analysing data and presenting research results. Those following the quantitative path will need to have high levels of skill in areas such as survey design, sampling methods, and statistical analysis; those following the qualitative path may need to be skilled at conducting 'in-depth' interviews, making field notes, coding and interpreting transcripts, and so on. In Part III we give extensive guidance on the choice and application of qualitative methods, followed by a more limited review of possible quantitative methods.

GETTING STARTED

It is very rare for students to have a clear focus at the outset of their research, and yet many find the lack of a clear focus is a major impediment to getting started. It often takes research students a whole year to find an acceptable focus, and this may include false starts, drifting, and moments of despondency and elation. Indeed, the whole research project may be seen as a continuous process of focusing.

Those who are working on shorter, more applied, projects may be more fortunate in having a problem or question given to them by their supervisors, tutors or clients (we discuss the different influences on the research 'question' in Chapter 4). The situation for people working in the natural sciences is similar, because work and funding is often parcelled up into groups of related projects, which are largely predetermined.

Whatever one's situation, it is worth getting started as quickly as possible. This means defining a provisional area of interest, reviewing relevant literature and gathering some data relevant to the focus. One way of thinking about a topic is to produce a model or 'mind map' of the issues involved. An example of such a scheme developed in relation to a project Mark was planning on international organizational learning is shown in Figure 2.2. In a Masters project time is short and one may then need to launch directly into the main study. In a doctoral project there is usually time to carry out a pilot investigation to test methodologies and to assess the feasibility of initial ideas, which might then lead into a larger study, or be completely jettisoned at a later stage. Even if data and reading subsequently needs to be discarded it does not necessarily mean that time has been wasted. There are most likely to be indirect benefits in terms of the contacts, ideas, or techniques one encounters on the way, and at the very least one is invoking Austin's (1978) second principle of being 'in motion'.

Once possible topics have been identified it might be worth considering them in the light of the study conducted by Hucznyski (1996) which looked at why certain management ideas and theories come to the fore and gain popularity at the expense of equally well researched and valid alternatives. Following Huczynski, we list below four main prerequisites for the successful management idea:

1 It must be *timely* and address a problem that is seen as important at that moment.
2 It has to be *promoted* effectively via academics, consultants and the business media.
3 It must *relate to the needs and concerns of the managers* to whom it is addressed.
4 It must be *presented* in an engaging way.

Sooner or later it is worth writing a research proposal which summarizes what the project is about, and how it is to be investigated. Some institutions require a proposal from prospective research candidates before registration, others

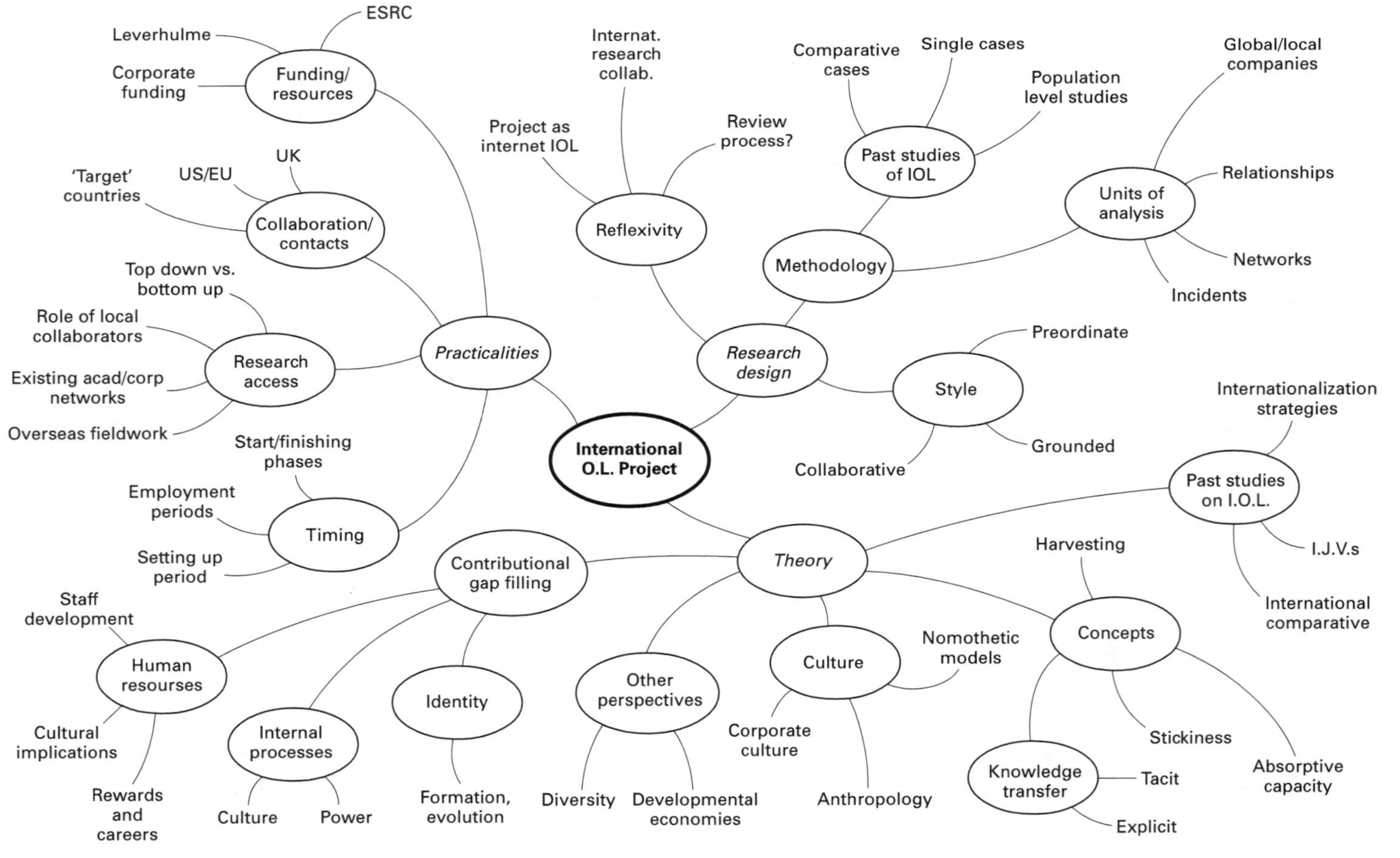

FIGURE 2.2 Preliminary mind map for international organization learning project

require a formal proposal after 12–15 months if a decision is required about upgrading registration from MPhil to PhD levels. Research Councils require detailed (but concise!) proposals before they will allocate money to major research projects; shorter proposals may also be required at the beginning of Masters projects. Even if there is no formal external requirement to produce a proposal, the exercise of producing one is a very good discipline for drawing together half-formed ideas in the early stages of research.

The main items that should go into a research proposal are as follows:

1. A statement of the focus of the research and the main questions to be investigated;
2. An explanation of how it relates to, builds on, or differs from previous work in that field, and hence how it will constitute a 'contribution';
3. A summary of the research design including a description of what and how data will be collected;
4. An explanation of how data will be interpreted and how this will relate back to the initial questions posed;
5. Comments on the practical value of the research, and any problems that may be encountered in its conduct.

The document should not normally exceed 3000 words although the amount of detail required will depend on the scale of the project and the time available. Likewise the emphasis and structure of the proposal will vary according to such things as the intended audience, the style of research and the methods to be used. As we suggested at the beginning of this chapter, there is no single formula for ensuring that research will be successful. One must always exercise judgement according to the particular circumstances that prevail. The next two parts of this book are intended to explain many of the factors that shape and constrain research, and thus to assist the researcher in making informed choices as he or she progresses.

PART TWO

DESIGNING MANAGEMENT RESEARCH

3 The Philosophy of Research Design

It is a capital mistake to theorise before one has data.

Arthur Conan Doyle

The relationship between data and theory is an issue that has been hotly debated by philosophers for many centuries. Failure to think through philosophical issues such as this, while not necessarily fatal, can seriously affect the quality of management research, and they are central to the notion of research design. The aim of this chapter is therefore to consider the main philosophical positions that underlie the designs of management research – in other words, how do philosophical factors affect the overall arrangements which enable satisfactory outcomes from the research activity?

There are at least three reasons why an understanding of philosophical issues is very useful. First, because it can help to clarify research designs. This not only involves considering what kind of evidence is required and how it is to be gathered and interpreted, but also how this will provide good answers to the basic questions being investigated in the research. Second, a knowledge of philosophy can help the researcher to recognize which designs will work and which will not. It should enable him or her to avoid going up too many blind alleys and should indicate the limitations of particular approaches. Third, knowledge of philosophy can help the researcher identify, and even create, designs that may be outside his or her past experience. And it may also suggest how to adapt research designs according to the constraints of different subject or knowledge structures.

Arguments, criticisms and debates are central to the progress of philosophy. But it is unfortunate that within the social sciences such debates sometimes take the form of denigrating the other point of view, or of completely ignoring its existence. We believe that it is important to understand both sides of an argument because research problems often require compromise designs which draw from more than one tradition. Thus we try to provide here a balanced view of the different philosophical positions underlying research methods and designs, and to do this we have had to return to some of the original sources of these positions. The chapter therefore starts by reviewing some key debates among philosophers of science and social science. We then go on to look at the implications of this for a number of fundamental choices in research design, and we conclude the chapter with a mapping of research designs in relation to philosophical alternatives.

TWO PHILOSOPHICAL TRADITIONS: POSITIVISM VERSUS SOCIAL CONSTRUCTIONISM

We start here with a straight debate between two contrasting views of how social science research should be conducted, and we will then broaden out the discussion in the following section. The two traditions are positivism and social constructionism. In the red corner is constructionism; in the blue corner is positivism. Each of these positions has to some extent been elevated into a stereotype, often by the opposing side. Although it is now possible to draw up comprehensive lists of assumptions and methodological implications associated with each position, it is not possible to identify any philosopher who ascribes to all aspects of one particular view. Indeed, occasionally an author from one side produces ideas which belong more neatly to those of the other side.

Also when one looks at the practice of research, as we shall see below, even self-confessed extremists do not hold consistently to one position or the other. And although there has been a trend away from positivism towards constructionism since the early 1980s, there are many researchers, especially in the management field, who adopt a pragmatic view by deliberately combining methods drawn from both traditions.

So what are these traditions? Let us start with *positivism*. The key idea of positivism is that the social world exists externally, and that its properties should be measured through objective methods, rather than being inferred subjectively through sensation, reflection or intuition. The French philosopher, Auguste Comte (1853), was the first person to encapsulate this view, as he said:

> All good intellects have repeated, since Bacon's time, that there can be no real knowledge but that which is based on observed facts.

This statement contains two assumptions. First, an ontological assumption, that reality is external and objective; and second, an epistemological assumption, that knowledge is only of significance if it is based on observations of this external reality. There follow from this a number of implications, although not all of them were proposed by Comte:

1. *independence*: the observer must be independent from what is being observed;
2. *value-freedom*: the choice of what to study, and how to study it, can be determined by objective criteria rather than by human beliefs and interests;
3. *causality*: the aim of social sciences should be to identify causal explanations and fundamental laws that explain regularities in human social behaviour;
4. *hypothesis and deduction*: science proceeds through a process of hypothesizing fundamental laws and then deducing what kinds of observations will demonstrate the truth or falsity of these hypotheses;
5. *operationalization*: concepts need to be operationalized in a way which enables facts to be measured quantitatively;

6 *reductionism*: problems as a whole are better understood if they are reduced into the simplest possible elements;
7 *generalization*: in order to be able to generalize about regularities in human and social behaviour it is necessary to select samples of sufficient size, from which inferences may be drawn about the wider population;
8 *cross-sectional analysis*: such regularities can most easily be identified by making comparisons of variations across samples.

It is worth repeating that these propositions are not simply the view of any single philosopher; they are a collection of points that have come to be associated with the positivist viewpoint. Some 'positivists' would disagree with some of these statements. Comte, for example, did not agree with the principle of reductionism. Wittgenstein argued strongly in his early work that all factual propositions can be reduced into elementary propositions which are completely independent of one another. But in his later work he challenged his earlier view on the grounds that elementary propositions such as colours, could still be logically related to each other (Pears, 1971). So philosophers within one school not only disagree with each other; they also disagree with themselves over time.

The view that positivism provides the best way of investigating human and social behaviour originated as a reaction to metaphysical speculation (Aiken, 1956). As such this philosophy has developed into a distinctive paradigm over the last one and a half centuries. This term 'paradigm' has come into vogue among social scientists, particularly through the work of Kuhn (1962) who used it to describe the progress of scientific discoveries in practice, rather than how they are subsequently reconstructed within text books and academic journals. Most of the time, according to Kuhn, science progresses in tiny steps, which refine and extend what is already 'known'. But occasionally experiments start to produce results that do not fit into existing theories and patterns. Then, perhaps many years later, a Galileo or Einstein proposes a new way of looking at things, which can account for both the old and the new observations.

It is evident from these examples, and from the illustrations given in Chapter 2, that major scientific advances are not produced by a logical and rational application of scientific method. They result from independent and creative thinking which goes outside the boundaries of existing ideas. The result of this is a 'scientific revolution' which not only provides new theories, but which may also alter radically the way people see the world, and the kind of questions that scientists consider are important to investigate. The combination of new theories and questions is referred to as a new paradigm.

The new paradigm which has been developed by philosophers during the last half century, largely in reaction to the application of positivism to the social sciences, stems from the view that 'reality' is not objective and exterior, but is socially constructed and given meaning by people. The idea of *social constructionism*[1] then, as developed by authors such as Berger and Luckman (1966), Watzlawick (1984) and Shotter (1993), focuses on the ways that people make sense of the world especially through sharing their experiences with others via the medium of language. Social constructionism is one of a group of approaches that Habermas (1970) has referred to as interpretive methods. We will touch on these, and a number of other approaches, in the course of this and the following chapter, and at the end of this chapter we provide a map to summarize the main concepts introduced so far.

What, then, is the essence of social constructionism? First, is the idea, as we have mentioned above, that 'reality' is determined by people rather than by objective and external factors. Hence the task of the social scientist should not be to gather facts and measure how often certain patterns occur, but to appreciate the different constructions and meanings that people place upon their experience. The focus should be on what people, individually and collectively, are thinking and feeling, and attention should be paid to the ways they communicate with each other, whether verbally or non-verbally. One should therefore try to understand and explain why people have different experiences, rather than search for external causes and fundamental laws to explain their behaviour. Human action arises from the sense that people make of different situations, rather than as a direct response to external stimuli.

The methods of social constructionist research can be contrasted directly with the eight features of classical positivist research. They are summarized in Table 3.1. Again, it should be emphasized that these represent a composite picture rather than the viewpoint of any single author.

TABLE 3.1 *Contrasting implications of positivism and social constructionism*

	Positivism	**Social Constructionism**
The observer	must be independent	is part of what is being observed
Human interests	should be irrelevant	are the main drivers of science
Explanations	must demonstrate causality	aim to increase general understanding of the situation
Research progresses through	hypotheses and deductions	gathering rich data from which ideas are induced
Concepts	need to be operationalized so that they can be measured	should incorporate stakeholder perspectives
Units of analysis	should be reduced to simplest terms	may include the complexity of 'whole' situations
Generalization through	statistical probability	theoretical abstraction
Sampling requires	large numbers selected randomly	small numbers of cases chosen for specific reasons

Some of the distinctions in the table above should be self-evident, but others require more explanation. We will therefore elaborate further on issues such as interests, units of analysis, theoretical generalizations and sampling as the story of Chapters 3 and 4 unfolds.

The implications of holding these different views may be seen, for example, in the way researchers might study managerial stress. The social constructionist would be interested in the aspects of work that managers consider 'stressful', and perhaps in the strategies that they develop for managing these aspects. He or she would therefore arrange to talk with a few managers about their jobs, about the aspects they find more, or less, difficult, and would attempt to gather stories about incidents that they had experienced as stressful. The positivist, on the other hand, would start with the assumption that occupational stress exists and then would formulate measures of stress experienced by a large number of managers in order to relate them to external causes such as organizational changes, interpersonal conflicts, negative appraisals, etc. Measures of stress could be based on standardized verbal reports from the managers, or on physiological factors such as blood pressure.

BROADENING THE PHILOSOPHICAL DEBATE

In the discussion above we have referred to debates among scientists as well as social scientists, and we have also mentioned in passing the links between terms such as ontology and epistemology. This is because methodological choices for social scientists can be located within broader debates on the philosophy of science. Unfortunately, some philosophical terms are used interchangeably and consequently there is confusion about their meaning. So, although these wider issues are not central to the design of management research some clarification seems in order, and hence in this section of the chapter we expand on them before returning to management research *per se*.

We start in Table 3.2 with some definitions which are our own distillation of common usage among researchers. Since the third part of the book is concerned with the choice and application of individual methods we will concentrate on the first three terms now.

TABLE 3.2 *Ontology, espistemology, methodology and method*

Ontology:	assumptions that we make about the nature of reality.
Epistemology:	general set of assumptions about the best ways of inquiring into the nature of the world.
Methodology:	combination of techniques used to enquire into a specific situation.
Methods:	individual techniques for data collection, analysis, etc.

It is the first term, ontology, which is the starting point for most of the debates among philosophers. Although there have been strong parallels between the debates within science and social science there have also been differences. Thus among philosophers of *science* the debate has been between realism and relativism. Realists come in several varieties. Traditional realists start with the position that the world is concrete and external, and that science can only progress through observations that have a direct correspondence to the phenomena being investigated. This extreme position has been modified by philosophers of science in recent decades who point out the difference on the one hand between the laws of physics and nature, and on the other hand, the knowledge, or theories, that scientists have about these laws. This position is labelled by Bhaskar as *transcendental* realism, which assumes that 'the ultimate objects of scientific inquiry exist and act (for the most part) quite independently of scientists and their activity'(1989: 12). Internal realists concentrate more on the processes of observation (epistemology) which have emerged in response to advances in physics. They point out that whether or not phenomena are concrete, it is only possible to gather indirect evidence of what is going on in fundamental physical processes (Putnam, 1987). The classical example is the Indeterminancy Principle, formulated by Werner Heisenberg in 1927, which states that it is never possible to obtain full and objective information about the state of a body because the act of experimentation itself will determine the observed state of the phenomenon being studied. Thus any attempt to measure the location of an electron will, for example, affect its velocity.

Internal realists do accept, however, that scientific laws once discovered are absolute and independent of further observations. The relativist position goes a stage further in suggesting that scientific laws may not be quite so immutable. It has been strongly influenced by the work of Latour and Woolgar (1979) who have studied the evolution of scientific ideas within research laboratories and noted how ideas only gain acceptance as being 'true' after much debate and discussion which is also tied in to the personal careers and statuses of the main protagonists. Furthermore, Knorr-Cetina (1983) points out that the acceptance of a particular theory, and hence the 'closure' of a scientific debate, may be highly influenced by the politics of business and commercial resources.

Many traditional scientists have responded vigorously to the relativist challenge by arguing that even if scientists work through social and political networks, the veracity of scientific laws is quite independent of the process of discovery. Richard Dawkins, the biologist, famously comments that even the most dedicated relativist does not believe, when flying at 40,000 feet in a jumbo jet, that the laws of physics which hold the jet in the air are mere constructs of the imagination (Irwin, 1994).

The arguments among *social scientists* can, in some respects, be mapped onto the scientific debate. Here we expand on the view developed in the previous section by looking at three main ontological positions: representationalism, relativism and nominalism. The first two correspond roughly to the internal realist and relativist viewpoints of science, although, as we will see below, the implications in terms of methods vary because the subject matter of social science is people rather than physical objects. The position of nominalism includes the view that it is the labels and names we attach to experiences and events which are crucial. The strongest debate occurs between the two more extreme positions with the sharpest attacks coming from the nominalist end (Cooper and Burrell, 1988; Cooper, 1992). The relativist position, in both science and social science, assumes that different observers may have different viewpoints and that, 'what counts for the truth can vary from place to place and from time to time' (Collins, 1983: 88).

A more recent variant of the relativist position is the idea of 'critical realism' which starts with the realist ontology of Bhaskhar and then incorporates an interpretative thread (Sayer, 2000). Critical realism makes a conscious compromise between the extreme positions: it recognizes social conditions (such as class or wealth) as having real consequences whether or not they are observed and labelled by social scientists; but it also recognizes that concepts are human constructions. There are also differences in the way the quality of types of research should be judged. For example, the representationalist asks whether the research results are an accurate reflection of reality; the relativist will want to ensure that a broad sample of viewpoints has been taken into account; and the nominalist will be interested in where the labels came from and who influenced their acceptance. We will return to this point later when we discuss different forms of 'validity'.

TABLE 3.3 *Ontologies and epistemologies in science and social science*

Ontology of science	**Traditional Realism**	**Internal Realism**	**Relativism**	
Ontology of social science		**Representationalism**	**Relativism**	**Nominalism**
Truth	is established by correspondence between observations and phenomena.	is determined through verification of predictions.	requires consensus between different viewpoints.	depends on who establishes it.
Facts	are concrete.	are concrete, but cannot be accessed directly.	depend on viewpoint of observer.	are all human creations
Epistemology of science	**Positivism**		**Relativism**	
Epistemology of social science		**Positivism**	**Relativism**	**Social Constructionism**

In Table 3.3 we have tried to summarize the overlapping discussion of ontological positions in science and the social sciences, and to indicate a link to epistemological positions – which also overlap in the central positions. The reason why some of the positions have been left blank is that these represent distinctions which are not generally seen as significant within each of the two domains.

The acceptance of a particular epistemology usually leads the researcher to adopt methods that are chacteristic of that position. Conversely, where a given range of methods is employed in a particular study it is possible to infer that the researcher holds, perhaps implicitly, a corresponding epistemology. Table 3.4 summarizes the likely correspondence between the three main epistemologies and methods in the social sciences.

TABLE 3.4 *Methodological implications of different epistemologies within social science*

	Social Science Epistemologies		
	Positivism	**Relativism**	**Social Constructionism**
Elements of Methods			
Aims	Discovery	Exposure	Invention
Starting points	Hypotheses	Suppositions	Meanings
Designs	Experiment	Triangulation	Reflexivity
Techniques	Measurement	Survey	Conversation
Analysis/interpretation	Verification/falsification	Probability	Sense-making
Outcomes	Causality	Correlation	Understanding

We will comment briefly on a few of these concepts since this should help to clarify the epistemological distinctions and their links to ontological positions. And we shall return to a number of them later in the chapter. In both the positivist and relativist positions it is assumed that there is a reality which exists independently of the observer, and hence the job of the scientist is merely to identify, albeit with increasing difficulty, this pre-existing reality. From the positivist perspective this is most readily achieved through the design of experiments in which key factors are measured precisely in order to test predetermined hypotheses. From the relativist position, the assumed difficulty of gaining direct access to 'reality' means that multiple perspectives will normally be adopted, both through 'triangulation' of methods and through surveying viewpoints and experiences of large samples of individuals. Even so, it is only a matter of probability that the views collected will provide an accurate indication of the underlying situation.

The story from the constructionist perspective is different again. In starting from a viewpoint which does not assume any pre-existing reality, the aims of the researcher are to understand how people invent structures to help them make sense of what is going on around them. Consequently, much attention is given to the use of language and conversations between people as they create their own meanings. Furthermore, the recognition that the observer can never be separated from the sense-making process means that researchers are starting to recognize that theories that apply to the subjects of their work must also be relevant to *themselves*. Such reflexive approaches to methodology are recognized as being particularly relevant when studies are considering power and cultural differences (Anderson, 1993; Easterby-Smith and Malina, 1999).

These three philosophical positions are, of course, the 'pure' versions of each paradigm. Although the basic beliefs may be quite incompatible, when one comes down to the actual research methods and techniques used by researchers the differences are by no means so clear and distinct. Moreover, some management researchers deliberately use methods which originate in different paradigms, and there is something of a debate as to whether this is an acceptable strategy. We will come back to this debate later, but in the meantime we shall look at some classic examples of management and organizational research which are widely acknowledged as representing one or other of these points of view. As we shall see, none of them can be considered as completely pure applications of their assumed paradigms.

RESEARCH PHILOSOPHIES UNDERLYING MANAGEMENT RESEARCH PRACTICE

In this section we will review a number of 'classic' research studies which have ostensibly adopted one or other of the three philosophical positions identified for social science research in Tables 3.3 and 3.4. In each case we will consider to what extent the studies have been consistent with the principles of the respective paradigms.

Positivist Studies

The first example of positivist research is the work of Pugh and his colleagues at Aston into organizational structure. From 1961 onwards, the research team conducted a number of major studies of organizations in the West Midlands of England, and in other parts of the world. Their initial, and best-known, study involved a sample of 46 organizations with manufacturing or service operations in Greater Birmingham, each one employing at least 250 people. Organizations were selected to provide a good range of sizes and product types. The researchers used a highly structured interview schedule in order to gather data on a total of 132 measures which characterized the structure and context of each organization. From an analysis of the data across their sample, they were able to come up with a number of general conclusions, for example, that size is the most important determinant of organizational structure, and that organizations which are closely dependent on other organizations tend to centralize as many decisions as possible.

These studies achieved international fame when the results were written up in a series of articles that appeared in *Administrative Science Quarterly*, and which were subsequently collected together in a book (Pugh and Hickson, 1976). Possibly their main significance is the way they highlight the authority structures within organizations as key factors to consider when attempting to change, or understand, organizational behaviour. Pugh (1988) feels that this provides a useful counterbalance to the prevailing emphasis on individual and group-related factors.

In a separate account of the ideas and methods behind this work, Pugh (1983) describes himself as an 'unreconstructed positivist'. The key principles that he applies to his work include: focusing on hard data rather than opinions; looking for regularities in the data obtained; and attempting to produce propositions that can generalize from the specific example to the wider population of organizations. He states his view that facts and values can be clearly separated, a view that would of course be hotly disputed by Habermas; but he also adopts a 'systems' view which attempts to examine the full complexity of the data, rather than simply reducing it to its simplest elements. This latter point is perhaps a modification of the positivist view which has arisen partly as a result of developments in the biological sciences (Von Bertalanffy, 1962), and partly as a result of the ability of modern computers to conduct very sophisticated multivariate analysis of data, provided it is expressed in quantitative terms. Thus Pugh, by his own admission, sticks fairly closely to the positivist paradigm described above, although in his own research programme he also found it necessary to conduct more detailed case studies of individual organizations in the later stages of his research in order to give a fuller understanding of what was taking place inside (Pugh, 1988).

The second example of positivist research is the classic study of Hofstede (1984, 1991) into the effect of national cultures on social and work behaviour. This was based on 116,000 questionnaires completed between 1967 and 1972 by approximately 88,000 employees of IBM. Hofstede's data was totally quantitative and it was processed through a factor analysis to yield four dimensions indicative of national culture:

DIMENSION	FEATURES RESULTING IN A HIGH SCORE:
individualism	whether a society emphasizes individual autonomy as opposed to responsibility to the group;
masculinity	how far roles in society are differentiated between men and women;
power distance	the extent to which inequality is accepted by the less powerful people in society;
uncertainty avoidance	the amount of concern about law and order in a society.

Each of these dimensions was statistically independent in the sense that a high score on one would imply neither a high nor a low score on any of the other dimensions. Hofstede, as the researcher, was also distanced and independent from the respondents of the questionnaires. Thus, in terms of how it is presented, Hofstede's highly quantitative research appears to conform closely to the positivist paradigm.

But in the light of his own account of the research process (Hofstede, 1984), the degree of fit with the positivist paradigm is much less clear. For example, he accepts that he is dealing with mental constructs rather than hard objective facts. The four main dimensions of national culture were not formulated as initial hypotheses, but only after considerable *post hoc* analysis of the data and much reading and discussion with other academic colleagues. The labels attached to the dimensions were his words; they did not emerge through some disembodied process from the data. Third, he is fully aware of the importance of avoiding making assumptions about culture which imply that any one culture is superior to another; and therefore he accepts that his results are not necessarily value-free. Fourth, he recognizes that different methods will provide different perspectives on what is being studied, and therefore it is worth 'triangulating' where possible by using a combination of both quantitative and qualitative methods. Thus, in practice, some of Hofstede's methods show signs of the relativist paradigm.

Relativist Management Research

The first example we offer here comes from a recent international study into Human Resource Management (HRM) practices in 10 different countries for which the authors published a detailed review of the methodology, both as intended and as it worked out in practice (Teagarden et al., 1995). The study was co-ordinated in the USA, but implemented through collaboration with academics based in each of the countries covered by the survey. The main aims were: to identify which HRM practices were most commonly used in a range of companies, countries and industrial sectors; to establish which HRM practices were linked to organizational performance; and to determine to what extent both practices and their effectiveness were situation-specific, or whether there were some universal principles that could be applied. To this end the researchers designed a standard questionnaire which was to be mailed to a random sample of approximately 800 companies in each country. Completed questionnaires were to be returned to the project co-ordinators for analysis and interpretation.

Within this design one can see most of the features of the relativist position as we have characterized it in Table 3.3. It starts with the ontological assumption that there are 'HRM practices' within companies, and that with a bit of ingenuity the researcher will be able to identify and group these practices both within and across countries. Some ingenuity will be required because the HRM practices are not immediately evident, hence the need to conduct surveys across substantial samples of companies in order to be able to describe the typical patterns and to have a good understanding of the likely degrees of variation. There is also the suggestion that correlations will be required in order to establish relations between particular patterns, their assumed outcomes in terms of organizational effectiveness, and a range of contextual variables.

That was how the project was intended to work. In practice, the researchers found that they had to make a number of substantial adjustments to cope with the problems of cross-national empirical research. Translations of the core questionnaire not only had to deal with linguistic equivalence (through using back-translations), but they also had to be adapted for local cultural differences – for example, the German managers felt insulted by the range of salary levels provided from the translation of the US version, and these had to be adapted accordingly. The researchers also found that they could not achieve random sampling of companies because in some countries, such as the UK and Mexico, companies would not respond to anonymous questionnaires. Hence the local contacts had to use their personal networks to obtain responses, which meant that the samples were, by definition, not going to be random.

Teagarden and her colleagues saw these factors as threats to the overall quality of the project, and experienced themselves to be caught in the dilemma of wanting to present the project as a rigorous, positivistic study, and yet recognizing the practical limitations on this aspiration. They question themselves as follows: 'How far can a study deviate from the normal rules of scientific rigour and still make a contribution? Is it advisable to strive for positivistic methods, or should alternative approaches be granted more legitimacy? How can researchers compensate for such disadvantages?' (1995: 1276). Evidently the relativist position can be uncomfortable for researchers, especially when they operate within an academic tradition which gives primacy to positivistic methods.

Another recent study, still within the relativist tradition, but on a smaller scale than the above study is provided by Tsang (1997, 1999). The researcher aimed to discover what and how Singaporean companies learn from direct investments in China (FDIs) and from conducting joint-ventures with Chinese companies (IJVs). His research design involved a sample of 19 Singaporean companies with business experience in China, and he then carried out approximately 80 interviews with both Singaporean and Chinese managers working for these companies. In addition he examined records of meetings and reports of visits by members of these companies whenever he could gain access to them. On the basis of his data he was able to conclude that Singaporean companies rarely learn much from their business links in China, although in most cases there was evidence of considerable transfer of technological and managerial systems to the Chinese partners. He was also able to infer a number of reasons for this one-way traffic. First, most Singaporean managers felt that their systems were superior to those in China, and therefore they did not have much to learn from Chinese partners; second, although managers seconded to the Chinese operations generally learnt a lot during their stay (especially if they were assigned full-time for a substantial period of time) it was hard for them to transfer this learning back to the parent company because no institutional structures were set up for this purpose.

This study has a number of features of the relativist tradition. First, there is an ontological assumption that specific practices and structures exist which will lead to organizational learning taking place, and that it is possible for the researcher to map these out. The methodology involved semi-structured interviews, which meant that, as far as possible, the same questions were asked in each of the interviews. This provided a structured and standardized set of data from which associations between variables could be investigated. There was also a questionnaire which was analysed using probabalistic statistics which was described in the earlier publication but was not mentioned in the later publication (Tsang, 1999). Together it is therefore possible to see a number of methods and viewpoints being used in order to be able to identify and represent, as accurately as possible, the phenomena under investigation. This form of triangulation is another hallmark of a relativist design.

Social Constructionist Management Research

We consider two examples of social constructionist research here, both focusing on what managers do in practice, but separated by a period of over 30 years. The reason for choosing studies that look at the same substantive topic is to show that this general type of research is by no means a new invention, and that nevertheless ideas and methods have evolved significantly over this period. First we will look at the pioneering work of Melville Dalton (1959), and then at the more recent study of Tony Watson (1994).

Dalton conducted an early study into managerial work from the perspective of an insider. This was published as a major book in 1959, and he then followed it up with a paper reviewing his methodology (Dalton, 1964). In the review he describes the ideas and philosophies that guided his work, and discusses some of the ethical dilemmas that were encountered. For a start Dalton rejects the classical 'scientific method' as inappropriate to his work (in this case, the sequence of hypothesis, observation, testing, and confirmation or disconfirmation of hypotheses). He points out that not only is this method rather idealistic in the sense that natural scientists do not usually follow it themselves (except in the school laboratory), but it was also not feasible to use it in the situation he had chosen. He is opposed to the tendency to quantify and to reduce variables to their smallest components on the grounds that this loses most of the real meaning of the situation.

Dalton therefore decided to study the behaviour of managers while he worked in the same organization as a manager. Curiously enough, although he is quite open about his methods and some of the dilemmas this caused, he does not say precisely what his role was, but he remarks that this allowed him 'much unquestioned movement about the firm'. While working in the company he gathered data from his own observations and from those of a number of informants. The informants were clearly aware to some extent of Dalton's purposes, but the rest of the people in the company were largely ignorant of what he was doing – his role was therefore partly overt and partly covert. This clearly meant that he was not in a position to establish any formal experiments to test his ideas, although curiously enough he comments that some of his informants who were aware of his general purpose, occasionally deliberately set up situations for Dalton to observe. Thus in no way was Dalton an independent observer of what was taking place; his presence certainly had some impact on the company, even though the nature of that impact is one of the things about which Dalton does not greatly speculate.

Although much of his data was qualitative, in the form of observations by him and comments from his informants, he was not averse to collecting a certain amount of quantitative data such as that of the salaries of managers in the company. This he obtained informally from a secretary in the personnel department in exchange for counselling about whether or not she should marry her boyfriend (in the end she did marry him, despite Dalton's counselling!).

It is quite clear that Dalton did not start the research with any clearly preconceived set of hypotheses and theories to test; his research grew out of his own 'confusions and irritations'. Rather than trying to formulate explicit hypotheses and guides for his work, he contented himself with framing simple questions about things that were taking place and which he did not clearly understand. After looking at a number of specific topics such as the reasons for conflict between different groups of people or the way people accounted for the success of some managers, he finally settled on the overall scheme of attempting to understand the distinction and relationships between official and unofficial action within the organization.

Dalton was also aware that having looked at only one organization in depth this could limit the generalizability of his conclusions. So he supplemented his work with studies through other contacts in several other organizations in the same area. That at least gave him the confidence that the things he had observed in his own company, Milo, were quite likely to be taking place in most other organizations, at least in that part of the United States.

Dalton follows many of the precepts of the social constructionist paradigm, in the sense that he took an open minded view of what he wanted to find out, and then engaged in extensive conversations with people backed up by observations and access to documents. Most importantly he was trying to make sense of what he had observed and to link this to existing theories, such as the distinction between the formal and informal organization. However there are a number of subtle differences between Dalton and the more recent study of managerial behaviour conducted by Tony Watson (1994), which we will describe below.

Watson starts by acknowledging his debt to Dalton, but his study is also useful for us since it gives an indication of how this kind of research has progressed in the intervening period of over 30 years. Watson entered his host company, ZTC Ryland, overtly as an academic researcher, although he also agreed to conduct a project for his sponsors at the same time. He thus had a mixed agenda, which was reasonably explicit. The official project was to develop a listing of competencies required of managers who would be able to function effectively in the new business environment in which the company was operating. Unofficially he was interested in several things including the impact of modern management theory on a company which had gone to considerable lengths to introduce topical ideas like total quality management, team working, performance, related pay, etc.

His book differs from Dalton's in several ways, particularly in the degree of reflexivity that he offers about his motives and methods. Here he is influenced by ideas from ethnography, and comments on the importance of 'reveal(ing) the hand behind the text' (Watson, 1994: 7). This is done by offering portions of transcripts which show his contribution to discussions, which demonstrate his personal relationship with informants, and which occasionally discuss explicitly why informants give him stories that are different to those offered to their bosses. This enables him to develop theoretical observations about the differences between 'official' and 'unofficial' discourses in the company, and the way that exchanges are strategically shaped. Also, in constrast to Dalton he does not seek additional sites for his observations, recognizing the distinction that has arisen between theoretical and empirical generalizations.

Mixed Methods and Philosophies

The above studies were selected as relatively pure examples, but as we have shown, in practice the researchers involved do not hold scrupulously to any single approach. Although the distinction between paradigms may be very clear at the philosophical level, as Burrell and Morgan (1979) argue, when it comes to the choice of specific methods, and to the issues of research design, the distinction breaks down (Bulmer, 1988; Punch 1986). Increasingly, authors and researchers who work in organizations and with managers argue that one should attempt to mix methods to some extent, because it provides more perspectives on the phenomena being investigated. Fielding and Fielding (1986), advocate the use of both quantitative and qualitative methods, and provide examples of how they have been able to combine these different forms of data to good effect in researching organizations such as the National Front in Britain.

The examples they give, however, show how to combine quantitative and qualitative data where the overall direction and significance of the two sources are fairly similar. A problem they do not confront is what to do when different kinds of data say contradictory things about the same phenomena. This problem was encountered by Morgan Tanton and Mark (personal communication) in a comparative evaluation study of two executive management programmes (courses A and B), held in two different business schools (respectively, Institutions A and B). Observations during the course and qualitative data obtained from follow-up interviews showed quite clearly that Course A was superior to Course B, but the quantitative data in the form of student ratings about the two courses showed to a high level of significance that Course B was preferred to Course A. Was this discrepancy caused by the methods used, or could it highlight some unusual features of the two courses being examined? It seemed that the best way to tackle the dilemma was to show the discrepancy to some later course participants and ask whether they had any explanations.

Two reasons emerged as most probable. First, participants commented that they tended to be rather cautious when filling in multiple choice rating forms, because they could never be sure what the data would be used for; therefore, they usually avoided extreme responses in either direction. Second, it seemed that the course designs and institutional settings affected the criteria that participants used for evaluating the two courses. In Institution A the emphasis was on the longer term application of what had been learnt; in Institution B the emphasis was on the immediate quality of sessions conducted within the classroom. Thus it was not surprising that the rating forms which were completed at the end of the course showed one pattern; whereas follow-up interviews conducted some months later showed another pattern. Ironically, it was only through talking further to some of the participants (i.e. through using a qualitative method) that we were able to come up with a satisfactory explanation of the discrepancy.

There are two morals from this story. First, be wary of mixing methods simply for the sake of getting a slightly richer picture, because they may lead to contradictions and confusions. Second, remember that the reality of what is being investigated may be considerably more complex than the data collection methods are capable of demonstrating.

Before we leave the discussion of how paradigms may underlie practical examples, it is worth summarizing from a pragmatic view what are seen as some of the strengths and weaknesses of each position. This should help the researcher to choose which methods and aspects are most likely to be of help in a given situation. In the case of quantitative methods and the *positivist* paradigm, the main strengths are that they can provide wide coverage of the range of situations, they can be fast and economical and, particularly when statistics are aggregated from large samples, they may be of considerable relevance to policy decisions. On the debit side, these methods tend to be rather inflexible and artificial; they are not very effective in understanding processes or the significance that people attach to actions; they are not very helpful in generating theories; and because they focus on what is, or what has been recently, they make it hard for the policy-maker to infer what changes and actions should take place in the future. As Legge (1984) points out, they may only provide illusions of the 'true' impact of social policies. Most of the data gathered will not be relevant to real decisions although it may be used to support the covert goals of decision makers.

The strengths and weaknesses of the *social constructionist* paradigm and associated qualitative methods are fairly complementary. Thus they have strengths in their ability to look at how change processes over time, to understand people's meanings, to adjust to new issues and ideas as they emerge, and to contribute to the evolution of new theories. They also provide a way of gathering data which is seen as natural rather than artificial. There are, of course, weaknesses. Data collection can take up a great deal of time and resources, and the analysis and interpretation of data may be very difficult, and this depends on the intimate, tacit knowledge of the researchers. Qualitative studies often feel very untidy because it is harder to control their pace, progress, and end points. And there is also the problem that many people, especially policy-makers, may give low credibility to studies based on apparently 'subjective' opinions.

It is tempting, then, to see the relativist position as a useful compromise which can combine the strengths, and avoid the limitations, of each. But life is not that simple: the *relativist* position is distinct and has its own strengths and weaknesses. The main strengths are that: it accepts the value of using multiple sources of data and perspectives; it enables generalizations to be made beyond the boundaries of the situation under study; and it can be conducted efficiently, for example, through outsourcing any survey work to specialized agencies. The weaknesses are that: large samples are required if results are to have credibility, and this may be costly; the requirement for standardization means it may not be able to deal effectively with the cultural and institutional differences found within international studies; and it may be hard to reconcile discrepant sources of data which point to different conclusions.

RESEARCH DESIGN: SOME CHOICES

As suggested at the start of this chapter, research designs are about organizing research activity, including the collection of data, in ways that are most likely to achieve the research aims. There are many potential choices to make when developing a research design, and there are few algorithms which can guide the researcher into making the ideal choices for a particular situation. However, many of these choices are allied quite closely to different philosophical positions, and an awareness of this can at least ensure that the different elements of a research design are consistent with each other.

In this section we shall describe six choices that are of particular significance. The first five relate fairly closely to the basic dichotomy between the use of positivist and social constructionist approaches; the last is a debate located mainly within the positivist paradigm, but it also has more widespread implications for the way people approach management research. These six choices are listed in Table 3.5 and are then discussed below in more detail.

TABLE 3.5 *Key choices of research design*

Researcher is independent	vs	Researcher is involved
Large samples	vs	Small numbers
Testing theories	vs	Generating theories
Experimental design	vs	Fieldwork methods
Universal theory	vs	Local knowledge
Verification	vs	Falsification

Independence or Involvement of the Researcher?

The first choice is around whether the researcher should remain distanced from, or get involved with, the material that is being researched. Clearly this choice stems from one's philosophical view about whether or not it is possible for the observer to remain independent from the phenomena being observed. The traditional assumption in science is that the researcher must maintain complete independence if there is to be any validity in the results produced. Although, as we have noted above, it has recently become evident in areas such as nuclear physics that this ideal is not always possible.

In social sciences, where claims of the researcher's independence are harder to sustain, there are those who have tried to turn this apparent 'problem' into a virtue. This is the tradition of *action research* which, as we have explained in Chapter 1, assumes that social phenomena are continually changing rather than static. Action research, and the researcher, are then seen as part of this change process itself. The following two features are normally part of action research projects:

1 a belief that the best way of learning about an organization or social system is through attempting to change it, and this therefore should to some extent be the objective of the action researcher;

2 the belief that those people most likely to be affected by, or involved in implementing, these changes should as far as possible become involved in the research process itself.

Although it is possible to conduct action research in a positivist way, for example by attempting to change the organization from the outside and then measuring the results, in most respects it derives from ideas that are alien to positivism. Many people schooled in positivist research methods are sceptical about the value of action research, but as Susman and Evered (1978) point out, action research is *bound* to be found wanting if it is measured against the criteria of positivist science; whereas it is perfectly justifiable from the viewpoint of other philosophies, such as social constructionism.

The involvement of the researcher is taken a stage further in what has come to be known as *co-operative inquiry* (Reason, 1988; Heron, 1996). This has been developed for researching human action more at an individual, rather than at collective or organizational levels. It adopts as a starting point the idea that all people have, at least latently, the ability to be self-directing, to choose how they will act and to give meaning to their own experiences. It rejects traditional positivist methods where people are studied as if they were objects under the influence of external forces. Co-operative inquiry not only focuses on the experiences and explanations of the individuals concerned, it also involves them in deciding in the first place what questions and issues are worth researching. Thus the 'subjects' become partners in the research process.

Large or Small Samples?

A second design choice is whether one attempts to sample across a large number of organizations or situations, or whether one focuses on a small number of situations and attempts to investigate them intensively, possibly over a period of time. An important concept here is the *unit of analysis*, which is the entity that forms the basis of any sample. Thus, samples may be formed from any of the following: countries, cultures, races, industrial sectors, organizations, departments, families, groups, individuals, incidents, stories, accidents, inventions, etc. In general, research adds power to everyday observations due to the rigour and focus which is brought to bear on a particular aspect of social or organizational life. Any single study will need to be conceptualized around a single unit of analysis, and it is important for the researcher to clarify whether he or she is basically interested in phenomena at the level, for example, of organizations, groups or individuals. Once the level of analysis has been clarified, then the next issue is whether to sample widely, or whether to go for depth.

Studies that sample widely are often known as cross-sectional surveys in the sense that they usually involve selecting different organizations, or units, in different contexts, and investigating how other factors vary across these units. For example, Lyles and Salk (1996) were interested in the conditions that led to greater transfer of knowledge from foreign parents into international joint ventures. So they selected a sample of 201 joint ventures that were regarded as small or medium-sized across four manufacturing industries in Hungary. Through comparing indicators of performance across the whole sample, they were able to conclude first, that there was a strong link between knowledge transfer and performance, and second that this transfer was most likely to take place when the foreign and domestic parents had equal (50/50) equity stakes in the new venture. This sample size was sufficient for them to demonstrate that the results were statistically significant, but one of the key problems for researchers using cross-sectional designs is knowing how large the sample needs to be in order to be adequately representative. This is discussed further in Chapter 6, which considers the use of quantitative methods.

Cross-sectional designs, particularly where they use questionnaires and survey techniques, belong either to the relativist or positivist traditions. As we have noted earlier they have undoubted strengths in their ability economically to describe features of large numbers of people or organizations. But a major limitation is that they find it hard to explain *why* the observed patterns are there. Thus, although Lyles and Salk were confident that balanced equity stakes led to the highest chance of knowledge transfer their study itself could not explain what mechanisms or processes led to knowledge being transferred. This kind of question can only be answered by looking in depth within the organization. One study that attempts to answer this question is currently ongoing (Easterby-Smith and Wu, 2000), and looks at the processes within a single joint venture which aid or impede the transfer of knowledge. From interviewing a number of managers within this company over a period of several years it is possible to understand how contextual variables such as culture and social identity have an impact on knowledge transfer. It is also evident that external measures such as relative equity stakes may not be a good guide to the power balance because other factors such as control over R&D, or strategic business contacts, or local influence over the labour market may be of greater significance. Another study recently carried out within an Australian research organization (Andrews and Delahaye, 2000) has shown how the quality of relationships can affect the exchanges of knowledge/information between individuals. In brief, it was found that people were only willing to share information with others if they trusted them; but they sought information, not from people whom they trusted, but from people whose scientific expertise they respected.

A couple of points are important about these in-depth studies. First, they are based on direct observation and personal contacts, generally through interviews. Second, they take place within single organizations, but then involve sampling from numbers of individuals. Third, the collection of data takes place over a period of time and may include both live observations and retrospective accounts of what has happened. Thus the unit of analysis is either the individual, or specific events such as the exchange of a piece of knowledge, or strategies employed to transfer or retain control of knowledge.

So there are some similarities between apparently in-depth and cross-sectional studies in that they all look at multiple instances, but that the level of unit of analysis is 'higher' in the case of the latter types. Even still, the number of observations will differ between the two types since cross-sectional studies will typically require hundreds of instances, whereas in-depth studies may only require tens of observations. The reason why different sizes of sample are appropriate is linked to the processes of generalization which employ different forms of logic for positivist and constructionist research, as will be explained below.

Theory or Data First?

The third choice is about which should come first: the theory or the data? Again this represents the split between the positivist and constructionist paradigms in relation to how the researcher should go about his or her work. In the latter case there is the approach known as *grounded theory*, which was first formulated in a classic book by Glaser and Strauss (1967).

These authors see the key task of the researcher as being to develop theory through 'comparative method'. This means looking at the same event or process in different settings or situations. For example, the researcher might be interested in the workings of appraisal interviews and would therefore study a number of interviews handled by different managers, in different departments, or in different organizations. As a result of the studies it might be noticed that most appraisal interviews either focus on reviewing performance in relation to last year's objectives, or they focus on future goals and how the subordinate may be helped to achieve these. They might then be labelled as 'judgemental' or 'developmental' interviews, and the distinction would represent a *substantive theory* about appraisal interviews.

However the theorizing could be taken further. For example it might be observed that neither form of interview has much effect on the individual's performance nor on the relationships between the managers and their subordinates. Thus one might conclude that both forms of interview are simply organizational rituals which have the function of demonstrating and reinforcing hierarchical power relations. This would be the beginning of a more generalized *formal theory* about power and organizational rituals. Glaser and Strauss consider both kinds of theory to be valuable, and they propose two main criteria for evaluating the quality of a theory. First, it should be sufficiently *analytic* to enable some generalization to take place, but at the same time it should be possible for people to relate the theory to their own experiences, thus *sensitizing* their own perceptions.

It is important to note that 'I'm doing grounded theory', should not be used as a justification for doing some vaguely qualitative research without any clear view of where it is supposed to lead. Grounded theory contains precisely articulated methods and presuppositions. The problem is, as Locke (1997) explains, that methods have evolved and developed since their initial exposition, and at the heart of this is a rather acrimonious debate between Barney Glaser and Anselm Strauss. In essence, Glaser now believes that researchers should start with no pre-suppositions, and should allow ideas to 'emerge' from the data (Glaser, 1978, 1992); whereas Strauss recommends familiarizing oneself with prior research and using structured, and somewhat mechanistic, processes to make sense of the data (Strauss, 1987; Strauss and Corbin, 1998). The implication for the researcher is that he should now be aware of the major contemporary variants of grounded theory and be able to explain to what extent he adheres to one or other view. A further problem is that the methods of grounded theory have been developed mainly within educational and health settings where the 'white coat brigade' can have relatively easy and flexible access to data and cases; but research within managed organizations means that access is far more difficult and therefore some of the assumptions of grounded theory have to be amended further to deal with this kind of situation (Locke, 2001) .

The Straussian view of grounded theory assumes that pre-conceptions are inevitable. After all, it seems common sense to assume that someone will not be interested in a research topic or setting without knowing something in advance about it. Hence he argues that the researcher should make herself aware of previous work conducted in the general field of research before starting to generate her own theory. This might be seen as a small move in the direction of the approach within positivist social science which assumes that one should start with a theory, or hypothesis, about the nature of the world, and then seek data that will confirm or disconfirm that theory. Thus, continuing with the above example, one might hypothesize that the prevalence of 'judgemental' or 'developmental' appraisal interviews depends on the personality of the boss, and that 'authoritarian' bosses will be more likely to conduct interviews in a judgemental manner. To test this hypothesis one needs to classify the bosses according to their authoritarian tendencies and to classify the appraisal interviews by type. If the data shows that most of the authoritarian bosses do indeed hold judgemental interviews then this will support the initial hypothesis. (We discuss in Chapter 6 methods and problems in interpreting statistical data such as this.)

The main practical advantage of the hypothesis-testing approach described above is that there is initial clarity about what is to be investigated, and hence information can be collected speedily and efficiently. Clarity of method means that it is easier for another researcher to replicate the study, and hence any claims arising from the research can be subjected to public scrutiny. The disadvantages are that its contribution may be quite trivial: confirming what is already known. And if the results are inconclusive or negative, the approach can give little guidance on why this is so. By contrast, the grounded approach is flexible and is good at providing both explanations and new insights. However it may take more time, and researchers often have to live with the fear that nothing of interest will emerge from the work. Some people regard grounded theory to be suspect because of the lack of clarity and standardization of methods, but that concern stems largely from a positivist perspective on the importance of 'finding the truth'.

Experimental Designs or Fieldwork

Experiments are one of the key elements of scientific method, although they are not necessarily an essential item of positivist methods. Classic experimental method involves assigning subjects *at random* to either an experimental or a control group. Conditions for the experimental group are then manipulated by the experimenter in order to assess their effect in comparison with members of the control group who are receiving no unusual conditions. In studies of social and human life, such experiments still remain quite popular amongst psychologists, particularly where there is a ready supply of undergraduate students upon whom to conduct the experiments. They are very much harder to conduct within real organizations, or where one does not have a captive population from which to draw volunteers. Occasionally, if one is as lucky as Melville Dalton (1964) was, the researcher might find people who are prepared to set up small artificial experiments for them when they are studying within organizations, but this is obviously a rarity.

Some researchers still working from within the positivist paradigm recognised the practical difficulties of producing pure experimental designs, and thus the idea of *quasi-experimental* designs was developed. The classic exposition of this is given by Campbell and Stanley (1963), where they evaluate a range of designs which make use of multiple measures over time in order to reduce the effects of control and experimental groups not being fully matched. One of the most common methods is the 'pre-test/post-test comparison design'. For example, the effects of a course on a group of managers might be evaluated by measuring the managers' knowledge or attitudes before and after the course, and by comparing the differences with those from a similar group of managers who did not attend the course but who completed identical tests at the same times.

This design is illustrated in Figure 3.1; but the problems of using it in real organizations are substantial. For example the design assumes that 'nothing' happens to the control group during the period that the treatment (course attendance) is being given to the experimental group. This is a naive assumption as Mark found when attempting to evaluate a project-based management development programme held at Durham University Business School (Easterby-Smith and Ashton, 1975). While the 'chosen few' were away on the course several members of the control group seized the opportunity to improve relationships with their bosses and strengthen their political standing in the

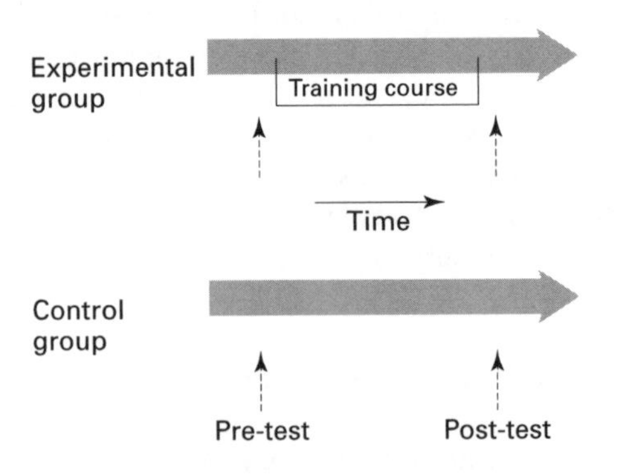

FIGURE 3.1 Quasi-experimental research design

company, thus effectively shutting out a number of managers who had attended the course.

The approach that stands in direct contrast to experimental and quasi-experimental designs is *fieldwork*, which is the study of real organizations or social settings. This may involve the use of positivist methods which use quantitative techniques, or it can be much more open-ended and constructionist. One of the distinctive research styles in the latter case is *ethnography*. Here the researcher tries to immerse him or herself in a setting and to become part of the group under study in order to understand the meanings and significances that people put upon the behaviour of themselves and others.

Most outsiders who are new to an organization or group will encounter things that they do not understand. These are what Agar (1986) calls 'breakdowns': events or situations where the researcher's past experience gives him no help in understanding what is going on. This breakdown therefore represents something unique about that organization, and previously unknown to the researcher. For example, most groups have 'in-jokes', based on experiences shared only by members of the group. In order for an outsider to make sense of the breakdown provided by an in-joke it will be necessary to track back to the original experiences. The breakdown provides a kind of window into exploring aspects of the experiences and meaning systems of groups and organizations. It will only be possible to resolve the breakdown when the researcher has understood these meaning systems. In this way the ethnographer is able to extend conventional wisdom, and to generate new insights into human behaviour.

Recent developments in organizational research have led to a wide range of designs, some of which extend the range of fieldwork methods, and others which provide intermediate positions between the two extremes. A group which goes under the general label of *case study* methods occupy an intermediate position. Robert Yin is probably the best known exponent of this approach (Yin, 1993, 1994), but others have also made significant contributions including Stake (1995), Eisenhardt (1989) and Hamel et al. (1993). Essentially the case study looks in depth at one, or a small number, of organizations generally over time. One example would be the longitudinal study of Organization Development within ICI during the 1970s and early 1980s, where the researcher stresses the importance of understanding both contextual and historical settings (Pettigrew, 1985). Another would be the comparative study of investment decisions in Chinese and UK companies (Lu and Heard, 1995) in which case studies of 16 decisions in 8 companies were compared and contrasted in order to establish the cultural and institutional variations in business decision-making between China and the UK. The latter study, in particular, collected both qualitative and quantitative data, and this is one of the features that distinguishes it from purely qualitative or grounded research. Yin (1994) is also at pains to demonstrate that case studies may contain the same degree of validity as more positivist studies and therefore his exposition of the method contains both rigour and the application of careful logic about comparisons. Hence it is in some senses quite similar to quasi-experimental methods. In contrast, Stake (1995) sees case method being much closer to action research: he is less concerned with issues of validity and more concerned with the potential for the researcher to aid change within the research setting.

A second group go under the label of *narrative* methods (Boje, 1995, 2001; Czarniawska, 1998; Hatch, 1996). These contain both an ontological spin, which is the view that the verbal medium is crucial to understanding behaviour within organizations, and hence the researchers should pay particular attention to collecting stories about what takes place. This may involve participant observation, or simply asking people for the stories that they have heard about particular events. In essence, the method relies on literary theory (Hatch, 1996) and hence both the position of the narrator and the role of the analyst are very important.

Universal Theory or Local Knowledge?

One of the key requirements of positivist methods is that for any research or knowledge to be useful it should have *universal* validity. Thus, Newton's Laws of Motion will have equal validity whether applied in New York, Bogota or Xi'an. If they do not apply in the same way everywhere then there should be a clear way of understanding how they vary in different circumstances. Thus Einstein was able to explain why, under certain circumstances, Newton's Laws appear not to work, and his Theory of Relativity is able to account for variations in these Laws and predict the behaviour of bodies when they are moving at relative velocities near to the speed of light. Within studies of management and organization, the aim is similarly to identify regularities in the pattern of organizations that have some kind of universal validity. Thus the Aston studies, which have been described earlier in this chapter, sought to identify general rules between organizational structure and other variables such as size. Similarly Hofstede (1984) attempts to develop a universal set of principles against which any culture can be measured – in the hope that this will provide a basis for predicting the behaviour of individuals and organizations in almost any country.

The contrasting position assumes that attempts to develop generalized theories may result in frameworks being forced inappropriately on others. The most obvious examples come from post-colonial theory, which claims that many theories of race, economic development and culture are constructs of scholars in Western countries which typically cast non-Western culture and institutions as being somehow inferior to their own (Said, 1978). Similarly, from feminist theory there is a strong view that many of the dominant theories of social behaviour are blind to the effects of gender and patriarchy which may have far greater significance (Ahmed, 1998). In both cases the argument is that any generalized statement about the social world is likely to contain within it assumptions which mask relations of power between those who formulate theories and those to whom they are applied. This is itself a generalized statement, which in a purely logical sense, detracts from the power of their arguments. Nevertheless, it links to a wider movement which claims that significant social theory should be understood in relation to the context whence it is derived.

There are two other variants of the case for local knowledge which have particular relevance to management and organizational research. First, is the view that the practical knowledge used by managers when going about their work is essentially contextually bound, and that it is learnt through engaging in practice (Brown and Duguid, 1991; Cook and Brown, 1999). If this is the case then it follows that for research to have theoretical value it should focus on these local practices – which may well be unique to that situation. This is the ontological variety. Second, is the idea that managerial behaviour is culturally relative, and that these cultures can be seen as both national and organizational cultures (Boyacigiller and Adler, 1991). Hence researchers should formulate their ideas separately within each cultural context, and should not try to generalize across cultures. For example, there is a growing literature on 'transitional economies' and one of the key areas of interest in these cases is in privatization processes. But there are two main groups of literature on transitional economies, one dealing with Eastern European countries and the other dealing with China. Although there are superficial similarities in context, in that they were all in centrally planned economies, there are much deeper differences between China and Eastern Europe which mean that both the issues and the ideal procedures are very different in the two cases. Moreover, as Nor (2000) found out, theories of privatization drawn either from transitional economies, or from Western countries such as the UK are largely irrelevant to a country like Malaysia which has its own unique cultural, political and institutional circumstances. This is the pragmatic variety. Common to these views is the point that generalizable knowledge always privileges the more powerful over the less powerful actors, and hence one should try to focus on the local actors' meanings, symbols and values. Naturally this perspective would include the examples of feminist and post-colonial research given above, and falls most neatly under the heading of critical management research (Alvesson and Deetz, 2000).

Verification or Falsification

As indicated at the start of this section, this final choice is slightly different from the five preceding ones in that it is not linked to resolving the broader debate between positivist and constructionist views. But it is very important both for researchers and for managers, as we will explain below. The distinction between *verification* and *falsification* was made by Karl Popper (1959) as a way of dealing with what has become known as Hume's 'problem of induction'. This is the philosophical problem that, however much data one obtains in support of a scientific theory it is not possible to reach a conclusive proof of the truth of that law. Popper's way out of this problem is to suggest that instead of looking for confirmatory evidence one should always look for evidence that will *disconfirm* one's hypothesis or existing view. This means that theories should be formulated in a way that will make them most easily exposed to possible refutation. The advantage then is that one only needs one instance of refutation to falsify a theory; whereas irrespective of the number of confirmations of the theory it will never be conclusively proven.

The example often given to illustrate this approach takes as a start the assertion that: 'all swans are white'. If one takes the verification route, the (non-Australian) researcher would start travelling around the country accumulating sightings of swans, and provided that he or she did not go near a zoo, a very high number of white sightings would eventually be obtained, and presumably no black sightings. This gives a lot of confidence to the assertion that all swans are white, but still does not conclusively prove the statement. If, on the other hand, one takes a falsification view, one would start to search for swans that are *not* white, deliberately looking for contexts and locations where one might encounter non-white swans. Thus, our intrepid researcher might head straight for a zoo, or perhaps book a flight to Australia where most swans happen to be black. On making this discovery, the initial hypothesis would be falsified, and it might then have to be modified to include the idea that 'all swans have either white or black feathers'. This statement has still what Popper calls high 'informative' content because it is expressed in a way that can easily be disproved; whereas a statement like 'all swans are large birds' would not be sufficiently precise to allow easy refutation.

Much of the debate about verification and falsification fits within the positivist view because ideas of 'truth' and 'proof' are associated mainly with that paradigm. But there are also important lessons that the constructionist might take from this discussion. For example, Alvesson and Deetz (2000) advise 'critical sensitivity', and Reason (1988) advocates 'critical subjectivity', which involves recognizing one's own views and experiences, but not allowing oneself to be overwhelmed and swept along by them. If the idea of falsification is to be applied more fully to constructionist research then one should look for evidence that might confirm or contradict what one currently believes to be true. This advice not only applies to researchers but also to managers who are concerned to investigate and understand what is taking place within their own organizations. Most managers are strongly tempted to look for evidence which supports the currently held views of the world. This is not surprising if they are responsible for formulating strategies and policies within a context that is very uncertain, and hence they will be looking for evidence that demonstrates that their strategies were correct. The logical position that follows from the above argument is that, even if *disconfirmatory* evidence is unpopular, it is certainly both more efficient and more informative than confirmatory evidence. Moreover, if managers adopt the falsification strategy and fail to come up with evidence that disconfirms their current views, then they will be able to have far more confidence in their present positions.

BUT HOW DO WE KNOW THAT IT IS VALID?

There is an underlying anxiety amongst researchers of all persuasions that the research will not stand up to outside scrutiny. This is very understandable since research papers and theses are most likely to be attacked on methodological grounds, and one of the key claims of 'research' is that it is somehow more believable than common everyday observations.

The technical language for examining this problem includes terms such as validity, reliability and generalizability. It should be no surprise by this stage to realize that the meaning of these terms varies considerably with the philosophical viewpoint adopted. Table 3.6 summarizes some of the differences between positivist, relativist and constructionist viewpoints.

TABLE 3.6 *Perspectives on validity, reliability and generalizability*

	Viewpoint		
	Positivist	**Relativist**	**Constructionist**
Validity	Do the measures correspond closely to reality?	Have a sufficient number of perspectives been included?	Does the study clearly gain access to the experiences of those in the research setting.
Reliability	Will the measures yield the same results on other occasions?	Will similar observations be reached by other observers?	Is there transparency in how sense was made from the raw data?
Generalizability	To what extent does the study confirm or contradict existing findings in the same field?	What is the probability that patterns observed in the sample will be repeated in the general population?	Do the concepts and constructs derived from this study have any relevance to other settings?

As Kirk and Miller (1986) point out, the language of validity and reliability was originally developed for use in quantitative social science, and many procedures have been devised for assessing different facets of each. Classic text books on methodology distinguish between three main kinds of validity: construct, internal and external validity. The former asks whether the instruments are accurate measures of reality; the second asks whether the research design is capable of eliminating bias and the effect of extraneous variables, and the third involves defining the domains to which the results of the study may be generalized. In Table 3.6 our definition of validity is similar to the concept of construct validity, and the notion of generalizability is similar to the traditional definition of external validity.

Text books have less frequently addressed the issues of validity in relation to the 'relativist' position, as we have defined it here. But it is still an important issue within this perspective because it still operates from a realist ontology – and therefore is concerned with issues of whether the research procedures can provide an accurate representation of reality. Robert Yin (1994) appears to operate from a realist ontology when he defends case method against attacks, specifically in relation to the three forms of validity mentioned above. A key suggestion for dealing with construct validity is to use multiple sources of evidence; for internal validity he stresses the importance of building cases over time in order to eliminate alternative explanations: and for external validity he points out that case studies rely on analytic rather than statistical generalizations. In the first two instances he is aligned with the relativist position, although in the third instance he moves towards the contructionist position.

There has been some reluctance to apply ideas of validity and reliability to interpretative and social constructionist research, because they might imply acceptance of one absolute (positivist) reality. However, as qualitative methods become increasingly mainstream, there is growing realization of their importance – because constructionist research must develop the power to convince examiners, professionals and the wider public that their results should be taken seriously.

David Silverman (2000) believes that qualitative methods in general are in danger of being dismissed as undisciplined journalism because there are few safeguards to prevent researchers from picking evidence out of the mass of data to support their particular prejudices. In defence against this kind of 'anecdotalism' he suggests several principles, including the following: refutability, constant comparison, comprehensive data treatment and tabulations. Refutability is a matter of using Popperian logic and looking for examples which might disconfirm current beliefs; constant comparison follows the principles of grounded theory in looking for new cases and settings which will stretch the current theory; comprehensive data treatment involves carrying out an initial analysis of all of the data available before coming up with conclusions; and tabulations imply greater rigour in organizing data, and accepting that it can also be useful to add up the occurrence of phenomena sometimes.

Whatever the strategies finally adopted, we consider that the results of constructionist research should be believable, and they should be reached through methods that are transparent. Thus it is very important for the researcher to explain how she gained access to the particular organization, what processes led to the selection of informants, how data was recorded, what processes were used to summarize or collate it, how the data became transformed into tentative ideas and explanations, and so on. These are the procedures that will be considered more fully in Chapter 6.

DRAWING THE THREADS TOGETHER, OR MAPPING RESEARCH DESIGNS

In this chapter we have covered a wide range of methods, issues and concepts. Our presentation has tried to follow a coherent logic and holistic logic because so many of the issues are so closely intertwined that it seemed wrong to treat them separately. We have therefore avoided, up to now, what one might call a taxonomic approach to discussing philosophies and research design. However, in this final section we will try to summarize most of the positions we have described through a mapping exercise. Like all good management theories, our map has two dimensions. The first dimension is the key ontological difference between realism and nominalism. This is a fundamental divide, even if, as we have noted, there are many intermediate positions. The second dimension corresponds to the first of the choices we have described in the preceding section of the chapter: it refers to the style, or the role, of the researcher which can vary from independence from, to involvement with, the subject(s) of the research.

We have sometimes used the analogy of fictional detective work to symbolize the differences in research designs that can be depicted by the resulting matrix (see Figure 3.2). For this analogy we have to thank Gummesson (1988). In this instance we might contrast the scientific approach of Sherlock Holmes with the more intuitive style of the Agatha Christie character Miss Marple. Whereas Holmes relies on detailed observation of evidence, and a process of logical deduction about the circumstances of the crime; Miss Marple operates as an insider to the scene of the crime and depends on her intuitive 'feel' about the crime and potential suspects. Thus Holmes is typically portrayed as representing the positivist side, and Miss Marple represents the constructionist, the ethnographer who operates from the inside. More recently, the central characters in the *X-Files* have been designed to represent precisely this tension, although the stereotype is reversed, because it is the man who is sensitive and intuitive, while the woman is the cold analytic scientist. Perhaps the continuing difficulty for the two characters in forming any more than a professional relationship, indicates the problems of those who would like to see positivism and constructionism as bedfellows.

It is also possible to identify characters who personify the vertical dimension in Figure 3.2. Thus, the other famous Agatha Christie character, Hercule Poirot

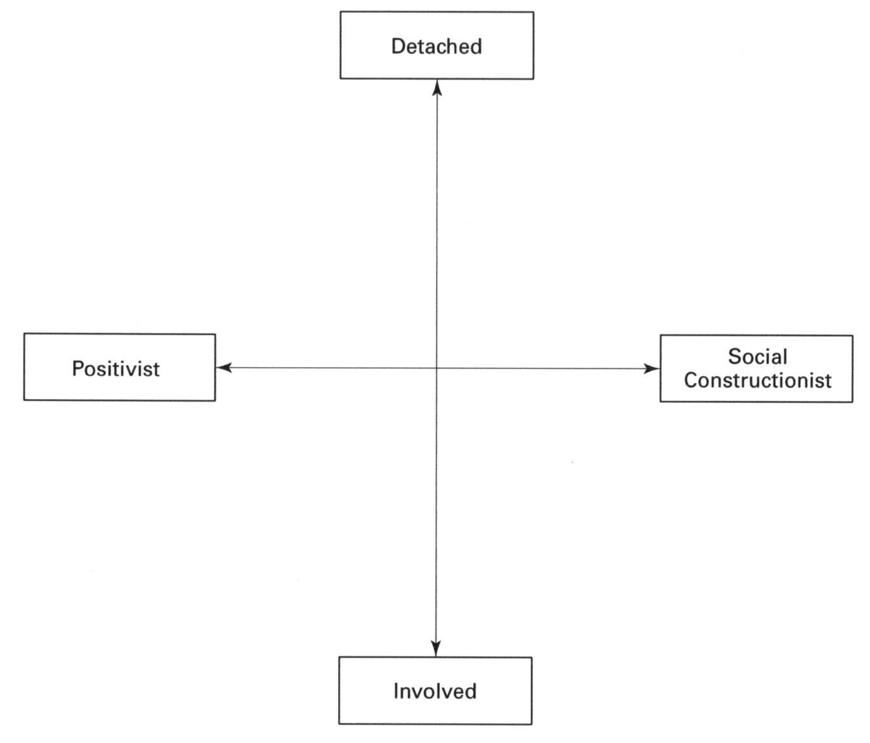

FIGURE 3.2 Matrix of research philosophies

is a classic example of the detective who is totally untouched and unruffled by the mayhem that inevitably surrounds his progress through high society. His only concern is his apparent inability to solve the crime immediately, although it is his superior intellect, those 'little grey cells' that always enable him to get there in the end (and well before Inspector Lestrade). Poirot stands in sharp constrast to many of the Hollywood detectives who operate very close to the world of the criminals they hunt, and who regularly end up engaged in violent exchanges with their quarries. Clint Eastwood's portrayal of Dirty Harry would be one such example, and Cagney and Lacey would be an example of an action-packed pair who prefer to shoot first and ask questions later.

Now we would like to suggest a little exercise aimed at drawing together the various threads that have been considered in this chapter. The task is for you, the reader, to map as many as possible of the buzz words we have used this far onto the matrix above. Overleaf we provide our view of the answers – although we would emphasis, as dedicated social constructionists that this is merely our interpretation of where things fit. You may feel that your classifications are better – which is fine with us, provided you are clear about why this is so. The list of possible research styles and buzz words is given below in Table 3.7.

TABLE 3.7 *Some typical research designs*

1	Action research	8	Grounded theory (Glaser)
2	Case method (Yin)	9	Grounded theory (Strauss)
3	Case method (Stake)	10	Narrative methods
4	Co-operative inquiry	11	Quasi-experimental design
5	Critical inquiry	12	Participant observation
6	Ethnography	13	Survey research
7	Experimental design	14	Survey feedback

We have not included everything because we couldn't fit them all onto the map, but we hope this provides a start for discussion and active reflection. One positioning that may seem a bit odd is the way experimental design has been located below quasi-experimental design. The reason for this is that social science experiments are normally rather interventionist in that they require setting up separate groups, the introduction of artificial treatments, and so on. These are very difficult to arrange when there is not a ready supply of psychology undergraduates available, and virtually impossible within managed organizations. On the other hand quasi-experimental methods try to make more use of naturally occurring groups and events and hence we have classified the role of the researcher as less involved in these cases.

CONCLUSIONS

In this chapter we have discussed some of the key philosophical debates underlying research methods in the social sciences, and we have looked at the

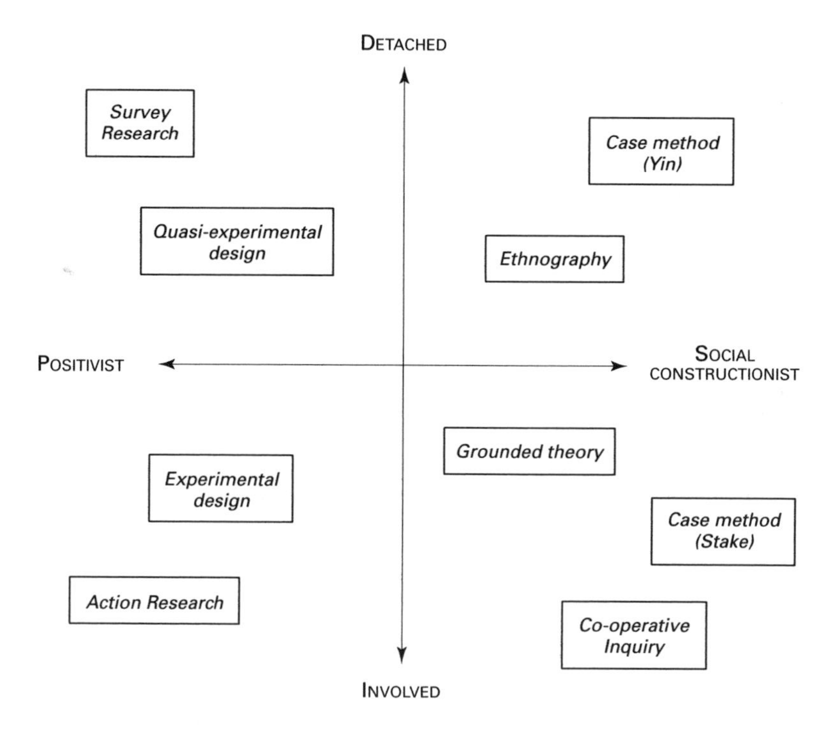

FIGURE 3.3 Matrix of research designs

implications these have for the design of management research. Although there is a clear dichotomy between the positivist and social constructionist world views, and sharp differences of opinion exist between researchers about the desirability of methods, the practice of research involves a lot of compromises between these pure positions.

The worldview held by an individual researcher or institute is clearly an important factor which affects the choice of research methods. But there are other factors, too. Within academic organizations senior members can exert pressure on junior people to adopt methods that they don't believe in. Governments, companies and funding organizations can exert pressure on institutions to ensure that the aims and forms of research meet with their interests. The politics of research are complex, and researchers neglect them at their peril. That is why we have chosen to devote the next chapter to a discussion of these issues.

NOTES

1 We use this term, rather than the expression of 'social constructivism' which is preferred by Guba and Lincoln (1989) and Knorr-Cetina (1983).

4 The Politics of Management Research

One of the myths about research is that it is an 'ivory tower' activity. According to this view, research is carried out by independent scholars dedicated to the pursuit of knowledge. Questions and issues are defined as interesting according to the current state of knowledge and the curiosity of the researcher's intellect.

It is doubtful whether there was ever much truth behind this myth. Scholars have regularly got themselves into trouble for following beliefs that were politically unpopular. Socrates was condemned to drink a cup of hemlock because he did not seem sufficiently respectful of current Athenian divinities; and Gallileo was forced to recant his belief, which was based on careful observation of sunspots and planetary orbits, that the earth moved around the sun. In China the first Qin emperor is reputed to have buried alive some 400 scholars because he did not like their opinions.

Although many academics have tried in the past to maintain their independence it has never been altogether possible to separate scholarship from politics. But what do we mean by 'politics'? Our basic premise is that it concerns the power relationships between the individuals and institutions involved in the research enterprise, plus the strategies adopted by different actors and the consequences of their actions on others. The crucial relationships may be between student and supervisor, funder and grant holder, authors and journal editors, companies and research institutes, project leaders and research assistants, researchers and managers, or between managers and their bosses. Influence within these relationships may be exerted over: what is to be researched, how, when, by whom; how information is to be used and disseminated; and how the products of research are to be evaluated.

In this context it is important to emphasize two major differences between management research and other forms of social and psychological research. First, 'management' is essentially about controlling, influencing and structuring the awareness of others. It is the central process whereby organizations achieve the semblance of coherence and direction. This process has, for some time, been recognized as political (Pettigrew, 1985; Hardy, 1996; Buchanan and Badham, 1999). Although 'management' is not the only arena in which politics is important, it does mean that political issues will rarely be absent from the research process.

The second difference is linked, and it starts with the observation that most empirical research in the social sciences is carried out on members of society who are less powerful than the researchers. That is why psychologists conduct their experiments on students rather than on professors, and sociologists tend to focus on people who are relatively powerless due to their low social or economic status (Taylor and Bogdan, 1984). It is 'the mad, the bad, and the ill' who have received most attention from social researchers in the past (Slater, 1989). This is no accident, however, for the more powerful members of society generally have both the awareness and the means to protect themselves from the prying eyes and tape recorders of researchers. It is rare to find researchers who have succeeded in studying powerful members of society without adopting methods of deceit, concealment or subterfuge.

Research into managers and management provides a case where the subjects of research are very likely to be more powerful than the researchers themselves. Furthermore, most organizations are both tightly structured and controlled, so that gaining access to the corporate boardroom is exceedingly difficult for most researchers. Managers are usually in a position where they can easily decline to provide information for researchers; they are also adept at handling face-to-face interviews and at managing interactions with strangers. In such circumstances they are fully aware of the significance of information and the importance of determining what use it might be put to, and by whom. So, in the case of managerial research the boot is firmly on the other foot.

We therefore begin this chapter with a discussion of the political factors that can influence the nature and direction of research. The next part focuses on some of the problems of gaining access to organizations and managers and offers some suggestions about how this can be handled. The third part considers some of the ethical dilemmas encountered in fieldwork, particularly those resulting from strategies to gain access, and which are contingent upon the utilization of data.

POLITICAL INFLUENCES ON THE RESEARCH QUESTION

Most positivist researchers are not keen on self-disclosure, because the admission of personal motives and aspirations might be seen to damage the image of independence and objectivity that they are at pains to cultivate. Hence they rarely explain precisely where their ideas and questions have come from. Fortunately things are beginning to change, for two reasons. First, because social studies of the development of scientific knowledge (Latour and Woolgar, 1979) have started to show that the formal view of scientific progress is at variance with what most scientists do in practice. Second, because there is a growing acceptance among social scientists of the need to be reflexive about their own work, and this has led to more autobiographical accounts of research in practice (Czarniawska, 1998). Consequently there is less reliance on traditional 'linear' models of scientific progress.

Although it is recognized that a thorough knowledge of prior research is very important, it is very rare for good research ideas to be derived directly from the literature. Indeed, as we shall note later in Chapter 8, qualitative researchers often develop *post hoc* theoretical rationales for their work, which are explained when the thesis, or learned paper, is submitted (Golden-Biddle and Locke, 1997). Our argument in this chapter is that there are many other factors that can influence the kind of questions that are seen as worthy of research, and that these include both the personal experiences of the researcher, the attitudes and influence of external stakeholders with whom he or she comes into contact, and the broader context within which he or she works and studies. These factors are summarized below in Figure 4.1.

We do not regard this as a mechanistic model, but rather, following Pettigrew (1985) we see research ideas evolving in an incremental way through a continual process of negotiation with these factors.

Before tackling each of these factors in turn we would like to offer a simple model which we have found useful in making sense of the politics of research. This is based on the study by Boissevain (1974) of social networks, especially in the Sicilian Mafia, where he identified two distinct roles played by participants: brokers and patrons. *Brokers* are social 'fixers' who use their secondary resources, such as information and a wide range of contacts, in order to achieve their ambitions. *Patrons* are people with direct control over primary resources such as people and money. But when they need information or the resolution of a problem they turn to brokers who have the contacts and a past record of solving problems. A skilful broker will also specify a tariff which is only part of the real cost – so that when the transaction is made he will have built up further goodwill with the patron. This will in turn increase the broker's overall credit for future problem-solving.

While we would not wish to suggest a direct correspondence between the worlds of Mafiosi and management researchers, there are a number of parallels. In the research world brokers are important because they know the way round the system, and are known by others. They may be able to advise on questions such as: how to obtain funds from Research Councils; which external examiners would be most appropriate for a thesis; which journal editor is most likely to be interested in a particular paper; which people are able to grant access to

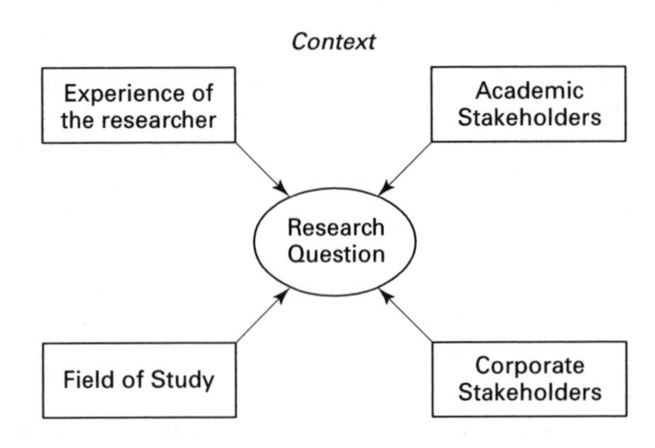

FIGURE 4.1 Influences on the research question

a particular organization. Within companies personnel and training managers can often act as brokers because, although they have little formal power, they usually have a wide range of contacts at all levels of the organization. Successful researchers can also develop brokerage skills. Thus a personnel manager is more likely to help provide access to her company if she thinks the researcher may be able to provide her with something in return – whether it be expertise, credibility, or other contacts.

The Experience of the Researcher

We have argued in previous chapters that direct contact with the subject of one's research is most important if one is to develop new insights about it. This can be illustrated from the research of people like Melville Dalton (1959) whose insights were based on personal experience as a manager at Milo, or Frederick Taylor who based his views of scientific management on his experiences first as a labourer, and then as a foreman, at the Midvale Steel Company in the 1880s.

The point we wish to make here is slightly different. It is that personal background affects what the researcher can see: experience acts both as a sensitizer and as a filter for the researcher. The motivations of individual researchers may be quite varied. As Platt (1976) has shown, many researchers in the early stages of projects are unclear about their aims and goals; others may have more precisely defined career goals, political aims, or agendas to create change in their own institutions and environments. When it comes to fieldwork, personal background, including social class, will affect the ease with which the researcher can gain access to different settings, and this may also pre-determine responses from different client groups. Those who conduct research on workers rarely get round to investigating managers, and vice-versa. This may be for ideological reasons, or merely for personal and social ease. Most organizations are highly sensitive to the possibility of researchers having any kind of political agenda, particularly if it differs from theirs. Amusingly, Beynon (1988) recounts problems that he and his colleagues have encountered in gaining access both to what he regarded as a 'right-wing' manufacturing organization, *and* to a 'left-wing' trade union organization.

The growth of executive MBAs and part-time Masters programmes has also resulted in many students carrying out research into aspects of their own organizations. This has several advantages since they generally will not have problems with access and they may also have direct experience of the issues they are investigating. So up to a point, their insights are likely to be deeper than those of researchers who arrive from outside the organization. But increasing use is also being made of teams within these programmes, especially full-time Masters or Batchelors programmes. These arrangements can provide added advantages through combining people with different backgrounds and interests, and the flexibility and synergy that this can create. Teams can sometimes be established to take advantage of the insider/outsider perspective. This, as developed by Bartunek and Louis (1996) follows the ethnographic principle that insiders will be able to see and understand things that will make no sense to outsiders, while outsiders will notice things that may have become quite invisible to insiders. Thus a team which balances perspectives, backgrounds and skills may be much more effective than individuals at conducting research.

But it is within teams that political and other problems can arise. In our own research we have found that the internal dynamics of a team can be affected by external pressures. In Mark's UK/China decision-making project the research team contained both Chinese and UK nationals. But on several occasions we found that UK companies where we were seeking access for fieldwork would only talk to the UK staff and would not respond to any communications from Chinese staff. These external pressures affected internal relationships, and they also created difficult decisions about who would be sent to carry out interviews at the companies (Easterby-Smith and Malina, 1999).

In a classic paper Hyder and Sims (1979) analyse the tensions between 'grant holders' who are awarded the funds, and 'research officers' who are hired to carry out the work. They suggest that the relationship is aggravated for three main reasons. First, there are different timescales: grant holders are generally tenured academics, while research staff on fixed term contracts are chronically insecure. Second, in terms of commitment, research staff are likely to be doing little else than working on the project while grant holders will have many other responsibilities and commitments. Third, most grant holders develop conflicting expectations of their research officers, expecting them on the one hand to be general factotums and dogsbodies, and on the other to be creative contributors to the research enterprise.

Barwise et al. (1989) also encountered the latter issue in the context of a multidisciplinary investigation of strategic investment decisions. Although the project was conceived and 'sold' to the funders by three senior staff, it was carried out by a half-time researcher who was recruited specifically for the project. The senior academics initially treated the researcher as their 'eyes and ears', but about half way through the project they were forced to recognize that she had developed a greater understanding of the project than they, and that she now had a major contribution to make both in the interpretation of data and in the overall direction of the project.

There is much potential for conflict here. The power of grant holders lies in their control of funds and their potential influence on the future career of the researcher; the researcher's power lies in intimate knowledge of the research process and the potential to withhold co-operation. Thus both parties are in a position to exert influence throughout the project, although the relative balance of this might vary as the project evolves. And things often come to a head when arrangements are made to start publishing the results, unless clear rules can be agreed in advance which are generally seen as fair to all parties. This is also a growing problem for research students where there is an expectation of one or two papers emerging from the thesis possibly with joint authorship from the supervisor. Increasingly, Mark has found it necessary to clarify this issue before research students register for research degrees – currently the principle is that author order is determined by who does most of the work, and no-one should expect a 'free ride'!

Academic Stakeholders

The relationship between supervisors and research staff or students is a key power dynamic. But there are many other dynamics within the academic world. Research Councils exert influence on the direction of research through control of funds; disciplinary associations determine quality criteria in their own fields; journal editors, referees and conference organizers act as final arbiters of academic quality; and senior academics may act as mentors, but they also control career rewards. In almost all circumstances, members of the academic community operate with a high degree of probity and professionalism; nevertheless, given the amount of competition for relatively few prizes, there are bound to be criteria and processes which are not totally transparent. Our aim in this section of the chapter is to make these criteria and processes more visible.

Starting at the top, academic funding bodies cannot entirely ignore the agendas of their political masters. These often require some explicit links to be made between research funding and national well-being. Consequently, in a number of countries, Research Councils have adopted policies of targeting resources towards specific initiatives which may generate sufficient critical mass to provide rapid development of theories and practical applications. Research proposals therefore stand greater chance of funding if they can demonstrate how they are meeting the priorities of their respective Councils. Even in the case of charities, which are theoretically not under the thrall of political pressures, there are still likely to be 'steers' given by boards of trustees, and hence it is important to check out policy statements (and perhaps scrutinize the range of projects already funded by the agency) while crafting any proposals for funding. Like it or not, the days of 'blue skies research' are over.

But there is also a danger if funding becomes *too* responsive to political priorities and pressures, because research results may be used by one group directly to harm another group, and it is very easy for researchers to become compromised in the process. An extreme example of this is the work carried out by scientists in Nazi Germany on concentration camp inmates. The majority of those involved appeared to be highly principled, as scientists, and strongly denied any anti-semitism. Yet in a review of a careful study of surviving evidence, Billig (1988: 476) comments:

> In *Murderous Science*, we see academics continually writing grant applications, guessing what projects the controllers of the funding agencies will be considering socially useful: is it the Gypsies, or the degenerates; or the ability to withstand cold, which will bring the grants this year?

He who pays the piper not only calls the tune, but can also define what a good tune is. One hopes that exercises such as these would never take place in or around modern organizations. But the personal and social consequences of losing a power struggle, or a job, can be very profound indeed. Researchers should therefore be very wary of the ends that they may be serving, whether wittingly or unwittingly.

Funding bodies always receive more proposals than they can accommodate.

Proposals in the UK are given an *alpha* rating if the independent referees consider them to be technically worthy of funding, but the Economic and Social Research Council only has funds for 30 per cent of the alpha-rated proposals. Thus decisions about the awards often have to take other information into account. Chief among these are whether the researcher has a good 'track record' of prior funded research, whether he or she is known to those involved in making the decision, and whether the research appears to be aligned with current funding council priorities. For those with international reputations and many years successful research experience, this is an advantage; but for the newcomer it is a major obstacle to getting started on funded research.

For newcomers we can offer three main bits of advice. First, make the best use of your own experience through highlighting any related work or publications you may have. It is also important to show that one has a record of delivering according to one's promises. Second, get known by key people in the field by going to conferences and submitting papers for publication. Third, make use of networks, possibly by submitting proposals jointly with people who are already established, and by sending drafts to potential referees. In both of these cases, senior colleagues may be able to act as brokers by establishing initial contacts, or they may be willing to collaborate directly.

For those working on projects or research degrees, the main pressures come from supervisors, colleagues and gatekeepers. Supervisors, for example, will normally try to influence the research so that it stays fairly close both in terms of content and methodology to their own research interests. If the research is being conducted for a doctoral degree, the supervisor will increasingly be anxious about whether the work will be completed successfully within a given time; this is because both academic departments and whole institutions are now being judged upon completion rates for research students and will have funding withdrawn if the 4-year completion rate falls below 60 or 70 per cent. The consequence of this is that both institutions and supervisors are tending to push students into limiting the scope of their research topics so that they are easily completed within the prescribed time, and hence there is some concern about the 'dumbing down' of the PhD.

The rise of professional doctorates in subjects such as education, psychology, social administration and business has added another form of stress to the system. At the time of writing, in the UK there are no nationally agreed criteria for a DBA (Doctor of Business Administration), other than the general belief that it should be 'equivalent' to a PhD. So entry qualifications, research training requirements, assessment criteria, and overall standards are still left up to individual institutions, which has resulted in the impression that some universities might be abusing the qualification. Even if standards and criteria are eventually agreed there is still unease about professional doctorates because they are intended to make a 'contribution' in both the practical and theoretical senses. While the latter aspect is fully within the domain of academic competence, the former is less so. Essentially it is a hybrid qualification, which is still awarded solely by academic institutions.

The nature and direction of research can be influenced by other forces, too. Most academic departments have their own house-styles which support and encourage particular kinds of work, whether quantitative or qualitative and there is also much pressure on departments to prioritize their research interests. This can make it hard to find the right supervisors and examiners. The ideal external examiner not only needs to share the same research philosophy as the candidate, but also needs to know a lot about the subject of investigation. It is advisable in most cases to start looking for potential external examiners at a fairly early stage in a research degree. This helps to focus the research project, because it requires the candidate to be clear about the boundaries of the field in which he or she is operating, and also to know who are the key movers and shakers in the field. Although the supervisor will need to approach the external examiner, it is important that the candidate is able to provide a list of potential examiners. If the candidate does not have such a list that is a worrying sign because it suggests that they may not be sufficiently on top of the field.

Conferences, as we have mentioned above, provide a valuable form of contact within the academic community, and it is essential for anyone doing a doctorate to get onto the right conference circuits. Most conferences are not too competitive, and will accept papers on the basis of 1–2 page abstracts; those that are more competitive, such as the US or British Academy of Management, will usually give preferential treatment to doctoral students.[1] The benefits of conference participation should be obvious, but here is a list of points: they provide visibility for you and your ideas; they enable you to get feedback on papers which you will subsequently submit to journals; they enable you to identify others working in your own field; you will get early copies of publications that may not appear in journals within two or three years; and you may be able to spot potential external examiners. In addition, conferences act as recruitment fairs, explicitly in the USA and implicitly in the UK. Gibson Burrell (1993:75) provides an entertaining account of how the system works at the Academy of Management Conference:

> Doctoral candidates, looking for university positions, are glaringly obvious in the hotel lobbies. The males dress in blazers and grey trousers, the women in blue suits. Prestigious professors dress in Bermuda shorts and sandals. One's position in the hierarchy therefore is marked by dress, so the 'smarter' the attire, the lower is one's standing.

We offer this quote partly for those who agonize over what to wear at conferences – the message being to dress down rather than up – but also to highlight aspects of power within the academic game, which is often expressed through (not so subtle) symbols. And if you are tempted to wear Bermuda shorts and Hawaiian T-shirts, remember that they should be well ironed.

Material presented at conferences is often published in the form of proceedings or as edited books, normally on more of a selective basis than the conference itself. Conference organizers often take on the editorial roles for these publications. Although peer review is normally used to support decisions, one of the easiest ways of getting included in such publications is to offer to co-edit the proceedings. You too can become a gatekeeper! But this is by no means the end of the road, because conference proceedings and book chapters only achieve modest ratings in the increasingly hierarchical world of academic publishing. The gold standard is the academic journal, and this is where some of the strictest hierarchies operate. There are two simple ways of judging in advance the standing of an academic journal. First, rejection rates indicate how much demand there is to get into the journal. Top journals will have rejection rates of up to 95 per cent, lesser journals may be around 50 per cent. Journals that take almost everything will not be considered as serious journals (but then they are unlikely to publish their rejection rates). Second, the citation indexes (SSCI) produce annual rankings of journals based on the frequency with which papers from a given journal are cited within papers published in other respectable journals.[2]

Beyond that, one must make up one's own mind, by reading past papers in the journal, or by submitting something to it. If you want to get something published quickly or easily then start with one of the more lowly journals. Top journals have much greater lead time, often running into several years. This is not because they are slow or inefficient, more that they will be dealing with a very large volume of material and they will be very exacting in their standards. For example, a paper that Mark recently had published in the *Academy of Management Journal* (Easterby-Smith and Malina, 1999) was initially submitted in March 1996 (and that was based on earlier conference papers given in 1993 and 1995). The initial rewrite offer from *AMJ* arrived 11 weeks after submission and contained 8 single-spaced pages of comments and advice from the editor and referees. Over the next two years the paper then went though 4 rewrites, and on each occasion the guidance from the editorial office ran to 4 or 5 pages. Thus by the time the paper was accepted in July 1998 the length of comments from the editorial office was greater than the eventual length of the paper. On occasions such as this, as Golden-Biddle and Locke (1997) comment, one starts to wonder whether the referees should be included as co-authors of the paper!

As we said at the outset of this section, it is important for people carrying out academic management research to understand some of the hidden rules and procedures, because these may determine whether they are eventually successful. Despite efforts to be fair and transparent, these hidden rules and procedures are inevitable. We have tried to provide some insight into the more obvious aspects but feel there is much more that could be told. Our general advice is to be alert, and don't accept stereotypes too easily. For example, one stereotype is that US journals tend to be very narrow in their criteria and somewhat ethnocentric. Our experience recounted above shows that it is possible for foreigners to get accepted, but also that the degree of rigour and general efficiency of a journal like the *AMJ* is much in excess of any UK journals.

Corporate Stakeholders

We use the term corporate loosely here, to include companies, public organizations and others generally within the 'user community'. These are becoming very significant because they are both sponsors and users of management research. One of the largest routes of sponsorship is through funding managers to attend MBA and other programmes, either held in traditional university business schools or in the new breed of corporate 'universities'. Most MBA programmes involve in-company projects: for part-time programmes they will normally be carried out within the sponsoring organization; for full-time programmes most institutions will have a list of companies that regularly sponsor projects for their students. The other route of sponsorship is where companies fund research programmes or Chairs in business schools, often as members of consortia.

In the case of Masters projects, there are several potential sets of expectations. A production manager attending a part-time MBA might, for example, want to set up a 3-month project in the marketing department. This means that the main stakeholders will include: the project sponsor in the marketing department, the academic supervisor, the training department that has organized sponsorship in the first place, and the manager herself. The strongest divergence will be between the sponsor who will be looking for the solution to a problem, and the academic supervisor who will be looking for a well argued case which takes account of existing literature supported by tangible evidence obtained with a well-explained methodology. The student-manager and the training representative will have the task of reconciling the two. Sometimes it is necessary to write two separate reports; ideally the two sets of expectations can be met with one report which blends academic theory with practical action. It may be possible to do this in a 'seamless' way; alternatively the 'sandwich' model is where the client report is prefaced by an academic introduction and literature review, and then followed by a methodological and substantive critique.

As we will see in the section below on access, it can be difficult to obtain formal sanction to carry out research in companies; but our impression is that the number of points of contact are increasing. With more exchange and interpenetration taking place, sponsorship decisions are becoming more decentralised and hence a wider range of opportunities are opening up for research. Within the much-vaunted knowledge economies of the 21st century, this is as it should be.

One residual consideration is whether research which is conducted for corporate clients will become 'contaminated' because of the funding relationship. There are two ways in which this might happen. As we have already noted, funders are likely to exert some influence on the direction of research and the kinds of questions that are considered to be significant. But this is likely to be the case with all forms of funded research, whether following a positivist or constructionist approach, and we think that the differences consequent upon corporate or non-corporate funding are merely a matter of degree. The other form of contamination may come from people within the organization deliberately feeding information into the project which is likely to support their political agendas. Again, the same thing can happen with any kind of organization, for example a school or a hospital, whether or not there is also a funding relationship.

Given that contamination inevitably arises from political factors, the question is how best to deal with it? Our view is that these political factors and their consequences should not be kept hidden; but they should be incorporated explicitly into the reports of the research process. The researcher's own interests, the process of gaining access or funds from organizations, or discussions about dissemination of results: these may all be relevant. Thus we would advise researchers to keep regular records not only of formal research data, but also to chronicle their own views and moods, and the processes of organizing and conducting the research. Further, we think it important that researchers are prepared to reflect critically on all of these influences on their research, and to make these thoughts available to others. Ultimately this should increase, rather than decrease, the credibility of the results.

The Subject of Study

The general subject or topic of study may also exert considerable influence on the nature and direction of the research enterprise. By the 'subject' we mean the problems or issues to be considered – rather than the people and data that will be looked at within the study.

Each academic discipline, whether it be mathematics, engineering, sociology, or organizational theory, tends to have a number of key debates and issues at any one time. Despite the relevance of this advice to the individual researcher, it does raise a problem of more general relevance to research as a whole. There is a marked tendency amongst researchers to follow fads and fashions with regard to both method and focus. As Scarbrough and Swan (1999) point out, fads often become popular because they appear to provide the solution to some contemporary problem, but they are also based on simple but ambiguous ideas. Thus both their nature and foundations are often quite shaky, and this can also account for their rapid disappearance.

For example, in the early 1990s when the first edition of this book was published some of the fashionable debates stimulated by academic management researchers in Europe were: postmodernism, ethics and critiques of enterprise culture. A decade later some of the hottest areas are knowledge management/creation, globalization and e-commerce. There are clear advantages to situating one's work close to the mainstream: there will be a lot of other interest in the subject, debates will be lively, and there are likely to be conferences and special issues of journals being commissioned on the topic. So there are plenty of opportunities for the researcher. On the other hand there will be a lot of competition for space and to establish ownership of new ideas. And the fashion may also turn, so that unless the research topic is defined in a flexible way there is a danger of being stranded with good ideas and materials that excite no further interest.

A 'strategic' approach may be to try to spot issues that are currently regarded as mundane, in the hope that they will suddenly pick up interest. This is another reason for working the conference circuit to find out what the 'industry leaders' think will be important issues for the future. At a wider level, though, the focus on fashion may result in other important or 'ordinary' issues being overlooked. Very often it is the ordinary and commonplace that can be most revealing. Ryave and Schenkein (1974), for example, describe a study of the relatively trivial topic of how people walk. Their results show how a number of social rules can be identified with regard to space, control and propriety – which are by no means mundane, and which can easily be related to other contexts.

If the research is to be carried out in a corporate setting it is always worth talking to practising managers to find out what they consider to be the emergent issues for them. Often practitioners are ahead of mainstream academics, partly because new ideas may be getting promoted by consultancies direct to companies, and the academics will be left out of the loop until they realize that there is a new fad in town which requires critiquing. Sometimes this can lead to tension between corporate sponsors and academic supervisors around the questions they consider to be important. But there are plenty of examples of the appropriate combination being achieved. One research student was asked by her sponsoring company to investigate how appraisal systems were working in practice in different parts of the company. The researcher was able to answer this practical question to the satisfaction of the company. At the same time she was able to use data from her interviews to show how organizational systems, such as appraisals, are a product of wider cultural value systems in those parts of the organizations; and conversely how such systems are a channel for the transmission and articulation of value systems, particularly as defined by senior members of the organization.

Thus there is no particular reason why academic and practical goals should not be achieved simultaneously; indeed we have also found that many practitioners will become enthusiastically involved in theoretical debates created from the academic perspective. Such managers are not only likely to be familiar with academic debates about culture and values; they also wish to contribute substantially to these debates. This increasingly leads to the possibility of managers, sponsors, and gatekeepers being seen as collaborators in the research process itself (Heron, 1996).

Context and Models of Research

We now come to the effect of the broad context within which the research is taking place. By context we include both the national setting and the extent to which resources and attitudes are likely to be supportive of research. We will then look at four different models of the role of the researcher. These are not derived theoretically from philosophical positions, as in the last chapter, but based on observations of different forms of research in practice.

The national setting is important both because of the way resource availability affects what is possible, and because different countries and cultures may have different views regarding what constitutes 'good' research. David Hickson (1988) provides a nice description of the contrasting resources that he found when conducting research in oil-rich Alberta, compared to his subsequent experiences of research at the University of Bradford which was at that time reeling from severe government cutbacks. Also, Pugh's (1988) account of the early period of the Aston research programme sounds almost unrecognizable today. Thus he and his team were able to spend a whole year reading books and discussing what the focus of their research would be, with no expectation that they should rush off and get data or produce preliminary reports within this first year.

The case for the localization of management research is argued by Davila (1989) on the grounds that North American models of research, which require large samples and substantial data analysis, are largely irrelevant both methodologically and substantively in the context of Latin America. He advocates paying far more attention to case studies which can draw more extensively upon local culture and problems – many of these problems being quite different from those considered significant in more highly developed countries. Teagarden et al. (1995) also found that US research methods could not be applied uniformly in their major cross-national study of HRM practices. The potential for co-operation from companies and managers varied greatly between countries, and it was simply not possible to adhere to the rigorous criteria for sampling and data collection that they had assumed from the USA.

Thus we believe that it is important for the researcher to be at least aware of the constraints and opportunities posed by the context within which he or she is currently working. This leads us to propose four archetypical research models, which although they are not comprehensive, offer different ways of tackling contextual variations. The first is what we call the *military model* which involves: teams of people; substantial preparation and planning; some differentiation of roles between those who design the research, those who gather data and those who make sense of the data. This is most appropriate in a resource-rich environment as in the case of the work of Pugh and his colleagues at Aston, or Hickson and his colleagues in Alberta. There are also downsides to the military model because, as noted above, teams that contain hierarchies of roles can find it hard to operate within the unpredicability of the research environment.

Whereas the workers in the military model are generally hired for the job, in the second model, the *private agent*, one is more likely to find students and lone academics. This involves individuals operating independently, developing their own ideas using their own resources, and making the best of whatever opportunities are available. Occasionally there may be an element of co-ordination, or networking, amongst the lone researchers through the Internet and conference links. Institutions that run doctoral programmes may also establish arrangements whereby students, although conducting their research quite independently, are also members of action learning sets that provide support and guidance to each other. Indeed the existence of academic communities of sufficient size is one of the necessary conditions for government funding of research studentships in the UK.

A third and somewhat controversial possibility is the *investigative* model. This starts from the assumption that powerful organizations and individuals will always try to control and repress research conducted on themselves, and hence some deception is both legitimate and necessary. This implies that researchers should be opportunistic, they should use any means necessary to gain access and gather data, and they should publish their findings quickly regardless of consequences. One of the main proponents of this model, sometimes known as conflict methodology, is Douglas (1976). Beynon's classic study of life on and around the assembly line at the Ford plant in Liverpool also had elements of investigative journalism in it (Beynon, 1973). But this subsequently attracted the comment from the company that: 'It's extreme left-wing propaganda . . . we don't think it merits serious discussion as it's not a serious attempt at sociology or education.' There is much sympathy for the investigative model because it can expose fraud, injustice, the misuse of power and organizational myths. But there are also concerns because of the potential backlash and the effect it may have on the opportunities for future researchers who might wish to gain access for non-investigative reasons.

The fourth research model is what we might call an *appropriate technology* model. This is most useful in situations where the normal trappings of the research environment such as computers, photocopiers, easy communications and transport can not be taken for granted. Increasingly, developing countries are appreciating the need for management practices which are based upon indigenous research. In these cases research methods must adjust to the realities of the developing country's situation, and they should not appear to be inferior in comparison to those of the far more munificent environments of developed countries.

All four of these models to some extent pre-determine the kind of research questions that can, and should, be investigated in their respective cases. Thus one might expect grand theoretical issues to emerge from the military model, for the private agent to be focusing on detailed and small-scale processes and issues, for the investigator to concentrate on exposing wrongdoings, and for the appropriate technology researcher to use ethnographic methods to identify the actual processes of management or managing within their own cultural context.

POLITICS OF ACCESS

Here we consider two kinds of access, first the formal access, or permission from senior management, to gather data from within the organization (generally within specific constraints), and then the informal process of gaining access to people and documents. Like Buchanan et al. (1988) we would argue for an opportunistic approach. Most researchers seriously underestimate the amount of time and patience that can be required to gain this initial access. In the following paragraphs we provide some 'war stories' of how hard it can be, and offer some advice on how access may be eased. The good news is that although there are currently far more people trying to gain access to organizations for their research there seems to be a growing acceptance of the value of in-company projects – possibly because a growing number of middle managers have now been through business schools themselves. Consequently they are not so likely to be threatened, and they may be genuinely interested in what is being investigated.

In our experience 'cold calling' is a waste of time and it is essential to start with some kind of personal contacts, however tenuous. If one's supervisor or institution does not have the right links then it is often worth trying the relevant trade or professional associations, or using contacts in related organizations. We have found associations to be very helpful here, and they rarely object to being mentioned as the source of the contact – because, of course, brokerage is the lifeblood of most trade and professional associations.

Once the initial contact has been made by phone or letter (sometimes an e-mail works better), the gatekeeper is likely to consider two questions: (a) is this individual worth supporting, and (b) will it be possible to 'sell' the project to patrons higher up the organization. The latter question hangs on a consideration of whether the potential benefits will outweigh the likely costs, or potential risks, of the project. Given that information about costs and benefits will be very imprecise it usually helps at this stage if:

1 the time and resources requested are minimal;
2 the project appears not to be politically sensitive; and
3 the individuals concerned, and their institution have a good reputation.

Two examples at Lancaster can illustrate these points, both projects being funded by the Economic and Social Research Council (ESRC). The first project aimed to examine the relationship and corporate performance in 60 major UK companies over a 15-year period. The methodology required analysis of financial indicators over this period (from public databases), and interviews with up to 5 key actors in each company. Gaining access to the latter was relatively easy since the research question was seen to be important and we were not asking for much ('an initial interview of 1 hour with a senior personnel manager, with the possibility of a small number of other interviews subsequently'). Consequently, we only had to approach 85 companies in order to reach our final sample of 49. In keeping with the above points, success was more likely when we had a warm contact, someone who already knew a member of the research team. To this end we used contacts from the Association of Management Education and Development (AMED), an academic-practitioner association to which we all belonged.

The other example was less successful. This involved trying to gain access to British Steel for a research project comparing decision-making processes in Chinese and UK organizations. British Steel was important to us because several of the potential Chinese companies were large steel manufacturers. We pursued them over a period of about two years and gradually collected a network of supporters first amongst central training staff, and then amongst senior line managers in operating companies. What we were asking for was access for about a week for two researchers who would carry out about ten interviews in connection with two major decisions. Unfortunately none of our contacts had the authority to commit the organization, and the decision was referred up to the Main Board and an unequivocal letter of reject followed shortly.

We never established exactly why we had failed to get into British Steel. The initial reason was that the company was in the process of privatization and hence it would be inappropriate to grant access to outsiders at that time. Perhaps China was not seen as 'flavour of the month' at that time. But also we suspect that British Steel could not see how contacts with academics, or with the Chinese, were in their interests. Certainly the UK companies to which we subsequently gained access had very clear ideas about what they wanted to gain from the project. These included identifying market opportunities, establishing contact with potential business partners, and obtaining information on the company's own image in China.

There is a principle of reciprocity evident in the above examples. The more the company gives, in time or money, the more it expects in exchange. Another feature that is common to the above examples is that the initiative usually comes from the researcher, and organizational brokers may then be used to reach the patrons. However there are occasions when patrons themselves may wish to initiate some research. At least five reasons for sponsoring research are common.

First, the sponsor may wish to gain political support for a new idea that he wants to initiate. The mere presence of an outside adviser, or researcher, may lend credibility to this idea, and preliminary data produced by the researcher may lend further support. Second, the sponsor may wish to demonstrate, largely to an internal audience, the success of a venture with which he has been associated. This is a common reason for sponsoring evaluations of training or development programmes. The third reason is when the potential sponsor or his unit is under attack from others in the organization. When a department or project is under threat of closure a possible line of defence is to introduce a researcher who can demonstrate how valuable the unit's work is. In our experience this stratagem rarely works, and the researcher must hope that the unit is not closed before he or she gets paid! Fourth, the sponsor may simply wish to test his ideas against some external validation, by using the researcher as a sounding board. Finally, there are a few enlightened sponsors who are sufficiently curious about the world in which they work to support research for its own sake.

As we have suggested above, official access is only the start of the story: the next problem is to obtain co-operation and trust inside. This depends mainly on the personality of the researcher, and whether he or she is genuinely curious about what is happening; it is also a function of the researcher's skills in dealing with what are sometimes very complex interpersonal relationships. In our experience these complex interpersonal relationships derive largely from the political issues within the organization, and we divide these into micro-issues, which are about relationships with individual managers, and macro-issues which are to do with the wider political conflicts within the organization.

At a *micro political* level it is important to be able to develop a co-operative relationship with each informant. With most managers the relationship begins when you try to negotiate an appointment either directly or through a secretary. Most managers will be protective over their time and will also be making assessments of the personal costs and benefits of co-operating. Some managers will get interested in the topic during the interview and will want to keep talking, others will give very short replies, and you will wonder how you are going to get through the allotted hour. We will discuss the dynamics of interview situations in more detail in Chapter 6; but for the time being we note how they may make things difficult for the researcher.

Barbara Czarniawska (1998) provides a fascinating account of her experiences in Warsaw, where she had obtained agreement to conduct a 10 day observational study of the Director of Finance of the City Council. Most of this period seemed to be taken up with the Director finding excuses not to talk to her, or to exclude her from virtually every meeting. Even when the Director, in a moment of helpfulness, tried to arrange for Barbara to meet the Deputy Mayor she only managed a passing contact and never managed to schedule an actual interview.

Barbara is a senior professor with an international reputation, so perhaps it was hard for the Director to resist her openly. With younger researchers more direct 'put downs' may be used. One technique is for the interviewee to cross-examine the interviewer at the outset in order to establish that he has very little relevant experience of the organization or context that he is apparently studying, and is very naive about the realities of anything outside the academic environment. Having established who is really in control of the interaction, the senior manager may then be prepared to sit back for forty or fifty minutes and respond honestly to questions. Even experienced researchers occasionally get caught out by this tactic. Beynon (1988) provides a nice example of a senior NCB manager attacking the credibility of an expert academic witness involved in a colliery enquiry by asking such direct questions as 'Are you qualified to manage a coalfield?', 'What practical management experience have you had in operating?', 'Have you any personal knowledge of selling to commercial buyers?' This form of discrediting the external expert provides a very effective form of corporate defence, and perhaps the minor 'put downs' given to researchers by senior managers may be an anticipatory form of defence just in case the 'wrong' results are produced by the study.

Beynon (1988) also recalls being pumped for information by a plant manager during an interview about the reasons why a particular group of workers with whom he had also held interviews were proving to be rather obstructive. He was put in the position that if he acceded to this request he would probably lose the confidence of the workers, but if he directly refused it he would be ejected from the plant by the manager involved. In the event, it appears that he played for time and staged a strategic retreat to the university on account of 'pressing business', until this particular crisis had blown over.

This is, however, an example of what we would call a *macro political* problem, because the researcher is becoming trapped between two major groups or factions. A similar example occurred when Mark was asked by the Works Manager of a major chemical plant to conduct a study into the consequences of a large plant closure exercise. This exercise had apparently been handled very successfully and had led to the voluntary redundancy of over 1000 workers, without any overt industrial relations strife occurring. About a week after starting the study he noticed that people were starting to become less available for interview, and people with access to personnel records were suddenly too busy to deal with requests. He was however very much reassured to be invited to lunch one day with a General Manager from that site: discussion ranged over the research project which had recently started, and the manager showed much interest in some initial observations. It was later the same day that he met one of the personnel managers from the site who informed him regretfully that a meeting had been held that same morning to discuss the research project, and that one person had been very insistent that the project be stopped – this was the General Manager with whom he had just had lunch.

This was very unexpected since nothing had been mentioned at lunchtime. It was even more surprising that the personnel manager thought there was nothing exceptional about this behaviour. It later emerged that the decision to ban the project was the focal point in a major battle between the Works Manager and the General Manager with regard to the appropriate management style on the site. The former was backing a rather paternalistic line of management, and the results of the study would no doubt have helped him in his argument. His protagonist was arguing for a much harder form of managerialism, and unfortunately for the research project it was an argument that he won. Like many organizational researchers faced with similar problems Mark was forced to complete the study by interviewing people in their homes about the closure, and by using networks of internal contacts provided for another project who would accept some surreptitious questioning about the closure themselves.

The lesson from these political examples is that the researcher needs to be aware of conflicts that may be far deeper and more complex than will be evident to a relative newcomer in the organization. We can offer three pieces of advice on how to deal with such politics. First, try to identify one or two 'key informants' who may be prepared to help in a disinterested way. They themselves need to be well-informed but not directly concerned with the issues under investigation. Informants may be able to advise on whom to talk to, and they should be able to explain why things are, or are not, happening. Second, deliberately look for people who have different perspectives on key issues. Talk further to them and others in order to understand *why* they hold different views. Third, always assume that there is more than meets the eye. People may withhold information because they believe it is irrelevant, or they may genuinely have forgotten things. In organizations that have a policy of moving people around every two years, the collective memory may be very short. The departmental secretary may be the only person who knows that your topic has already been researched and written up twice in the last five years.

ETHICS

Up to this point we have made no mention of ethics. This is because it is most frequently linked to the responsibilities of more powerful people against those who are less powerful. It should be quite evident from the examples given above that it is the researcher who is likely to be in the less powerful position. The most likely ethical dilemma may therefore be to betray the confidences given by junior managers, when one is cross-examined by more senior managers.

Informants who are politically adept, often read a great deal into the question that the interviewer is asking. For example, on one occasion Mark happened to be interviewing the Director of a national investigatory organization about the longer term effects of a particular management development programme. He happened to ask a carefully focused question about how the reward system was working, to which the Director immediately came back with, 'I take it you have been talking to John Dawson about that . . . Well in that case . . .'. Even though they may not be professionally trained as investigators, managers will often be able to work out the nature and sources of information already collected by researchers who are sufficiently unfamiliar with the detailed political context of the organization to be aware of the significance of the questions that they are asking.

According to Punch (1986), ethical issues frequently arise from a clash between personal and professional interests. In other words, when the researcher for the sake of his or her career badly wants to obtain some data, he or she may overstep the bounds of personal privacy or confidentiality. Another point worth noting is that discussions about research ethics are most frequently held in relation to the use of qualitative methods. This may be simply because qualitative researchers are more sympathetic and sensitive to human feelings and responsibilities. On the other hand, it may be that when using qualitative methods, such as open interviews or participant observation (see Chapter 6), the researcher has far more control about what information is gathered, how it is recorded, and how it is interpreted. With quantitative methods it is generally the informant who provides the information directly, through completing questionnaires or whatever, and the researcher simply has to accept what is provided by the informant without having much opportunity to question it. The paradox is that the use of qualitative research methods may put the researcher in a considerably more powerful position in relation to individuals – and hence the additional concern with ethical issues in this case.

Two particular ethical issues frequently concern organizational researchers. The first arises from the use of participant observation research methods which, as Ditton (1977) says, are essentially deceitful. That is, if you are participating in a situation, and at the same time observing and recording (perhaps later) what has taken place, you cannot avoid some deception about your real purposes. For as soon as you explain clearly to those involved precisely what you are doing you cannot continue as a 'normal' participant – unless, of course, you persuade participants to adjust *their* roles so that they become co-researchers. This is the paradox that is structurally woven into the role of the participant observer, and we discuss it further in Chapter 6 in relation to a wider classification of participant/observer roles. The ethical questions for the researcher then concern how much deception in a situation is acceptable, and how far the researcher should go in not betraying the trust of any particular informants.

Our view on this dilemma is that one should only deceive people as far as it is necessary to 'get by'. We agree with Taylor and Bogdan (1984: 25) when they suggest that the researcher, on being asked about the nature and purposes of his work, should, 'Be truthful, but vague and imprecise'. This seems to have been the approach adopted by Dalton in his pioneering study of the processes of management. He comments that he was prepared to explain to most of his informants about the nature and purposes of his study, and that in the long run this did not inhibit the majority of his informants (Dalton, 1964).

The second ethical issue is around the control and use of data obtained by the researcher. In most cases we can assume that it is the researcher who has this control and ownership, and that therefore she must exercise due ethical responsibility by not publicising or circulating any information that is likely to harm the interests of individual informants, particularly the less powerful ones. There is an interesting story however where this particular assumption was neatly turned upon its head. A senior academic happened to be interviewing a member of the British Royal Family, and at the end of the interview he offered to have the tape transcribed and to send a transcript to the interviewee who would then be asked to strike out any passages to which he objected. Whereupon the Important Person stretched out a hand saying 'No. I shall retain the tape and will let you have the portions that I am prepared to have published'.

Finally, there is an on-going debate about the value, or otherwise, of ethical codes in relation to research. It is argued that at least some codes need to be made explicit in order to ensure that people are alerted to some of the likely ethical dilemmas that they may face. Such codes should also provide some kind of sanction in cases of blatant abuse and exploitation. But there is a problem here. As Snell (1993) points out, ethical issues are extremely complex. They involve not only the dynamics of power but also the competing claims of different ideologies. The danger is that ethical guidelines will not only be too rigid and simplistic to deal with real cases; they will also contain the biases that are inherent in one or another ideological position.

Mason (1996) makes a similar point about ethical codes being generally written in abstract terms, aimed at preventing serious and unambiguous cases of abuse. The problem is that most of the ethical issues faced by the researcher are small-scale, incremental and ambiguous. Hence she argues that researchers should operate as thinking, reflective practitioners who are prepared to ask difficult questions about the ethics and politics of their own research practice on a regular basis. And we will offer Melville Dalton (1964: 61) the final word: 'The social investigator must sort his values and obligations and weigh them repeatedly throughout the research process. In a democratic society, he cannot impose one fixed code on multiple conflicting codes'.

UTILIZATION OF RESEARCH

The link between research and action is often very weak, and many people find this extremely disappointing. Researchers themselves are only too aware of this feeling when they find that the fruits of several years' labour are gratefully accepted by the sponsoring organization, whether it be academic or industrial, and are simply filed away in a dust-proof cabinet. Likewise the impact of research on public policy has been rather limited, especially as Finch (1986) points out, when the methods are essentially qualitative. This is also true in the United States where a major AACSB-sponsored survey on management education commented on the widespread dissatisfaction of American companies with the usability of research produced by Business Schools (Porter and McKibbin, 1988).

To some extent this disappointment could simply be a result of different people having different expectations from research. Within the academic world, the expectations are fairly specific. Good research should lead to successful PhDs (completed within target dates), to the publication of articles in refereed journals, and to the timely production of research reports which demonstrate that the work has satisfactorily completed what it set out to do in the first place. Getting published in the appropriate academic journals is still very important for the career advancement of academics, and the main political problems are related to debates, cliques and paradigms within the academic world (as we have discussed earlier in this chapter). Fortunately, or not, most academic journals have a very limited circulation outside academia and commercial sponsors are not often concerned about what is likely to be published in these outlets as a result of studies that they have sponsored.

The same cannot be said for publication of books, as Punch (1986) found out to his cost. At the outset of his research with Dartington Hall Trust he had signed a piece of paper in which he committed himself only to publish with prior permission of the Trust. Initially he regarded this as a mere formality, and therefore he was greatly surprised when the document was used to prevent publication of a book about Dartington Hall School. Given the importance of publications to academic careers, Punch realized that his own career was effectively being blocked by what he regarded as the intransigent position of the organization he had studied. Conversely Dartington Hall felt that publication of Punch's findings would undoubtedly do harm to the School, and therefore that he should be stopped in his tracks.

The advice of Punch, then, is that the researcher should *never* sign away her rights of publication, and this view is also strongly supported by traditional researchers such as Bulmer (1988). On the other hand, Buchanan et al. (1988) take the more pragmatic line that organizational clients have a right to receive reports from those who research them, and that they should be allowed to comment upon the reports before they are published. This collaborative approach should enable both the quality of final reports to be improved, and may also contribute to the maintenance of positive relationships between researchers and clients.

One way of resolving this dilemma is to consider the research 'models' involved. Those adopting the *military* model will wish to have clear agreements about issues such as access, confidentiality and publication rights agreed well in advance. At the other end of the scale it is very important for the *investigative journalism* researcher not to sign anything that could be used in evidence against her. This would argue for fudging agreements and avoiding any formal commitments. The two other models, *private agent* and *appropriate technology*, would represent intermediate cases between these two extremes. If agreements are to be reached in these cases they should ideally specify both the rights that the researcher has to publish, as well as the right of the client to monitor and control certain kinds of output.

Issues of implementation and utilization become more serious when one considers the more practical and applied forms of research. When working directly for clients or patrons, as in evaluation research, we have found it very important to tie the research closely to the question that the sponsors or clients want to have answered. This is not a one-off process, but depends on a considerable amount of discussion and negotiation between the needs of the client and the capabilities of the researcher (Easterby-Smith, 1994). Many clients already have a fairly good idea of the likely results from a research study *before* they commission it, and therefore the researcher should pay particular attention to the possibility of disproving what the client thinks to be the case. Success in this respect will lead to the clients learning something new; failure will provide the client with much more confidence in his or her existing beliefs.

The problem of utilization is not confined only to academic research. Innovatory projects conducted within organizations can have just as much difficulty being accepted and implemented. One of the ways that the fast-moving company 3M deals with this problem is to formalize the role of 'sponsor' – usually a senior manager who is prepared to champion a particular idea or project. As Nonaka comments:

> Before a daring and promising idea can stand on its own, it must be defined and supported by a sponsor willing to risk his or her reputation in order to advance or support changes in intracompany values. (1988: 14)

Similarly, when in-company research projects have been incorporated into management development programmes it has been found that the close involvement of senior managers as clients is essential if results are to be acted upon (Ashton and Easterby-Smith, 1979).

What remains crucial is the nature and relationship between the researcher and the clients: this needs to be open and honest rather than sycophantic, and above all there should be a reasonable degree of mutual trust. Where the degree of mutual trust is limited we have noticed a marked tendency for clients and sponsors to try to push researchers into more of a 'technician' role where the researcher is expected to gather data, often quantitative, within a framework defined by the clients. Interpretation of the data is then under the control of the clients rather than the researchers.

To some extent we have assumed above that the responsibility for utilization and consequent action is the responsibility, and in the capacity, of these clients or patrons. In the case of policy-orientated research it is by no means as simple because one may be dealing with rather complex bureaucracies or political systems. In the case of research geared towards national (social) policy, Finch (1986) points to two distinct traditions, and assumptions, about the appropriate way of using such research. On the one hand there is the social engineering model which sees research as a linear and rational process where research studies are commissioned so that their results feed into specific decisions and supply the missing facts to enable decision-makers to take the right course of action.

On the other hand there is the enlightenment model which sees implementation as an incremental process with lots of diffuse viewpoints being introduced from different levels of the social system, hence providing an *indirect* link between the research and policy implications. The former model makes full use of quantitative methods, and the latter has a preference for qualitative methods.

As one might expect, most governments and sponsoring agencies prefer to use the social engineering kind of research because it gives them more power and control over what will take place. But the problem with the largely quantitative studies implied by this model is that they can only describe the situation as it is now, or as it was in the past; they can give very little guidance on what should take place in the future, and this is a limitation when research is supposed to be aiding policy formulation. This is where the more democratic enlightenment model can help to some extent by providing a much wider range of options and ideas in order to guide future action.

But it still remains unpopular amongst sponsors, and attracts criticism from some academic quarters. Gubrium and Silverman (1989) for example, argue that even when the enlightenment model is used to provide knowledge of alternative possibilities and problems to administrators, it is still acting largely in the interests of 'the establishment'. The simple idea that the fruits of the social sciences will lead to improvements of the human condition, serves as a justification for the distinction between those who make, and those who are affected by, the rules of society. This disguises the reality of power by suggesting that it is the property of one or other group in society – rather than it being implicit in all relationships, like capillaries in the social body.

CONCLUSIONS

So what are the implications for the researcher? First, it is important to recognize that power and political issues will be significant even when, or perhaps especially when, they are not obviously present. Second, there are no easy answers, nor solutions, to the political web. It exists in the form of ideologies, of personal interests (including those of the researchers), of power differences and of ethical dilemmas.

This suggests that the researcher needs both clarity of purpose, and much flexibility in tackling problems. Much clarity of purpose can come from self-awareness, both of one's own interests, and of one's assumptions about the world and how best to investigate it. We have discussed these issues in the last two chapters. In the next part of the book we turn to consider the range of methods and techniques that are at the disposal of the researcher. We stress consistently that these should not be seen as entirely free-standing; but they should be subordinated to considerations of purpose and philosophy that have been outlined above.

NOTES

1 We have added a list of some of the best-known academic associations and contact addresses in Appendix II. Our advice would be to join one general association and a specialist one initially, they are not expensive and you will often get journals included as part of your subscription price.
2 The latest ranking of journals in the Business and Management area from the SSCI is given in Appendix III.

PART THREE

DOING MANAGEMENT RESEARCH: GATHERING DATA, MAKING SENSE AND COMMUNICATING RESEARCH RESULTS

The three chapters in this part of the book consider ways of gathering data, making sense of it, and completing the research process. Chapters 5 and 6 respectively look at the use of quantitative and qualitative methods for data collection and analysis, and Chapter 7 looks at the problems of writing-up, and capitalizing on, research results.

Before embarking on these chapters we need to emphasize a general difference between positivist and constructionist methods. Within the positivist approach, which assumes that there is an objective truth as we have seen in Chapter 3, there needs to be a separation between data collection and data analysis. This leads to three almost discrete stages to the research process. First, collection of data where all the treatments have to be the same, and where close contact with respondents may lead to bias; second, analysis which is undertaken at a time and place separate from the collection process, usually after having recourse to statistical analysis of the data; and third, the writing-up process which declares the finding thus produced.

Qualitative data collection methods are altogether different, both in terms of the philosophy of the approach and the skills required to carry them out. First, there is no clear separation between the different stages identified above. Unlike the quantitative approach above, it is perfectly legitimate to change the questions asked as a consequence of the information gained. Ideally it is useful when new themes appear to check those in earlier interviews if the opportunity is there. What we can see is a more iterative process than the quantitative study, where some analysis takes place while interviews are in progress, and these understandings are incorporated into future interviews to check out the emergent ideas and understandings. Similarly, as the method of declaring qualitative studies relies on quotations, illustrations or vignettes, these have to be accurately collected at the time of the study and as a consequence, noted and reported so that they can be reproduced later.

The implication for the organization of the two following chapters is that we have several choices. If we were to follow the positivist viewpoint we would discuss qualitative and quantitative forms of data collection, and then follow this with a separate chapter on data analysis. If, on the other hand, we were to follow the constructionist route then we would discuss data collection and interpretation in an integrated way. But there is also the added complication that quantitative methods are not fully synonymous with positivism, and qualitative methods are not totally synonymous with constructionism. So, in the qualitative chapter we have separate sections for data collection and analysis, but we also discuss issues of interpretation as we go through the earlier part of the chapter. However in the quantitative chapter we try to maintain the separation between issues of data collection and analysis.

5 Qualitative Methods

In this chapter we consider techniques primarily associated with qualitative methods: interviews, observation and diary methods. Questionnaires and survey methods are tackled in the following chapter, not because they are always quantitative methods, but because they are easily used in a quantitative way, and they therefore provide a framework around which to discuss issues of quantitative methods.

Many of the qualitative methods discussed here are simply devices whereby the researcher, once close to organizational members, can gain the sorts of insights into people and situations she requires. Others are useful as aids or tools to help respondents themselves to think about their own worlds and consider the way, possibly for the first time, they construct their reality.

Van Maanen (1983: 9) defines qualitative techniques as 'an array of interpretative techniques which seek to describe, decode, translate and otherwise come to terms with the meaning, not the frequency, of certain more or less naturally occurring phenomena in the social world'.

The most fundamental of all qualitative methods is that of in-depth interviewing, and it is for this reason that we have examined its use in detail. But there is a range of lesser-known 'instruments' which provide useful ways of supplementing interviews and help to generate insights into how respondents see their world. We have chosen to present six of these instruments or approaches and have briefly discussed the use of each, pointing to further literature where appropriate. These are critical incident technique, repertory grid technique, projective techniques, protocol analysis, group interviews and cognitive mapping.

In the later part of the chapter, we examine the different ways in which qualitative data can be managed and analysed, including both manual and the rapidly advancing computer-based methods, and we also look at the circumstances under which each method is most appropriate.

INTERVIEWING

Before adopting any method of data collection, it helps to be clear about the overall objectives of the research. This applies to the choice of the interview as a method, as well as to the wide range of ways in which interviews may be conducted. They can be highly formalized and structured, for example, as in market research, or they can be quite unstructured, akin to free-ranging conversations.

Although interviewing is often claimed to be 'the best' method of gathering information, its complexity can sometimes be underestimated. It is time consuming to undertake interviews properly, and they are sometimes used when other methods might be more appropriate. If researchers wish to obtain answers to a number of fairly simple questions then a questionnaire might well be more appropriate. Face-to-face interviewing in this case only provides the researcher with access to the individuals to be asked the questions. These highly structured interviews are based on carefully prepared sets of questions piloted and refined until the researcher is convinced of their 'validity'. The assumption is made that the interviewer will ask each interviewee the same question in the same tone of voice. The simplest form of such interviews is where there are short answers to questions and the interviewer simply ticks boxes and no deep thought is required by either party. These are the type of interviews that take place in the shopping areas of towns and cities every Saturday morning and their primary aim is to gain a quantitative result from a carefully targeted sample. Within certain limits of accuracy we can infer that, for example, 20 per cent of a population think one thing, and 10 per cent think another. Large numbers (hundreds or thousands) are required in order to have confidence that the responses obtained can be generalized to the population at large.

As with most types of research, there are compromise positions. A positivistic approach can be retained where the interview follows a fairly standardized set of questions, whilst offering some flexibility, and allowing the views of the interviewee to become known. The type of interview might be appropriate, for example, when questions require a good deal of thought and when responses need to be explored and clarified. This process often gives an added degree of confidence to the replies which are not available in questionnaires. In addition, the interviewer does have the opportunity to identify non-verbal clues, which are present, for example, in the inflection of the voice, facial expressions or the clothes that the interviewee is wearing and these can be used to develop secondary questions. Sometimes these verbal clues may offer important reasons for misinformation (Sims, 1993). Although this type of research is conducted by interview, the standards by which it is judged are those that apply to quantitative questionnaires and readers should refer to the following chapter of the book when considering their use.

The present section deals primarily with interviews where the primary purpose is to understand the meanings interviewees attach to issues and situations in contexts that are not structured in advance by the researcher.

This method of data collection was much used by Rosemary Stewart in her research on the nature of managerial work. The importance of interviews is summarized by Burgess (1982: 107): '(the interview) is . . . the opportunity for the researcher to probe deeply to uncover new clues, open up new dimensions of a problem and to secure vivid, accurate inclusive accounts that are based on personal experience'. Most interviews are conducted on a one-to-one basis, between the interviewer and the interviewee.

The label 'qualitative interview' has been used to describe a broad range of types of interview, from those that are supposedly totally non-directive, or open, to those where the interviewer has prepared a list of questions which he or she is determined to ask, come what may. Jones (1985: 45) comments that: 'between these two extremes is an abyss of practice and therefore theory about the purpose and nature of the qualitative interview'. In her view the main reason for conducting qualitative interviews is to understand 'how individuals construct the reality of their situation formed from the complex personal framework of beliefs and values, which they have developed over their lives in order to help explain and predict events in their world'. Researchers must therefore be able to conduct interviews so that the opportunity is present for these insights to be gained. Failure to achieve this might well result in a superficial exchange of information, which might as well have been better achieved via a semi-structured questionnaire.

In order to be able to achieve these insights the researcher will need to be sensitive enough, and skilled enough, to ensure that he or she not only understands the other person's views, but also at times, assists individuals to explore their own beliefs. Later in this chapter, we will discuss a number of techniques that might help the researcher do this to advantage.

Interviews, both semi-structured and unstructured, are therefore appropriate methods when:

1. it is necessary to understand the constructs that the interviewee uses as a basis for her opinions and beliefs about a particular matter or situation; and
2. one aim of the interview is to develop an understanding of the respondent's 'world' so that the researcher might influence it, either independently, or collaboratively as in the case with action research.

In addition they are useful when: the step by step logic of a situation is not clear; the subject matter is highly confidential or commercially sensitive; and there are issues about which the interviewee may be reluctant to be truthful other than confidentially in a one-to-one situation.

Degree of Structure

Jones (1985) highlights a number of issues that researchers need to consider in order for interviews to be successful. The first is the problem which all researchers must resolve – how much structure to put into the interview. She makes the point that:

> . . . there is no such thing as presuppositionless research. In preparing for interviews researchers will have, and should have, some broad questions in mind, and the more interviews they do and the more patterns they see in the data, the more

> likely they are to use this grounded understanding to want to explore in certain directions rather than others. (1985: 47)

In a study conducted by Richard, employees and managers were interviewed together. By mixing the interviews he was able not only to compare the way different people viewed situations, but also to develop better lines of inquiry which provided the opportunity to check out emergent themes and patterns as the interviews progressed. On a purely practical note, as these interviews all took place within two days, he remembers being saturated with information, and a consideration might have been to spread them out over a longer period.

We would encourage researchers to make choices as they collect their data as to which line of questioning they should explore further, and which lines of inquiry to discard. Even still, they need frameworks from which to plot out the developing themes, but as Jones reminds us, although researchers are to some extent tied to their frameworks they shouldn't be 'tied up by them'. One way in which this can be achieved is to prepare a checklist, which can be used as a loose structure for the questions. Although there may be some deviation from the sequence in order to follow interesting lines of inquiry and to facilitate an unbroken discussion, the interviewer should attempt to cover all the issues mentioned.

Finally, on the subject of structure, the researcher should be warned against assuming that a 'non-directive' interview, where the interviewee talks freely without interruption or intervention, is the way to achieve a clear picture of the interviewee's perspective. This is far from true. It is more likely to produce no clear picture in the mind of the interviewee of what questions or issues the interviewer is interested in, and in the mind of the interviewer, of what questions the interviewee is answering! Too many assumptions of this kind lead to poor data, which is difficult to interpret. Researchers are therefore likely to be more successful if they are clear at the outset about the exact areas of their interest.

Interviewing Skills

Understanding issues from an interviewee's point of view can be extremely difficult, especially when the respondent himself may not have a clearly articulated view of the answers to the questions posed, or may not wish to divulge sensitive information. It is here that the skills of the interviewer come to the fore.

McClelland (1965) conducted careful studies about commonsense notions of 'motivation'. He concluded that people cannot be trusted to say exactly what their motives are, as they often get ideas about their own motives from commonly accepted half-truths. For example, a person may say that he is interested in achievement because he has made money. But a careful check using different probing methods may reveal quite a different picture. Often people simply aren't aware of their own motives. Mangham (1986) in his studies of managerial competence met this problem. He found that many managers complained that they needed subordinates who could better motivate staff, but when asked what, exactly, they meant by motivation, they gave ambiguous answers and became confused.

From a positivistic standpoint, the fact that there is ambiguity about the meaning of 'motivation' invalidates the research. But for the in-depth interviewer who probes, questions and checks, this is important data. The fact that people are confused and can't agree on what they mean by motivation or the way they construct particular situations is the essence of the research.

The skills of an interviewer centre around the ability to recognize what is relevant and remember it, or tape it, so that afterwards detailed notes can be made. This requires one to be perceptive and sensitive to events, so that lines of inquiry can be changed and adapted as one progresses. Above all, interviewers need to be able to listen, and to refrain from projecting their own opinions or feelings into the situation. This is more difficult than it sounds, since one of the ways of obtaining trust is to empathize with the respondent. The interviewer needs to listen to what the person wants to say, and what she does not want to say, without helping (Mayo, 1949). In recognizing these situations, non-verbal data might be crucial in providing clues, for example the loss of eye contact, or a changed facial expression.

From time to time as patterns or uncertainties arise from the interview, it is useful to check one's understanding by summarizing what has been said. This should be presented as a way of seeking clarification. The process of 'testing out' is a way of safeguarding against assuming too quickly that understanding has been achieved.

Social Interaction

Another important factor and skill which the interviewer must understand is the importance placed on the social interaction between interviewer and interviewee. Jones (1985) suggests people will attribute meaning and significance to the particular research situations they are in. The questions an interviewer may ask and the answers an interviewee gives will often depend on the way in which their situations are defined.

From the point of view of the interviewer, certain conclusions may be drawn from the dress, mannerisms, voice or language of the interviewee which can in part formulate the attitude we take to that person. Wrong assumptions made from non-verbals might also bias attitudes in other ways. Richard recalls one interview when the Union Convenor wore a sports jacket in complete contrast to the other men who wore overalls and boots. This raised questions in his mind about the convenor's relationship with both men and management.

Similarly Jones (1985) points out that interviewees will 'suss out' what researchers are like, and make judgements from their first impressions about whether they can be trusted and be told everything or whether they might be damaged in some way by data that could be so used. Such suspicions do not necessarily mean that interviewees will refuse to be interviewed, but it might mean, as Jones indicates, that they just: '. . . seek to get the interview over as quickly as possible, with enough detail and enough feigned interest to satisfy the researcher that he or she is getting something of value but without saying anything that touches the core of what is actually believed and cared about in the research' (1985: 50).

In extreme circumstances an interviewee may deliberately try to deceive the researcher, as in the classic case of the famous American anthropologist, Margaret Mead. The Australian scholar, Derek Freeman, carefully followed the trail of Mead's research five decades later, and managed to identify and interview the two women, who as young girls, had supplied her with material about the sexual behaviour of adolescent Samoan girls. According to these women, they talked with Mead for just one evening and deliberately engaged in what they called *taufa'a se'e*, or 'recreational lying', in which a person tries to convince the other of the opposite of the truth (Freeman, 1996). It was this information upon which Mead built her theory that if there is freedom of sexual life within a society then the 'adolescent crisis' will disappear. This theory formed the foundation of her fame and fortune.

For reasons such as this, Sims (1993) comments that being able to recognize when an interviewer is being misinformed is an important aspect of the interview process. Individuals will often select answers between complex truths, rather than providing the 'whole truth', simply because it would take too long to give all the nuances. The problem arises when they are providing a consistent and deliberate spin on the information so as to push the researcher in the wrong direction. With luck this kind of deception might be detected through such things as eye movements, discomfort, or general shiftiness. It can also be discouraged if the interviewer encourages complexity and potential contradictions in the data: this will make it harder for the prankster to spin a simple, and erroneous, yarn.

Obtaining Trust

An important factor underlying the effectiveness of social interaction within qualitative interviewing is therefore trust. This is a difficult issue, especially in one-off interviews where the people involved have not met before. Failure to develop trust may well result in interviewees simply resorting to telling the researcher what they think she wants to know. But an open and trusting relationship may not be possible or sufficient when dealing with particular elites or individuals in positions of power as we have discussed in Chapter 4. It often helps if the researcher is viewed as having equal status to the manager as we saw with Pettigrew's research on elites in Chapter 2, and also if the manager feels he might gain from the exchange. There are some practical ways to achieve this.

The first point is to ensure that one is well clued up about the company. A scan through the company's website will give a quick impression both of the issues that are currently considered significant, and of the extent to which their PR people are keeping up with communications technology. In addition, an online search of recent press coverage, or tracking down a couple of annual reports and recruitment literature in advance should enable you to appear 'on the ball'. When making initial contact our experience suggests that a quick e-mail followed by a phone call is often better than a formal letter. But be prepared to make two or three calls before the right contact is established. Contrary to common belief, managers are surprisingly ready to talk over the telephone and the 'voice' contact is a first opportunity to communicate enthusiasm for the project. Take full advantage of the opportunity, but beware that at the same time the manager will be weighing up the likely costs (and benefits) of the potential intrusion.

When talking about research it is important to use appropriate language. It is not a good strategy to baffle the possible gatekeeper by using too many theoretical concepts. Here are a few examples of the way words may be interpreted:

Student implies an unskilled 'amateurish' inquiry, which may be a waste of time, although unthreatening.

Researcher implies that there might be a more professional relationship, but that questions of access might need to be managed carefully.

Interview gives the impression of a formal structured interrogation, which is controlled by the researcher.

Discussion may make the manager feel more relaxed and less threatened, with the potential for genuine exchange.

Survey is often understood to be the kind of study where findings are aggregated at a very high level and are therefore of limited use to the practitioner.

Provided the gatekeeper has shown some interest then preliminary contacts are best followed up by letter. This fulfils three purposes. One is credibility, especially if this can be done on the headed paper of an independent body – a university, institute or college. Second, it may assist co-operation in the future; and third, it provides the opportunity to send further details about the research. This is the opportunity to set out in detail what is required. The phenomenal growth in business and management courses over the last two decades has had both negative and positive effects on the likelihood of gaining access. On the one hand there are now a lot of other students and institutions competing for access to a limited number of organizations; on the other hand, there are now large numbers of managers who have taken management degrees themselves (and some may still be studying on part-time schemes), and they are likely both to understand, and be sympathetic towards, the researcher's objectives.

A further piece of advice is to avoid being over-anxious about getting all the data in one go. Relationships take time to form. It may be better to undertake a series of short interviews from which a useful dialogue flows, rather than to act hastily and alienate the interviewees through lots of pushy questioning.

The location of the interview and the setting in which it takes place can also be important. Richard found in one project that by conducting interviews in the manager's office adverse results were produced because the employees being interviewed were uncertain as to the confidentiality of what they might say.

Interviewing on 'neutral territory', for example in a car or in the works canteen, might have alleviated the problem. Mark encountered the effect of geographical setting very forcibly when conducting research within Chinese companies. Most interviews with managers conducted on-site were highly formalized, rather like public performances, yet when invited off-site to banquets or the researcher's hotel, managers would open up with all kinds of opinions and indiscretions which would be inconceivable at work (Easterby-Smith and Malina, 1999).

One strategy used by a colleague of ours, which worked to his advantage, was conducted well away from the work place. When researching into aspects of management development, he undertook this fieldwork by sitting in the first class compartments of trains. He would sit next to executive-looking individuals armed only with a folder marked Management Development in the hope that managers would talk to him. This they usually did, and without prompts he was able to elicit their views on a range of management development issues. What struck Neil was the extent to which the views and opinions expressed by managers, off-guard and to a person they were unlikely ever to meet again, contradicted the 'reality' contained in much contemporary management literature. Had the interview taken place in the manager's office, the results might well have been quite different.

This example not only illustrates how a researcher managed to obtain data which the manager may have found hard to articulate in his office; it also shows how a method can be undertaken in a 'natural setting' where each views the other as having equal status. This kind of research would normally be extremely costly, yet it does illustrate the lengths that might be required to obtain data.

In another example, researching small business owners, we have found that relationships have often developed quickest when interviewees are first engaged in general discussions about their business. This is something which they know and understand, though care needs to be taken that this does not go on far too long. Whatever focus subsequent questions have, answers have a context that is useful and they will be answered with much less formality.

Finally, there is the question about the effects of using audio tape to record interviews. The decision on whether or not to use a tape recorder depends on an interviewee's anxiety about confidentiality and the use to which any information divulged can be put. Anxiety can be minimized, for example, by handing over the responsibility for switching the tape on and off to the interviewee, so that when he or she does not wish certain parts to be recorded, they can just switch off the machine. The main reasons in favour of using a tape recorder are that it aids the listening process and gives the opportunity of an unbiased record of the conversation. Good audio recordings are essential for accurate transcripts and also enable the researcher to re-listen to the interview, so she may well hear things that were missed at the time. On the other hand, if the existence of a tape recorder, for reasons of general anxiety or corporate security, creates strong inhibitions then the researcher will have to rely on good note taking at the time, followed as soon as possible afterwards by committing further reflections to paper.

Interview Bias

Readers will see in the next chapter on quantitative research that interview bias – where the process of conducting an interview might influence the responses given – is regarded as crucial. With in-depth interviewing the issue is slightly different. Since depth interviews derive from a social constructionist perspective, it follows that there is no one 'objective' view to be discovered which the process of interviewing may bias. However, there is a very real concern about interviewers imposing their own reference frame on the interviewees, both when the questions are asked and when the answers are interpreted.

The researcher is in something of a dilemma for, as has been suggested in an earlier section, open questions may avoid bias, but they are not always the best way of obtaining the information one may wish to know. Nor are they always the best way of putting an interviewee at ease. But the issue of bias gives a pull in the other direction. In order to avoid bias, there is often the tendency for researchers to leave questions open. There will be some occasions when researchers will want to focus on discovering responses to specific alternatives, and in this case 'probes' can be useful as a intervention technique to improve, or sharpen-up, the interviewee's response.

There are a number of alternative ways in which these can be used:

- the *basic probe* simply involves repeating the initial question and is useful when the interviewee seems to be wandering off the point;
- *explanatory probes* involve building onto incomplete or vague statements made by the respondent. Ask questions such as: 'what did you mean by that?', 'What makes you say that?'
- *focused probes* are used to obtain specific information. Typically one would ask the respondent,'What sort of . . .?';
- the *silent probe* is one of the most effective techniques to use when the respondent is either reluctant or very slow to answer the question posed. Simply pause and let her break the silence;
- the technique of *drawing out* can be used when the interviewee has halted, or dried up. Repeat the last few words she said, and then look expectantly or say, 'tell me more about that', 'what happened then';
- *giving ideas or suggestions* involves offering the interviewee an idea to think about – 'have you thought about . . .?', 'have you tried . . .?', 'did you know that . . .?', 'perhaps you should ask Y . . .';
- *mirroring* or *reflecting* involves expressing in your own words what the respondent has just said. This is very effective because it may force the respondent to rethink her answer and reconstruct another reply which will amplify the previous answer – 'what you seem to be saying/feeling is . . .'.

To avoid bias, probes should never lead. An example of a leading probe might be: 'So you would say that you were really satisfied?'. Instead of which the interviewer should say: 'Can you explain a little more?' or 'How do you mean?'.

The Relevance to Interviewees

The relevance of the research to interviewees is another factor that will affect the quality of the data provided. Maruyama (1981) has explored the attitudes of prison inmates to researchers, such as sociologists or newspaper reporters. Because they regard them to be exploiting their situation for reasons such as an enhanced reputation and career advancement they tend to invent plausible but untrue responses in order to minimize the intrusion such research often represents. This is a variant of the more 'innocent' amusement of the Samoan informants of Margaret Mead, which we noted above, and there are salutary lessons here for many researchers in management.

But not all interaction or questioning produces answers that are threatening or potentially damaging, particularly in management. On the contrary, many individuals find benefit in talking to an independent outsider about themselves or learning something about future changes in the organization as in action research. Researchers should be able to recognize and capitalize on these situations and offer them as benefits or advantages to interviewees in exchange for participation. This is the strategy which underlies much work in the tradition of participative action research (Reason and Bradley, 2000). The more they are willing to be open the more that both parties are likely to gain.

In addition, interest and commitment shown by the interviewer often produces far better results than clinical detachment. There are several practical ways in which this can be achieved. One way is by conducting more than one interview, or by offering the interviewee the opportunity to comment on the transcripts of the tape or on written-up field notes. Another is to offer interviewees a summary of the results or conclusions, and to make sure that they are sent. These strategies are not just 'ploys' to obtain compliance with a researcher's wishes, they can for example, form important ways of validating data and gaining new insights.

In some kinds of research there can be more immediate benefits to participation. In action research for example, where change is one objective of the research, the researcher's role can be viewed as a cross between an importer of new knowledge to organizational members and a medium through which individuals can express the way they view the organization or change. By working on the change process and by operating in this way, researchers and the organization will often gain the kind of contextual information, behavioural as well as structural, that can assist the change process, as well as enabling the participants in the research to gain a better understanding of their organization and their role within it. This is particularly important at times of change, as individuals have a natural concern about how change might affect them.

In other forms of action research, for example in the group interviewing technique which we discuss later called 'cognitive mapping', change is also seen as a primary objective, but in this case information is shared between the organizational members. With this technique, perceptions, views and beliefs can be explored, and facilitated by the researcher, in relation to particular organizational problems. Through such processes interviewees become involved in activities which are both meaningful and useful to them.

Ethics and Choices

In Chapter 4 we reviewed some of the main ethical issues that may be encountered in any form of management research. These are particularly pertinent in the case of interviewing because of the potential freedom within the interaction for exchanging information and interpretations. It is for this reason that organizations may be hostile to totally open interviews, and it is not unusual for researchers to be asked for a copy of the interview schedule before access is granted. In this way the organization, or factions within it, may feel they are reducing the potential risk involved.

The ethical issues relating to individual respondents concern the micro-politics of the organization. Despite assurances given about confidentiality, which normally mean not revealing raw data to anyone else in the same organization, it is virtually impossible to hide everything that has been said. In qualitative interviews the focus will inevitably be affected by data and impressions obtained from earlier interviews. As we noted in Chapter 4, it is not beyond the wit of managers to infer from the questions asked what kind of information has already been obtained by the interviewer, and from whom. Thus it is important for the interviewer to be aware of the possible interests of the interviewee, and how these could be harmed by indirect disclosures of the wrong information.

The same point applies to the style or degree of intervention that researchers should make overall, and many ideal situations will be tempered by such things as resource availability and the ease of access. However, much of what will be possible will depend upon the nature of the relationship that develops, and whether sufficient trust has been formed. What is important is that researchers understand these issues when dealing with interviews. By understanding the implications of the choices they make they will be better placed to recognize any effect they may have on the nature of the relationship formed, and therefore on the data that is collected.

WAYS OF SUPPLEMENTING INTERVIEWS

Critical Incident Technique

One method of teasing out information is the critical incident technique which was proposed by Flanagan (1954). He defines it as 'a set of procedures for collecting direct observations of human behaviour in such a way as to facilitate their potential usefulness in solving practical problems and developing broad psychological principles'. By 'incident', Flanagan meant any observable human activity that is sufficiently complete in itself to permit inference or prediction to be made about the person performing the act. To be 'critical' the incident must occur in a situation where the purpose or intent of the act seems fairly clear to the observer and where its consequences are sufficiently definite to leave little doubt concerning its effect.

An example that illustrates the technique was the way the American army investigated the large number of helicopter crashes that were occurring particularly when landing in groups. By concentrating their research only on what the pilot recalled of the 'critical incident' when control of the aircraft was lost they were able to build up a picture of the particular circumstances when most crashes happened. Control was invariably lost just before the helicopter landed, and the 'critical incident' was the occasion when the pilot viewed the ground through another helicopter's rotor blades.

In his writings, Flanagan describes his technique from a highly 'objectivist' standpoint, claiming its value as being able to bridge the gap between the observation, and the recording and interpretation of the reasons behind actions. One of the most famous uses of the technique which closely follows Flanagan's principles is the work of Herzberg into employee motivation. His study involved interviews with 200 engineers and salesmen about their experiences of work. They were asked to recall a time when they felt particularly good and particularly bad about their work, and once each incident had been identified the researchers probed for the events that had preceded these feelings. It was found that one group of factors very commonly preceded the good incidents, but a different list of factors normally preceded the bad incidents. From this Herzberg was able to conclude that the reasons for work satisfaction and dissatisfaction were different, from which it was but a small step for him to conclude that factors such as recognition and advancement acted as motivators, whereas other factors, such as poor supervision or low salary, would demotivate people (Herzberg, 1987).

But the technique has also been used by qualitative researchers to great effect, particularly in conjunction with in-depth interviews. Respondents might, for example, be asked to track back to particular instances in their work lives and to explain their actions and motives with specific regard to those instances. In Richard's research he has used the technique to ask owner/managers of small companies what had been their particular barriers to growth. At a given point in the interview he would ask if there had been any particular problems in the development of the company. He would then encourage the manager to explain that problem in some detail and illustrate how the problem was eventually surmounted. From this example he would begin to develop ideas about how individuals managed particular problems and about the information they used in doing this. It is important to use material that can be substantiated since there are criticisms of the technique relating to recall, and the natural tendency of individuals to use hindsight in rationalizing the past. One technique which overcomes this problem is protocol analysis, and we will discuss it later.

Mackinlay (1986), when undertaking research into a housing authority used the critical incident technique in a most unusual way. His 'open' questionnaire was targeted directly on householders; it was intentionally made simple, the number of questions being set at only six to enable easy completion. The phrases used in the questions were clear without any extensive technical or ambiguous wording. Each question allowed a third of an A4 page for a reply but some respondents added additional sheets. The questions concentrated on the primary area of interest and were preceded by the brief explanation: 'These questions are open-ended and I have kept them to a few vital areas of interest. All will require you to reflect back on decisions and reasons for decisions you have made'.

The questions themselves were short and to the point:

1 Please think about an occasion when you improved your home. What improvements did you make?
2 On that occasion what made you do it?
3 Did you receive any help? If yes, please explain what help you received.
4 Have you wanted to improve your home in any other way but could not?
5 What improvements did you wish to make?
6 What stopped you from doing it?

Data analysis was carried out using a grounded theory approach, which will be discussed later in the chapter, and proved most revealing. There were, he found, only two main 'triggers' for major house improvement, neighbours improving their homes in particular ways and the inheritance of significant amounts of money. So taken was he by the approach, that he also used photographs of different interior improvements (bathrooms, etc.) in order to understand better the kind of interiors householders preferred.

Repertory Grid Technique

Another useful technique for investigating areas that are hard to articulate is the repertory grid. The technique is used to understand individuals' perceptions and the constructs they use to understand and manage their world. A repertory grid is a mathematical representation of how an individual differentiates between objects or experiences in his or her world. Repertory grids can also be used with people who have low verbal ability, making them particularly useful for children and people with language difficulties. A colleague of Richard's piloting the repertory grid technique for his research, used it on his children to find out what they wanted for Christmas. The technique has a strong track record and has been used extensively in areas such as career guidance and job descriptions.

The repertory grid is based on the Personal Construct Theory of George Kelly (1955), who regarded individuals as 'scientists' in their own right, continually exploring and developing understanding of their worlds. In doing this they develop cognitive maps for all significant aspects of their experience – which then define, and limit, their potential repertories of behaviour. It follows from such a theory that if we can find ways of drawing a personal map then we are in a position either to understand behaviour, or possibly to alter the map and change behaviour. A repertory grid is a tool for uncovering an individual's view of the world, and it contains the following features:

1 *Elements* – or the objects of thought. These objects are usually the other people in the world about us, but they can be inanimate objects or abstract ideas such as, for example, the individual's view of the skills he or she possesses and how these skills were learnt.

2 *Constructs* – 'qualities' which the individual uses to describe and differentiate between the elements. These are the spectacles with which he or she views the world outside.
3 *Linking mechanisms* – there are various ways of indicating how the elements and constructs are linked, and of presenting the links in matrix form.

The standard procedure for generating a repertory grid is as follows: first, decide on the *focus* of the grid. This should be quite specific and the interviewee should be reminded of this focus at regular intervals. These might be qualities required of a manager in a particular function, the particular work content of a given job, or the features of products currently competing with one's own.

Second, select with the interviewee a group of *elements* (between 5 and 10) which are relevant to the chosen focus, and which are also likely to provide a good range. If, for example, the focus of the grid was on the skills required of a manager it would be appropriate to choose individuals who were familiar to the interviewee, some of whom he regarded as particularly able, some of average ability and some of below average ability.

Third, *constructs* are elicited, usually by asking the respondent to compare and contrast elements in groups of three, known as triads. Each element is written onto a card and then three cards are selected at random. The interviewee is asked to decide which pair of cards are similar in a way which also makes them distinct from the third. They are asked to provide a word or phrase which describes the pair, and a contrasting word or phrase to describe the remaining card. For example, in the case of a grid with the focus on the competencies required of a manager, someone might choose two cards of named people as similar because they see them both as *dynamic*, and the third as *staid*. In this case the construct elicited is a continuum on which *dynamic* is at one end and *staid* is at the other. This process is repeated with different triads of elements until a reasonable number of constructs (perhaps 6 to 10) have been produced.

Fourth, each of the elements needs to be *linked* to, or rated against, each of the constructs. This can be done in several different ways: by deciding which of the two 'poles' of the construct provides the best description of the element; by determining the position of the element on a rating scale (often 7 points) constructed between the poles of each construct; or by rank-ordering each of the elements along the dimension indicated by each of the constructs. The results of these ratings or rankings are recorded as ticks and crosses, or as numbers in a matrix.

Figure 5.1 shows a grid that was completed by one of the team managers at a food manufacturer. It was intended to explore the qualities required of team members and lead directly to the redesign of a system for their performance appraisal. The linking process in this case involves simply indicating which of the two poles is most appropriate.

Small grids can be analysed manually, or by eye, by looking for patterns of relationships and differences between constructs and elements. This can form the basis of an interesting collaborative discussion between interviewer and interviewee. With larger grids (say, 5 × 5, or upwards) it is more common to use computer analysis packages. There are two main families of these, based either on principal components analysis, or on cluster analysis. The former produces

	Skilled operator	**Skilled operator**	**Average**	**Average**	**Unskilled**	**Unskilled**	
Tick if this end applies	Leslie	Ann	Frank	Denise	Julie	David	*Cross if this end applies*
Timekeeping	✓	✓	✓	✗	✓	✓	Poor Timekeeping
Flexible	✓	✓	✓	✓	✗	✗	Unwilling to use skills
Quality awareness	✗	✗	✓	✓	✗	✗	Lacks awareness
Appropriate communi-cation with assistant manager	✓	✓	✗	✓	✗	✗	Not commu-nicative with manager
Suggest ideas for improvement	✓	✓	✓	✗	✗	✗	Does not want to improve
Competitive	✓	✗	✗	✗	✓	✗	Not competitive
Problem solving	✓	✓	✓	✓	✗	✗	Does not solve problems

FIGURE 5.1 Repertory grid completed by team manager

a map which plots the elements within dimensions, and axes, defined by the constructs. Figure 5.2 shows the principle component analysis of a grid completed by a manager which focuses on the competencies of himself and others at work. The constructs are numbered 1 to 17 and the two poles of each construct are plotted on the map. The labels given to each pole are listed above or below each of the quadrants of the map. The elements are listed as A to F, and they are also plotted on the map within the space defined by the 17 constructs. The map is structured around 'components', which are defined by clusterings of some of the strongest constructs (a strong construct has high mathematical variance and is shown as distant from the centre of the map). Thus component 1 is closely linked to constructs 16, 1 and 5 (understanding business problems, technical knowledge and making decisions). We might therefore choose to label this component as a 'task' dimension. Similarly, component 2 is closely linked to constructs 7, 8 and 9, which could therefore be summarized as a 'people' dimension. Thus we can say that the Ideal Manager (D) combines both people and task skills; Skilled Managers (B and C) have high task skills and low people skills; and he rates himself (E) as rather weak on both dimensions.

Figure 5.3 shows an example of a dendrogram which analyses the perceptions drawn from university students about the kind of skills they need to develop. The dendrogram should be read from right to left and splits firstly into two large clusters A and B which comprise *taking immediate action* to *being in a mess* and from *standing up for yourself* to *communicating* showing the closeness of the links between the different constructs. The greater the degree of similarity, the more the link is shown to the left of the dendrogram.

Advantages and disadvantages of the repertory grid technique are set out by Stewart and Stewart (1981). The main advantages being that:

1 it involves verbalizing constructs which otherwise would remain hidden;
2 it is based on the individual's own framework, not that of the expert; and
3 it provides insights for both the researcher and the researched.

13 Abdicates problems
2 Presentation skills
8 Delegates
9 Motivates team
4 Knows what is going on in team

7 Deals with poor performance
6 Faces up to poor performance
11 Presents options to customers
15 Selling what you do not agree with
3 Manages relationships with customers
14 Knowing what others do
1 Technical knowledge
17 Organized
5 Makes day-to-day decisions
10 Plans ahead
16 Understanding problems facing busines:
12 Openness to problems

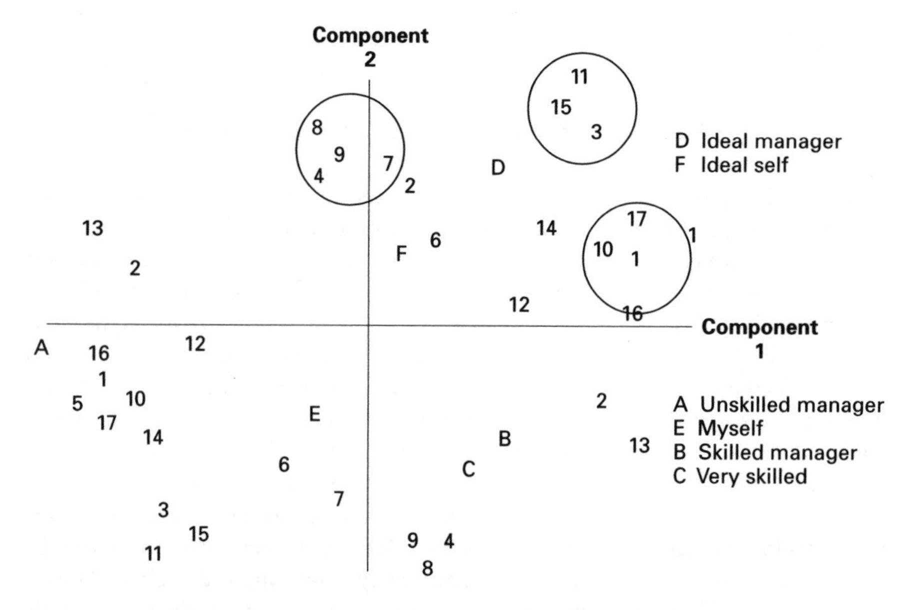

12 Covers up problems
16 Unaware of problems facing business
10 Does not plan ahead
5 Lets others take decisions
17 Unorganized
1 Low knowledge
14 Planning in isolation
15 Shifting the blame
11 Cannot say no to customers
6 Letting things slide
7 Not dealing with poor performance

4 Not aware of 'goings-on'
9 Antagonizes team
8 Holds on to problems
2 Poor presentation
13 Effectively deals with problems

FIGURE 5.2 Principal component analysis of competencies required by a manager

The main disadvantages are that:

1 grids are very hard work to complete and can take considerable periods of time: a 20 × 10 matrix can take up to one and a half hours to complete;
2 they require a high degree of skill from the interviewer if the interviewee's construct framework is to be fully explored;
3 they may be difficult to analyse and interpret, and there is some danger that people will rely on the structure of the technique to produce packaged, rather than meaningful results; and
4 the technique has become 'popular' and as a consequence is sometimes used mechanistically while forgetting the underlying theory of personal constructs.

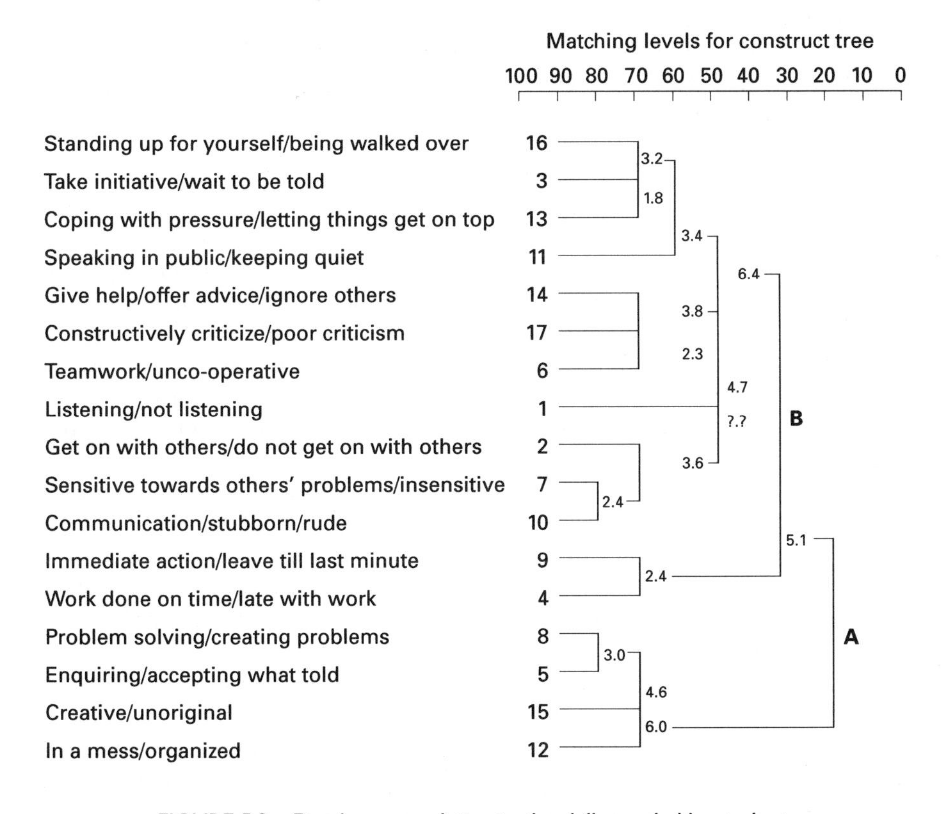

FIGURE 5.3 Dendrogram relating to the skills needed by students

For those interested in learning more about the repertory grid technique, it has been well written up in a number of publications. For example, Bannister and Fransella (1971) provide a classic overview of the theory and method; Stewart and Stewart (1981) review business applications; and Easterby-Smith et al. (1996) illustrate a number of applications in the field of management.

Projective Techniques

The rationale for these techniques is that individuals will reveal hidden levels of their consciousness by reacting to different types of stimuli, such as drawings. These stimuli are intended to be very ambiguous in the hope that the respondents will 'project' their own meaning and significance onto the drawings. In so doing they declare aspects of their innermost motives and feelings, which can be interpreted by trained psychologists.

Psychologists such as Freud (see Hall, 1954) and Rogers (1967) claim that there are at least three important barriers which provide blockages to the discovery of an individual's innermost motives: repression and the unconscious; self-awareness and rationality; and social influences. Projective techniques are regarded as effective ways to bypass these barriers.

Personally we see the value of projective techniques as being confined to specific applications since they always require 'expert analysis'. In many quarters they are also viewed with scepticism and suspicion. Projective techniques are useful exploratory devices which can reveal hidden aspects of personality or begin a dialogue between researcher and those researched. The technique is widely used in market research (Jobber and Horgan, 1987) in the attempt to establish deep-seated feelings about such things as the basic motivation to buy or not to buy, consumer reaction to colours, size and shape of packaging, or names of products.

A common form of projective test is the thematic apperception test (TAT) which asks individuals simply to write a story; the researcher's task is then to find themes in what people say. One way of prompting stories is by the use of photographs. The technique was first used by Henry Murray (1938) and has been developed by David McClelland (1961) as a means of measuring the strength of an individual's need for achievement. McClelland found that a distinctive achievement motive could be isolated and stimulated. The strength of the motive could be measured by taking samples of a person's spontaneous thoughts, such as making up a story about a picture which had been shown, then counting the frequency of mentions about, for example achievement and task accomplishment. Although the procedure involves subjective judgements at the analysis stage, researchers who have been trained in the procedure can reach a high degree of consistency in scoring stories.

Whereas the critical incident technique deals with past behaviour, projective tests focus on present behaviour, and this is often of more interest to management researchers as a predictor of future behaviour. For example, the approach has been used in the selection of public house managers for a large brewery chain. In the test to select pub managers a question is posed such as: 'Suppose somebody comes into your pub you know well, as a good and valued customer. He says, "Lend me £20 because I've got a certainty for a horse running in the 3.30" – What would you do?'

The candidate is asked to explain, or 'project', what he would do in that situation. The more desirable answers will indicate that the individual is sensible enough to decline in such a way the customer is retained along with the goodwill. The scanning for themes is very similar to employing a grounded approach to data analysis and content analysis, both of which will be described later in the section. The technique is used extensively in recruitment, and many consulting companies, particularly in the USA, offer a profiling service to aid recruitment and selection of staff.

A similar approach that can be used to elicit views is to introduce the idea of metaphors and to ask respondents to draw them and explain their significance. In research conducted in a large multinational, one of Richard's colleagues used this approach to explore how senior staff viewed their organization. The research was conducted using a series of focus group interviews, and on each occasion the group members were asked the following questions:

1 If the organization was a parent, how do you think it would relate to its children?
2 If you were asked to write an honest character reference for the organization, what would it say? Some guidance here included, how well it performed in its most recent job; its achievements; anything else that individuals thought was important.
3 Try to imagine the company as an old friend whom you have not seen over the last ten years. How would you judge if their personality had changed?

Finally, individuals were asked to draw a picture of the company as the 'person' is today. The questions produced very rich responses which were taped and analysed, but perhaps the most interesting aspects of this projective technique were the drawings individuals produced and their interpretation. An example of one is shown below in Figure 5.4.

Protocol Analysis

Protocol analysis provides another way of finding out the underlying logic of the way people think, and as such fits within the social constructionist perspective. It has been used successfully in the area of market research where researchers are trying to uncover the elements and stages (protocols) in the buying decision. By uncovering the considerations and values held by consumers, product mapping is possible and buying behaviour becomes better understood.

Protocol analysis seeks explanations as soon as possible after the event has occurred, and is therefore less affected than techniques such as critical incident by the tendency of people to rationalize and re-evaluate their past experience.

Episodes or protocols unique to an individual, for example during a decision-making situation form the focus of analysis, and the person is asked to comment on what is going on, either as it happens, or when that is difficult, from a tape recording of the incident. The 'analysis' refers both to the fact that the individual may be analysing events in his life, and that the researchers may analyse the taped discussions for themes that are relevant to their research.

Protocol analysis was used in research undertaken by Burgoyne and Hodgson (1983) which had as its aim the objective of describing and understanding

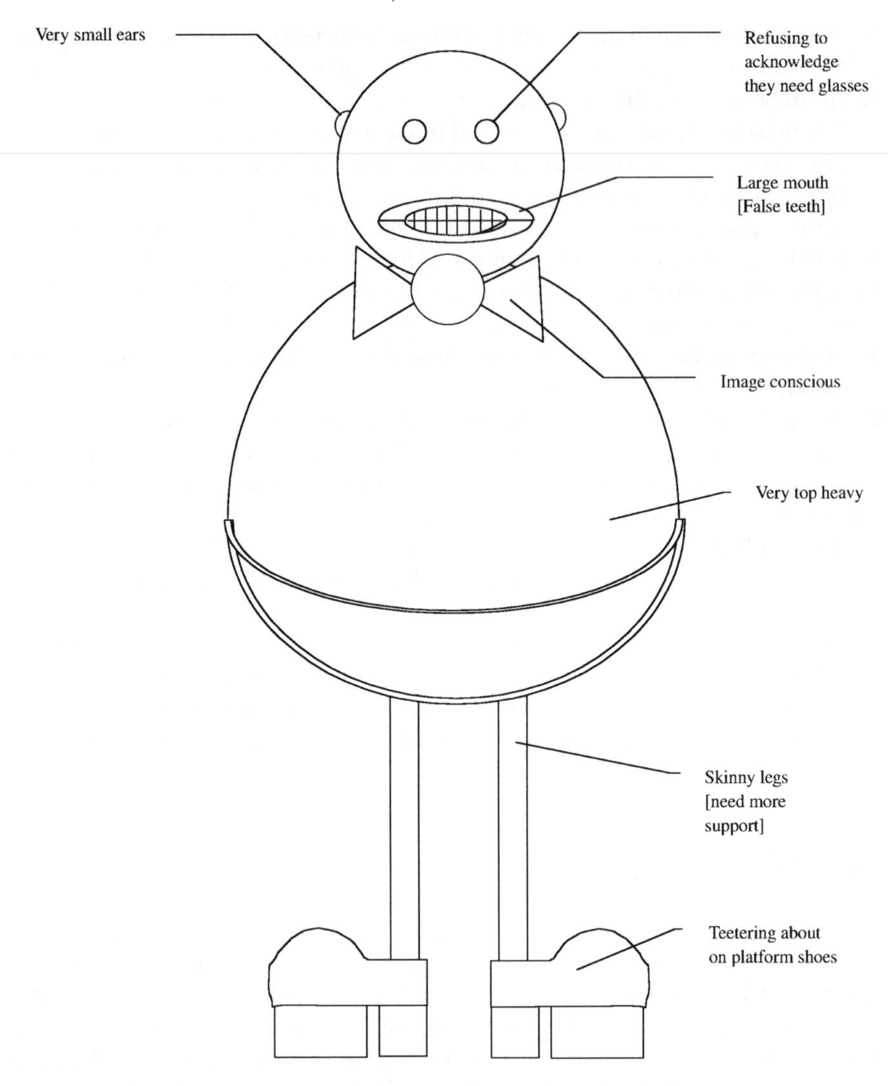

FIGURE 5.4 Example of 'the company' drawn as if it were a person.

managerial action and how managers learned. The method they adopted was as follows:

1 A general context interview was held to explore areas such as the manager's work, activities, role and use of time.
2 Actual incidents from his or her work life were observed and recorded, and where possible, he or she was asked to think aloud during the incident.
3 Shortly after recording the real time incident, the manager was asked to recall thoughts and feelings during the incident and to describe why he or she felt, acted or responded in the way they did.
4 A further meeting was held with the manager some weeks or months later about:

(a) further developments in the stream of events of which the episodes were a part;
(b) consequences of action taken, choice made or orientations adopted during the episodes;
(c) their current interpretation of phenomena, process and relationships pertinent to the incident.

Protocol analysis, in common with many techniques we have discussed so far, aims to get managers to talk. Of course, as we have acknowledged earlier, individuals might well censor their thoughts before articulation and the method may have limitations in understanding aspects that might be unconscious, semi-conscious or simply of a non-verbal form. However the immediacy of the process is a check against too much retrospection and the technique, providing trust can be developed, appears to facilitate open statements and descriptions. Burgoyne and Hodgson comment that the very act of discussing incidents or protocols with individuals actually facilitates the development of trust, so that in their study people found it much easier later on to explain what had been going on in their minds. Burgoyne and Hodgson cite two other methodological issues that arise out of such an approach. These are in common with all in-depth approaches: (a) the nature of the researcher/respondent relationship, which we have already discussed in the section on interviewing; and (b) the general problem of analysing experiential and descriptive data. Since this is a common problem in qualitative research it will be discussed in a later section.

Group and Focus Interviews

Interviews need not necessarily take place on a one-to-one basis, and for some types of investigation group interviews can be very useful. These take the form of loosely structured 'steered conversations'. They are used extensively in market research and increasingly in politics. Such techniques were used in the 1988 American Presidential election to establish the election strategy for the Republican Party, and they were used extensively by the British Labour Party in order to identify likely reactions to policies. Representative groups of voters are interviewed and their reactions to a number of major policy positions from both sides of the political debate were monitored.

The results of their reactions to these policy statements were used to strengthen or suppress aspects of the policy presentation in each case and led to the Republican victory in 1988 and Labour's sweeping election victory of 1997. These two uses of focus groups were seen as noteworthy since they were the first widespread use for political purposes in each country, and they were seen to provide a critical advantage in each case. Inevitably they have now been adopted as normal procedure by all political parties.

In any interview, the skill of the interviewer both as initiator and facilitator is of vital importance. In focus group interviews this role is called a moderator, and the added complexity of the situation means that the skills of initiating and facilitating are of particular relevance in a group interview. According to Walker

(1985: 5), 'The task of the group interviewer . . . is not to conduct interviews simultaneously but to facilitate a comprehensive exchange of views in which all participants are able to speak their minds and to respond to the ideas of others.'

Andy's experience of conducting interviews with lawyers (Lowe and Nilsson, 1989) endorses the view that the person carrying out the group interview needs to be particularly skilled. He suggests that two kinds of skill are required. First, initiator skills, which are those concerned with establishing and creating rapport before discussion takes off. Second, executive skills, which give the group members sufficient confidence in the moderator to allow him or her to steer the conversation.

Andy found that for each group interview lasting about thirty minutes an additional forty minutes was taken up prior to the discussion creating an appropriate climate for the main discussion to begin. This bias of time given to preparation may feel unnaturally long to inexperienced researchers but it does reflect the importance of preparation and the time it takes for people to feel sufficiently relaxed to be able to contribute fully to the interview.

Although the focus interview is loosely structured, it should never be entirely without structure. The format of the interview should be organized by using what is called a 'topic guide'. This is a résumé of the main areas of interest which are to be explored. It is designed so that whilst still covering the general areas of interest it should also allow unforeseen areas to emerge. In addition, the discussion venue needs to be chosen with care. Ideally, in common with in-depth interviews, it should take place in surroundings within which the participants feel relaxed and unthreatened. This can often be on their home ground, for example in a meeting or conference room close to the office. Alternatively it might be in neutral territory such as a business school, a club or a hotel.

However the problems of group interviews can sometimes outweigh the advantages. Social pressures can condition the responses gained, and it may well be that people are not willing to air their views publicly. Our own view is that criticisms such as this illustrate the mistake of applying the wrong criteria for assessing the technique. Focus group interviews can be extremely useful in applied market research studies and are used to great effect as an exploratory tool in other types of qualitative research. Curran and Downing (1989), for example, used the technique to good effect as a means of validating the questionnaire responses made by owner managers in a largely quantitative study which sought to understand the utility of the UK government's consultation strategies with small- and medium-sized firms.

Those wishing to know more about focus group interviewing or panel interviewing are recommended to read *Group Interviewing* by Alan Hedges (1985) which gives a clear account of how this technique might be practised and developed.

Cognitive Mapping

A further development of the group interview is known as cognitive mapping. This takes an action research perspective regarding any changes in individual attitudes and organizational policies as an important part of the research process. In cognitive mapping managers attempt to model the complexity of their organizational problems as *they* see them so that they can be subsequently analysed and solved.

A map can be a powerful way of analysing and presenting large amounts of qualitative data, but is also useful in planning next steps and identifying areas where more information might be required. Figure 5.5 shows a typical cognitive map from work by Baker (1996) into a comparative study of consumer perceptions in Europe, using running shoes as examples.

To read this map, the lines running between the numbers (content codes) represent the linkages. There are generally much fewer values at the top of a map than attributes (at the bottom of the map) and consequences (in the middle). The map would be interpreted in the following way. The dominant element in the map (primary value) is 26 *well-being*. Under this there are three further elements each of which have a large number of elements that lead to them, these are 2 *design*, 3 *weight/shape* and 14 *enhanced performance*. Baker and Knox (1995) comment that 'the design, enhanced performance, well-being chain can be seen to have a high number of relations among its respective elements which implies that the product was purchased for the perceived benefits it might deliver in terms of performance'.

In order to gain understanding and in order to interpret it, the interviewer needs to go through a process of laddering. Laddering is a way of exploring a person's understanding in more depth and relates back to the notion of constructs having a hierarchical relationship. Laddering helps the researcher gain a better understanding of a person's construct system. *Laddering down* (also called pyramiding) is where you explore the person's understanding of a particular construct. *Laddering up* is where you ask the person why a particular construct is important. 'Why' questions quickly leap to an exploration of a person's value system.

Returning then to Figure 5.5 and the data from which it was derived, an example from one respondent illustrates how the hierarchical map was formed.

Question: Anything else about the design?
Answer: I think the weight of the shoe is important. The shoe shouldn't be too heavy.
Question: Why is this?
Answer: Because a lighter shoe is more comfortable.
Question: Why is this important to you?
Answer: It means I can move around quickly at tennis . . .
Question: Tennis is important to you?
Answer: Yes . . . I like it . . . it means I get some fresh air . . . it's good for the heart, the nerves and your cholesterol . . . it makes me feel better. I feel good when I play tennis (from Baker and Knox, 1995: 89)

Cognitive maps are now being used by researchers in a whole variety of contexts. Clark and MacKaness (2001) suggest that the popularity of the technique emanates from its inherent simplicity (as compared to techniques such as repertory grids) and the attractiveness of using visual forms of data presentation

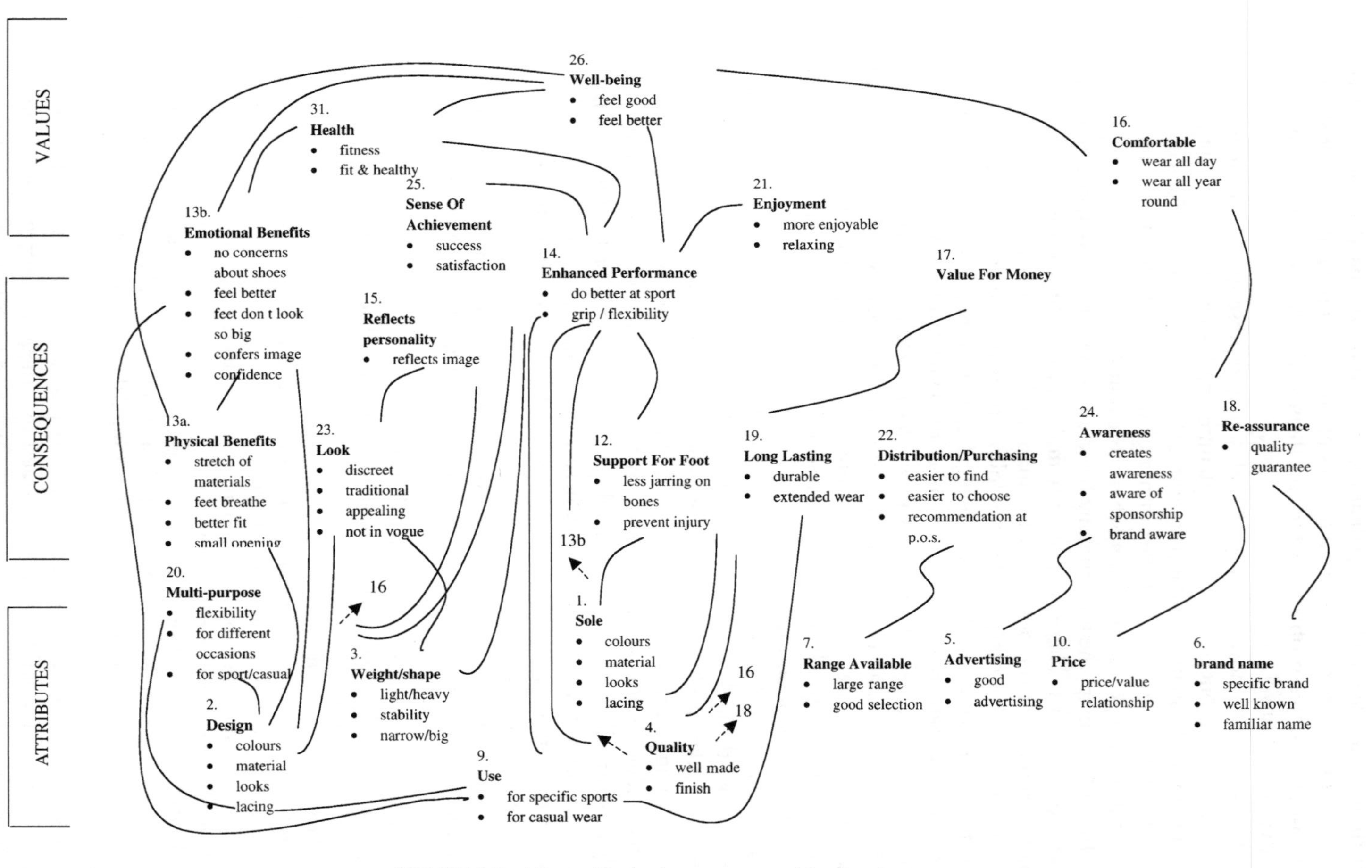

FIGURE 5.5 Hierarchical value map – combined trainers

when working interactively with managers – particularly senior ones. The argument being that they offer a holistic 'picture' without loss of detail and can enable researchers to move beyond the notion of developing 'internal consistency' to a more detailed assessment of specific concepts within maps (Jenkins and Johnson, 1997).

As a consequence, cognitive mapping methodologies have been increasingly used in action research, where groups of individuals, managers or employees collaborate together to attempt to model the complexity of their organizational problems as *they* see them so that they can be subsequently analysed and solved. One of the important areas where the technique has been used in this way is in the area of strategy development. Originally a manual system was employed, and some still feel this is preferable since using a pen and paper keeps everything out in the open. But computer packages have also been developed (Eden, 1990) to assist both the analysis process as well as providing powerful support for the exploration of an organization's strategic options. Eden argues that, for the most part, 'developing strategy has been viewed as an analytical activity devoid of urgency, fun or passion'. In addition he is critical of the traditional view that the formulation of strategy can be conducted quite independently from its implementation.

If strategic planning is actually about encouraging strategic thinking and encouraging individuals to take action, then the work of the strategic planner needs to be 'client-orientated' rather than 'plan-orientated'. Strategy formulation, therefore, needs to be seen as a social process where the main issues are behavioural, and there is a need to understand the nature of problems, threats and opportunities as viewed or perceived by key individuals in the organization. In the famous words of Thomas and Thomas (1928), 'If men define situations as real, they are real in their consequences.'

The approach is based on a modified form of repertory grid (see above). Senior managers who are concerned about particular problems are brought together in a room facing a large computer screen. The strategic problem or opportunity on which they are to work is presented by a member of the team. In comfortable surroundings and with a permanent supply of coffee the managers begin to consider all the aspects relating both to the existence and the solution of the problem. Each contribution made is stored by computer, and the unfolding cognitive map which represents the managers' perceptions of the problem, or opportunity, is presented on the screen for them to alter and refine.

Approaches such as cognitive mapping are particularly suitable for action research designs where organizational development is an important outcome of the research. The method allows not only individual managers to offer their perceptions of a problem, but gives those responsible for strategy formulation the opportunity to understand the perspectives of others. In this context interaction amongst participants and collaboration between researcher and researched is decidedly a good thing.

Researchers wishing to understand more about the techniques employed in cognitive mapping are recommended first to read *Messing about in Problems* by Eden et al. (1983) where the concept is very lucidly explained. Those wishing to read further, and learn more about the process as applied to alternative decision support systems are recommended to read *Tackling Strategic Problems: The Role of Group Decision Support* (Eden and Radford, 1990).

PARTICIPANT OBSERVATION

The method of participant observation has its roots in anthropological research, where a key element of the research training involves living within societies or tribes in far away places and attempting to understand the customs and practices of these strange cultures. Margaret Mead's studies in Samoa were part of a tradition which continues to this day. Hence there is a very extensive literature on participant observation and ethnography, particularly in sociology and anthropology. Since organizations can easily be viewed as 'tribes' with their own strange customs and practices, it is by no means surprising that observation has also been used in organizational and management research. Donald Roy (1952) used the method to great effect when working as a company employee in the machine shop of a large company. He was able both to show how workers manipulated the piecework incentive scheme, and to understand the motives behind this.

The role of the participant observer is by no means simple. There are many different ways of handling it. One commonly used classification of the possibilities is offered by Junkers (1960), and comprises a continuum of four main roles: complete participation, participation as observer, observer as participant, and complete observer. However we have found Junkers' scheme a little confusing when put into practice because of the way one role shades into another. Instead we propose here a different scheme, based more explicitly on the possibilities available in management or organizational research. These are: researcher as employee; research as explicit role; interrupted involvement; and observation alone.

Researcher as Employee

One role a researcher can take is that of employee. Here he or she works within the organization, alongside others, to all intents and purposes as one of them. The role of researcher may or may not be explicit and this will have implications for the extent to which he or she will be able to move around and gather information and perspectives from other sources.

This role is appropriate when the researcher needs to become totally immersed and experience the work or situation at first hand. Sometimes it is the only way to gain the kind of insights sought. For example, in a study conducted by Richard using this approach he was able to gain an understanding of how management's failure to cater for the motivational needs of the workforce led to disillusionment and apathy (Thorpe, 1980). Poor planning of work meant that men were often bored: by experiencing this boredom himself he was better able to understand its causes and the ways in which the employees attempted to alleviate it. His team developed a pattern of activity where they worked for the first hour or so, then they took a break, had a wash and a walk outside. On certain days they changed their overalls in the laundry which involved a walk of about 600 yards and a break of about half an hour. After mid-morning the pace became much slower, and after lunchtime very little work was done at all.

One Wednesday afternoon Richard saw that the conveyor belt was beginning to back-up for no apparent reason. On questioning co-workers about it, he learnt that they saw this as a good way to put pressure on management and guarantee themselves overtime on Saturday morning at time and a half. Since overtime working had to be notified to the employees three days in advance it was important to slow things down on Wednesday. By Friday the backlog had all but been cleared promising the department a fairly easy Saturday morning's work. Naturally his questioning didn't stop at just what was observed, for it then became of interest to know *why* the extra pay was required, why was this strategy used in preference to others, and so on.

In these examples, the research was conducted in a covert manner as far as the employees were concerned, but permission had been negotiated for entry via the company chairman and the works convener who saw merits in such 'academic' research. Gaining entry had been difficult and getting both management and unions to agree had not been easy. If this had not been possible it might have been necessary to apply for, and be successful at getting, a job in the factory. This strategy is increasingly used by research students who have to get part-time jobs in order to make ends meet, for example, in call centres, and they then realize that they are sitting on very rich research material.

As we commented in Chapter 4, participant observation invariably raises *ethical* dilemmas, particularly when conducted in a covert way. These dilemmas need to be considered carefully by researchers, preferably before they embark on fieldwork. People may be resentful when they learn of the presence of a covert researcher, but as more and more people study for management qualifications on a part-time basis there is a growing acceptance that employees may be researchers. Even still one has to be careful. In Richard's own case he thought a lot about deceiving individuals whom he had begun to think of as colleagues and friends. To overcome the conflict he developed an explanation for when he was asked what he was doing which wasn't a lie, but neither was it the whole truth.

This latter point, raises another issue related to complete participation: the problem of a crisis of identity. Getting to know people quite well, even being invited into their homes, and then reporting on them in a covert way is, for most researchers, regardless of ethics, a difficult task. Richard remembers his own experience vividly. He was some 300 miles from his academic base and unable to obtain help or support from colleagues and found it difficult not to experience a confusion of roles. For complete participation is not just a matter of being an employee for three months or so, keeping a diary, and analysing the results at a distance at a later date. It involves observing, participating, talking, checking, understanding and making interpretations, all of which are required if complete participant observers are to share and understand the employee's experience.

Linked to this is the time period over which this kind of activity has to be sustained. It is not unusual for studies to take several months with results taking a long time to produce. It must also be noted that the method is one of high risk. As we have discussed, studies are often extremely difficult to set up, anonymity is a problem, and considerable resources may be consumed in their execution with no guarantees that the method will yield the insights sought.

Finally, and this also applies somewhat to other qualitative methodologies, the complete observer role can be both a physical as well as an intellectual challenge. In Richard's case, he had to complete a day of manual work and then in the evening continue the process of interpretation so that new lines of enquiry could be continued the following day.

Research as the Explicit Role

A second way of managing the role is for the researcher to be present every day over a period of time; but this time entry is negotiated in advance with management and preferably with employees as well. In this case, the individual is quite clearly in the role of a researcher who can move around, observe, interview and participate in the work as appropriate.

This type of observer role is the most often favoured, as it provides many of the insights that the complete observer would gain, whilst offering much greater flexibility without the ethical problems that deception entails. Roy (1970: 217) describes the advantages of the approach as, 'the participant as observer not only makes no secret of his investigation: he makes it known that research is his overriding interest. He is there to observe. The participant observer is not tied down; he is free to run around as research interest beckons.'

A colleague of ours, Eileen Fairhurst (1983), used this type of approach in a study of employee's attitudes to organizational rules. She chose for her research a geriatric nursing ward, and this is where she met her first problem. It took a considerable amount of time to obtain agreement to conduct her research in a particular unit, for two reasons which illustrate a number of problems involved in this type of research. The first was that different consultants in the hospital viewed 'research' in two distinct ways. Some saw it as something in which they must become personally involved and 'vet'; others saw it as a self-indulgent activity of which they wanted no part.

Even after she had gained agreement for the location of the research, there were additional problems associated with the sensitive focus of the study. Old people are especially vulnerable, and there was real concern that researching them might be viewed as a form of exploitation. To experience delay in the setting up of this kind of study is not in any way unusual. Richard's researcher-as-employee study, and the diary study that will be discussed later, took a number of months. Researchers, as we have discussed with interviewing, must find strategies that will allay people's fears, and offer the organization or the managers and employees who control access either reassurance, or something in return. This might involve many meetings and even presentations to the employees about the aims and potential value of the research.

Once accepted, Eileen explained how a principal task was to move from a position of stranger to that of friend – someone who could be trusted. When she had achieved this she found individuals were very willing to tell her about the organization, whether they were nurses, cleaners or ward clerks. While on the wards, Eileen felt it appropriate to help make beds and assist generally, for example, with the distribution of food and drink at meal times, and to collect bed linen or clothes for patients. At such times she was not only participating but strengthening relationships. She also recalls that there were times when she simply had to observe, for example when patients were spending time with occupational therapists or physiotherapists, or on the occasions when she did not possess the technical qualifications to take any role in the work. People understood this and accepted it.

The key skill is to be sensitive enough to know just what role is required at each particular situation. This is influenced almost entirely by the circumstances appertaining at the time. For example, Eileen explains that it would have been conspicuous if she had stood or sat apart, rather than offering help when the wards were short staffed. On the other hand night staff were always short of work, and as a consequence she spent much of the time during this period observing, listening and talking with nurses.

Interrupted Involvement

A third kind of role involves the observer being present sporadically over a period of time, moving, for example, in and out of the organization to deal with other work or to conduct interviews with, or observations of, different people across a number of different organizations.

The essential characteristic of the researcher taking this role, is that the process is not one of continuous longitudinal involvement as we have described in the previous examples. In addition, the role is unlikely to contain much actual participation in work. Instead, it provides a model for what is often seen as participant observation method: spending a period of time in a particular setting, and combining observation with interviews.

Observation Alone

Finally, for completeness we offer the role of complete observer. In many ways, this is hardly a 'qualitative' method, since the researcher avoids sustained interaction with those under study. This type of observation is used in the field of management services where, for job design and specification purposes, requests are made for 'objective' accounts of the content of work; it can also be used in conjunction with other methods when lists of managerial competencies are being developed.

As a technique it is of very little use to those interested in a social constructionist view. Even when used in the discipline of management services, practitioners often fail to obtain people for accounts of their own actions because of the requirement for detachment. The observer role is often disliked by employees since it seems like snooping, and it prevents the degree of trust and friendship forming between researcher and respondent which, as we have noted, is an important component of the other methods. However, for trained practitioners, such techniques do give extremely accurate pictures of what takes place and how long they take, even if they fall short of giving a full account of why things are happening.

Choice of Roles

Clearly the choice of role is important. Here are some of the factors that may be taken into consideration:

The purpose of the research. Does the research require continued longitudinal involvement, or will in-depth interviews conducted over time give the kind of insights required?

The cost of the research. To what extent can the researcher afford to be committed for extended periods of time, and are there any additional costs involved such as training or housing costs?

The extent to which access can be gained. Gaining access where the role of the researcher is either explicit or covert, can be difficult, and may take time.

Is the researcher comfortable in the role? If she intends to keep her identity concealed, will she also feel able to develop the kind of trusting relationships that are important?

The amount of time available. Some methods involve a considerable commitment of time.

Whichever method is chosen, they all provide the means to obtain a detailed understanding of values, motives and practices. As Eileen Fairhurst comments 'the crucial personal skill is to be seen as someone who can be trusted no matter what role is adopted – this will enable much to become possible.'

DIARY METHODS

There is quite a long history of using diaries as a basis for social research in the UK, one of the most interesting examples being the Mass-Observation studies during the Second World War. Here a substantial number of ordinary people were recruited to keep diaries of everything they did for one day each month, and they were also asked to report on specific days, such as bank holidays. Analysis of these diaries was intended to show how the British population in general was reacting to different aspects of the war (Calder and Sheridan, 1984).

Diaries can be either quantitative or qualitative depending on the kind of information that is recorded. They can be useful in management and organizational research on a number of levels. At one level, diary keeping by organizational members can be a simple journal or record of events. A quantitative analysis might take the form of activity sampling from which patterns may be identified statistically. This approach is sometimes used by management services practitioners who wish to measure the frequency of certain activities so that they can reorganize or 'improve' the work; sometimes it is used by managers to reflect on aspects of their own work, as in time management analysis (see, for example, Stewart, 1967, 1982). At another level, diaries might take the form of a personal journal of the research process and include emergent ideas and results, reflections on personal learning, and an examination of personal attitudes and values which may be important at the data analysis and writing up stages. At yet another level they can provide a rich qualitative picture of motives and perspectives which allows the researcher to gain considerable insight into situations being examined. It is this latter use of a diary that we wish to explore in a little more detail here.

There are a number of advantages to using diaries. First, they provide a useful method for collecting data from the perspective of the employee. Whereas in participant observation the researcher cannot help imposing to some extent his own reference frame as the data is collected, in the diary study the data is collected and presented largely within the reference frame of the diary writer. Second, a diary approach allows the perspectives of several different writers to be compared and contrasted simultaneously, and it allows the researcher greater freedom to move from one situation or organization to another. Some detachment also prevents the researcher becoming too personally involved.

Third, it allows the researcher to collect other relevant data while the study is in progress and enables him or her to carry out much more analysis than the participant observer would be able to carry out in the course of their fieldwork. This is the opportunity to collect information not only from the perspectives of different individuals, but also through using different data sources. Finally, although diary studies do not allow for the same interaction and questioning they can sometimes be an alternative to participant observation when, for example, it is impractical for a researcher to invest the time in an extended longitudinal study as observer.

A number of important lessons were learnt from a multiple diary study conducted by Richard and a colleague in one organization during a national study into incentive schemes. First, it was found to be important to select participants who were able to express themselves well in writing. In cases where there was doubt and a group of associates had been asked to keep a diary a judgement had to be made as to the likely consequences of the individual taking offence if he was excluded.

Second, some structure was found necessary to give the diarist focus. To assist this a list of general headings developed from earlier pilot studies was provided. For example, the instructions for a one day specimen diary entry enquiring into aspects of the work in a North West England coal mine are given below.

Please write about the following:

1. Your relationships with other people, including your supervisor, your workmates, anyone you supervise and other people you come into contact with.
2. Any particular difficulties you encountered during the day with: machinery, raw materials or other people.
3. If the incentive bonus scheme affected you at work, and if so in what way.
4. Anything you were especially pleased about or made you feel angry.
5. Anything else you feel is important, especially if it is anything to do with the incentive bonus scheme.

A third lesson highlighted was the need for continued encouragement and reassurance during the study. An earlier pilot study had left diarists very much to their own devices, and they had continued to write for only four to six weeks. In the main study, where regular contact was maintained and feedback given in the form of additional questions or classification, almost two thirds of the sample kept writing into the third month, and more than a quarter completed the full three-month period. An improvement we might have made would have been to supplement the diaries with interviews. This would have enhanced the effect of maintaining interest as well as providing the opportunity to probe areas of interest further.

Fourth, the importance of the need for confidentiality was confirmed. In a pilot study, jotters had been issued to record instances that occurred during the day and this had led to problems. One particularly uncomplimentary entry in a respondent's jotter had been left in an accessible place and was read by the person described. This caused the relationships between the two people to be soured even though thoughts entered 'in the heat of the moment' did not generally reflect the opinions of the individual. It was therefore decided that even at the cost of a loss of spontaneity it was preferable for diaries to be written up away from the workplace.

Finally, the study confirmed individuals' willingness and enthusiasm for co-operating at every level. There was no evidence to justify the view that individuals might be nervous of participating in this kind of research. The experience showed that there was more nervousness among the researchers themselves who felt that they 'dare not ask' or that asking people to maintain a diary for up to three months would be unacceptable to those under study.

All diarists in the Coal Board study to which we refer (including those who stopped writing before the end of the three-month period) maintained that they had welcomed the opportunity to express their feelings, observations and opinions about their life and work to somebody who was interested. All maintained that they enjoyed writing them, and some confided that they were flattered that outsiders were taking an interest in them as individuals. No payment or other inducements were made, although pens and folders were regularly provided. This was sufficient reward for many and it reinforces the point, made in the section on interviewing, about how important it is to find out what individuals wish to gain from participating in the research.

As with participant observation, the setting up of a research study such as this involves considerable time and effort. There were numerous meetings required to gain access and our purpose had to be explained to management and union officials separately. The practicalities of undertaking diary research is fully discussed in Bowey and Thorpe (1986).

ANALYSING QUALITATIVE DATA

The big problem with qualitative data is how to condense highly complex and context-bound information into a format which tells a story in a way that is fully convincing to the reader. In the case of management research, this goes beyond the requirements of good journalism where sources are well referenced and interpretations are 'balanced'. It requires both a clear explanation of how the analysis was done and conclusions reached, and a demonstration of how the raw data was transformed into meaningful conclusions. This does not mean that all the data needs to be displayed, but at least a sample needs to be illustrated so that the reader can follow the same path, and draw their own independent conclusions if they wish.

To some extent the issues related to the analysis of qualitative data are a microcosm of those discussed in Chapter 3 between positivist and social constructionist approaches. If the researcher is undertaking his or her research from a social constructionist perspective, then they will attempt as far as possible not to draw a distinction between the collection of data and its analysis and interpretation. The nature of the problem being investigated and the philosophical stance taken will dictate the relationship of the research process. Exploratory research will place considerable emphasis on specifying research objectives. Research concerned with testing hypotheses will place emphasis on the data collection stage.

Researchers who prefer a more positivist approach will see a sharper distinction between data and the process of analysis, to the extent that the data collection and analysis may well be performed by different people. They will also be more concerned to examine frequencies within qualitative data which will enable them to turn it into numeric form. After all, numbers are both seductive and persuasive, and for many managers, or funders, the political need for numbers wins through against attempts to provide rich descriptions.

The debate leads to two distinct ways of analysing qualitative data which we label: content analysis and grounded analysis. In the first, the researcher 'goes by numbers'; and in the second, the researcher goes by feel and intuition, aiming to produce common or contradictory themes and patterns from the data, which can be used as a basis for interpretation. This second approach is more holistic: researchers need to stay close to the data and any observations made have to be placed carefully in context. Classically, the data used in this type of research remains available for scrutiny.

TABLE 5.1 *Qualitative data analysis: content versus grounded methods*

Content analysis	Grounded analysis
Searching for content (prior hypotheses)	Understanding of context and time
Fragmented	Holisitic
Objective	Subjective: faithful to views of respondents
More deductive	More inductive
Aims for clarity and unity	Preserves ambiguity and contradiction

Content Analysis

Methods of content analyis have been used very successfully in the examination of historical artefacts. In one such study, analysis was made of Caesar's accounts of his wars in Gaul. It involved certain key phrases or words being counted, and the frequencies were then analysed. The selection of these would depend on the hypothesis the researcher wished to prove or disprove. In the case of Caesar's accounts of his campaigns the hypothesis being tested related to the forms of money being used. A similar kind of content analysis has been used to try to determine the authorship of anonymous plays and even more recently to determine where criminals' statements have been added to, or amended, by others at some later date!

Earlier in his career Richard worked in a research team that used a similar kind of systematic approach. First, material was read and themes and statements were collected. Early problems were encountered as field notes had been used rather than verbatim tape recordings. It was therefore necessary to assume that if something had been mentioned then it had happened; if it wasn't, then it hadn't. This was far from satisfactory. Second, three substantial sets of interviews were examined by a researcher and coding was established from key interviews. Issues that the researcher wished to explore in further interviews were marked down one axis and the interviewees across the other.

Third, this frame, once established, was discussed with a number of researchers and modified in the light of apparent inconsistencies. And following the pilot study a workshop was organized where the researchers met to agree definitions of terms and ways of interpreting the three sets of interviews. A check then showed that errors had been reduced to an acceptable level between coders.

So far at least the information had all been derived from the data, although many of the themes for which we had searched had been assessed as relevant prior to analysis. Following this, all the interviews were examined for the presence of the themes which were coded on sheets for computer analysis. New themes that occurred in later interviews were handled in a flexible way and added into the framework. At a later date, using this method, it was possible to compare answers derived from interviews with those derived from questionnaires, moreover it was possible to separate these into definite responses and probable responses.

By far the most influential text on content analysis is by Miles and Huberman (1984/1994). Their book offers a proceduralized way of capturing the complexity of a mass of qualitative data in a whole variety of circumstances. At the heart of the process is a matrix format which identifies the constructs along one axis and the respondents or occurrences on the other. Although this method of data analysis is still essentially qualitative, it is still possible to introduce some element of quantification into the process.

An example from an analysis by Miles and Huberman is shown in Figure 5.6. The aim of the research was to predict the level of assistance provided by an organization at 12 field sites shown in the left hand column (column 1). The most likely predictors 'expected' were arranged across the top of the matrix. Note that the first three columns in this analysis matrix although being scored in a qualitative way (columns 2–4) have been bundled together to give some numerical value (column 5) presumably so as to signify the strength of these variables and provides more persuasive power. What follows (columns 6–8) are three more antecedents (scale of finding, central office commitment and administrative latitude). Note again that in this matrix all the variables are summarized this time qualitatively (column 9).

Miles and Huberman argue that displays of this type can help with another objective of the analysis, that of looking ahead to the consequences (column 10) for early implementation and then to column 11 for a summary of later implementation. They also explain what is happening in the matrix using very 'quantitatively derived' terminology. For example, they suggest that although the degree of assistance was the dependent variable for the earlier analysis, it is, in turn, the main predictor of the later consequences.

In this analysis they are going beyond a simple prediction into attempting to identify whether the predictors that had accounted for the degree of assistance make sense when combined with the level of assistance, to lead to different levels of later outcomes. So in this matrix, there is the beginning of a causal chain – going beyond a simple configuration to sort and order data, to an understanding of the causal linkages – very much in the same way that linkages are gained from manually analysed repertory grids.

Of course, this is only one type of matrix design constructed for one particular purpose and great flexibility is possible. They can range from those that simply count occurrences of the various phenomena of interest in the research study, to matrices that order variables against the dimension of time (for an example of this, see Miles and Huberman, 1994: 201), to those that simply display qualitative data.

Whatever the approach, the content analysis of qualitative data is time consuming, often costly and requires either good (written-up) field notes or verbatim transcripts to be available. Often in applied research where the focus of the investigation is relatively clear and a large number of interviews may have been conducted by different people, some standardization of the process may well be necessary. However tackled, the method should allow the researcher to draw key features out of the data, whilst at the same time allowing the richness of some of the material to remain so it can be used to evidence the conclusions drawn and help to 'let the data speak' for itself.

	Antecedent conditions				Assistance				Consequences	
SITES/ Scale of Assistance (1)	Actual size/ scope of innovation (2)	Required practice change (3)	Actual classroom/ organiza-tional fit (4)	Implementation requirements (5)	Scale of funding (6)	Central office commitment to change (7)	Admin. latitude (8)	OVERALL PRESENCE (9)	Smoothness/ roughness of early imple-mentation (10)	Practice stabilization (on later imple-mentation (11)
Substantial assistance										
Masepa(E)	large	major	mod. good	12	$30–50K	high	low	HIGH	very rough	mod
Plummet(L)	large	mod/major	good/poor	12	$300K	high	high	HIGH	very rough	mod
Carson(L)	large	major	mod/good	12	$969K	high	mod	MOD/HIGH	rough	mod
Tindale(L)	large/mod	major	mod	12	$87K	high	low	MOD/HIGH	rough	high
Perry Parkdale(E)	mod	mod/major	mod	10	$300K	mod	high	MOD/HIGH	mixed	mod/high
Banestown(E)	small/mod	major	mod	10	$5.6K	high	high	MOD	very rough	mod
Initial assistance, then minimal										
Lido(E)	small	mod	mod	7	$6.1K	low	high	LOW/MOD	mostly smooth	mod/high
Astoria(E)	small	minor	good	3	none	high	high	LOW/MOD	smooth	high
Carlston(E)	small	mod	poor	9	none	mod/high	mod/high	LOW/MOD	mixed	mod/high
Nearly none										
Dun Hollow (L)	small	minor	poor	7	none	low	mod	LOW	rough	low
Proville(L)	mod	minor	good	7	$180K	high/low	high	LOW	very rough	low
Burton(E)	small	minor	poor	3	$3.1K	mod/high	high	LOW	smooth	mod

FIGURE 5.6 Predictor-outcome consequences matrix (from Miles and Huberman, 1994:224)

Two other methods of content analysis are frequently used when the data is in the form of transcripts of naturally occurring conversations between two or more people. *Conversation Analysis* (CA) has been used extensively by Silverman (1993, 2000) to examine, for example, the way judgements are formed in selection interviews and how teachers converse with classes of schoolchildren. There are three fundamental assumptions to CA: (i) that all conversations exhibit stable, organized patterns irrespective of who is talking; (ii) that conversations are organized sequentially, and that it is only possible to make sense of a statement in relation to an on-going sequence of comments; and (iii) that analysis should be grounded in a detailed empirical examination of the data.

This emphasis on detailed empirical analysis has resulted in very precise conventions for transcribing tapes. We give some examples below:

Symbol	Example	Explanation
[	A: for quite a [while B: [yes, but	Left bracket indicates the point at which the current speaker's talk is overlapped by another's talk
=	A: that I'm aware of = B: = Yes. Would you confirm that?	Equal sign, one at the end of a line and one at the beginning, indicate no gap between the two lines.
.hhhh	I feel that .hh	A row of h's prefixed by a dot indicates an inbreath; without a dot, an outbreath. The number indicates the length of breath.
( )	future risks and ( ) and life ( )	Empty parentheses indicate an undecipherable word.
____	What's <u>up</u>?	Underscoring indicates some stress through pitch of amplitude.

FIGURE 5.7 Simplified transcription symbols (from Silverman, 1993: 118)

The second method, known as *Discourse Analysis* (DA), takes into account the broader social context in which the conversation takes place, and is therefore somewhat less concerned with detailed analysis of transcripts. Discourse analysis does not restrict itself to conversations alone, and may use texts such as newspaper articles, computer conferences or advertisements as the basis for analysis. *Critical* discourse analysis takes this further by emphasizing the power relations and ideologies that are created by and represented in language (Fairclough and Hardy, 1997). Discourse analysis generally requires some kind of naturally occurring text and is less relevant to interview transcripts, unless the aim is, for example, to identify the power relations within an interview. For further information on critical discourse analysis, see Fairclough (1995).

Finally under this section, mention should be made of Yin's work on Case Study Research (Yin, 1994). His books seem almost obligatory to cite in support of qualitative methods, yet like a number of other researchers in the United States, he adopts a very proceduralized approach to the analysis of qualitative research in his building of theory. This tradition is to establish 'the facts' of a particular case, and then design the kind of replication logic found in scientific experiments. This contrasts strongly with the ethnographic approaches to case studies which reserve a 'modest stance towards existing theory and a style of analysis that interweaves data collection and theory building so that as the research progresses, the analyst successfully redefines and narrows her focus of study' (Locke, 2001: 18–19). It is also quite distinct from the action research tradition built up by education researchers such as Stake (1995).

Grounded Analysis

Grounded analysis provides a more open approach which is closely linked to the idea of grounded theory. In quantitative data analysis an external structure is imposed on the data which makes analysis far more straightforward. With qualitative data, however, the structure has first to be derived from the data. This means systematically analysing it so as to tease out themes, patterns and categories. As Jones (1987: 25) comments, grounded theory works because 'rather than forcing data within logico-deductively derived assumptions and categories, research should be used to generate grounded theory, which "fits" and "works" because it is derived from the concepts and categories used by social actors themselves to interpret and organise their worlds'.

As we pointed out in Chapter 4, there is no single approach, and even the methodology proposed by Glaser and Stauss has undergone many changes and developments. Karen Locke (2001: 33) reminds us that the original methodological monograph was written 'as a polemic against hypothetical-deductive; speculative theory-building and its associated research practices that characterised the sociological context of the time'. Their work not only encouraged researchers to be more courageous in using imagination and creativity in developing theory but also to show researchers a rigorous method by which this could be done.

Since the late 1970s grounded theory practices have been developed in many different ways often drawing from methodological resources and traditions outside management and organization studies. Unfortunately many students merely resort to quoting Glaser and Strauss (1967) as a way of making their choice of a qualitative approach sound respectable. Often they misunderstand both the rigour that is involved in developing a 'grounded theory' and the hard work and intellectual challenge that is involved.

Glaser and Strauss were interested principally in the development of theory and the way this could be achieved by closely linking the theory to the data from which it was generated, the central feature being a method of constant comparative analysis in the same way as experimental and statistical methods used the logic of comparison. What is stressed in the method is process. Charmaz (1983) argues that this stress on the process of discovery and theory *development* leads grounded theory to characterize itself in certain ways. First, data collection and analysis proceed *simultaneously*. Second, both the processes and products of research are *shaped from the data* rather than from preconceived logically deduced theoretical frameworks. Third, grounded theorists do not follow the traditional *check and refine the categories* that emerge. Fourth, as well as undertaking a *process*, grounded theory assumes that making theoretical sense of social life is *itself a process*, rather than explicitly aiming for an ultimate and final interpretation of the phenomenon (Charmaz, 1983: 110–11).

In the first edition of our book we put forward a practical approach to sifting through volumes of non-standard data. In order to make the procedure more understandable we explained it in the way we and our colleagues had used it. The method assumes that one is working with transcripts of in-depth interviews – one of the more intractable analysis problems. We considered that there are seven main stages to such analysis:

1 *Familiarization* Re-read the data transcripts again. When reading, draw on unrecorded information as well as recorded. This is where the field notes and personal diary come into the analytic process. Note should be taken of, for example, the relationships established between the researcher and the people interviewed, the general attitude of the respondent, and the level of confidence felt about the data that was offered.

2 *Reflection* At this stage desperation may begin to set in. There is usually so much rich data that trying to make sense of it seems an impossible task. Often researchers find that they have missed some crucial issues which should have been explored, but which for some reason were not. Evaluation and critique become more evident as the data is evaluated in the light of previous research, academic texts, and commonsense explanations. The kind of questions researchers might ask themselves are:

- Does it support existing knowledge?
- Does it challenge it?
- Does it answer previously unanswered questions?
- What is different?
- Is it different?

3 *Conceptualization* At this stage there is usually a set of concepts which seem to be important for understanding what is going on. For example in an examination of performance these might include: management style, technology, absence rates, demographic qualities of the labour force, locus of power, and so on. These concepts which respondents mentioned are now articulated as explanatory variables.

4 *Cataloguing concepts* Having established that these concepts do seem to occur in people's explanations, they then can be transferred onto cards or a database as a quick reference guide. When this is done there is an issue of labelling. Do you use the language of the people concerned when labelling or do you use your own terms? Our view is that it is probably helpful at this stage to use your own terms providing a trace is kept of how they were derived.

Although it is tempting to use computer packages for qualitative analysis (see below), good old-fashioned methods are still worth considering with modest amounts of data. For example, Figure 5.8 shows an index card on which aspects to do with *labour turnover* have been written down. Each line on the card gives the source in the transcripts, and is further elaborated with a word or phrase which indicates the content.

Labour Turnover

Interview	Page	Line	
4	3	7	Other's motives
11	2	18	Effect on production
4	9	23	Management policies

FIGURE 5.8 Index card for cataloguing concepts in interviews

5 *Re-coding* Now that all the references to particular concepts are known, it will be possible to go back and check against the original data. At this stage, it may be found that the note about a particular concept was different to what the respondent actually said. Or that people in the same organization were interpreting similar concepts in different ways. In these cases re-coding will be necessary. For example, a number of people may have used the concept of flexibility as an explanation for why their organization survived the recession in the early 1980s. But on probing what people meant by flexibility, it might be found that some people were talking about labour mobility, some were talking about flexible working hours, while others were talking about flexibility in strategic directions.

6 *Linking* By now the analytical framework and explanations should be becoming clearer with patterns emerging between concepts. One can now begin to link the key variables into a more holistic theory. This involves linking empirical data with more general models, and it takes the form of tracking backwards and forwards between the literature and the evidence collected in practice. At this stage it is often worth producing a first draft which can be tried out on others, both colleagues and respondents so that the argument and supporting data can be exposed to scrutiny.

7 *Re-evaluation* In the light of the comments of others, the researcher may feel that more work is needed in some areas. For example, the analysis may have omitted some factors or have over-emphasized others. Following a consideration of issues such as these the first draft is re-written, taking into account the criticisms made and contradictions highlighted. This stage may go on for a considerable period of time, and as with the other stages it may have to be undertaken more than once.

This approach can be applied to almost any kind of qualitative data. As with other methods of data collection a critical peer group of researchers can be useful in the early stages of research to suggest new categories as well as assist with interpretation of the data. The researcher may well feel that for much of the time the analysis of qualitative data is chaotic and extremely messy. A colleague of Richard's had his dining room out of commission for some four weeks whilst cards littered the table and floor, and covered the walls. The themes he developed as a result were well worth the inconvenience.

As far as the literature is concerned, there are at least three sets of advice on how to conduct grounded analyses of data. A four-stage process was laid out in the original book by Glaser and Strauss (1967), a classification system employing three levels was developed by Strauss and Corbin (1990/1998), and a rejection of any such mechanistic process was proposed by Glaser (1992). The first of these goes as follows:

Stage 1: comparing incidents applicable to each category To do this, data has to be coded before it can be compared and the process of coding requires a process of naming. This is where researchers attempt to conceptualize and develop abstract meaning from the observations or transcripts studied. The writing of memos is also a feature of this stage and takes the form of jottings or notes which help to conceptualize categories. Later in the analysis this process of memoizing, it is argued 'captures these fresh theoretical musings and gives us analytical space to reflect and to work out these ideas' (Locke, 2001: 51).

Stage 2: integrating categories and their properties This is a process of arranging categories so that they begin to come together as a more conceptual whole. It is at this stage that the memoizing process again helps to articulate the significance of the categories.

Stage 3: delimiting the theory This is a stage where the ideas are bounded and the theoretical formulations composed. Glaser and Strauss suggest that the comparative process itself works to 'delimit' the theory both at the level of the broader framework and at the level of specific categories identified from data incidents selected at the earlier analysis stage. This delimiting of categories is the process of 'solidifying'.

Stage 4: writing the theory At this stage it is the memos produced at earlier stages that provide the theoretical substance for the output.

Since the early development of grounded theory there has been considerable development of the method, not least by Glaser (1978, 1992, 1998), by Strauss (1987), and by students of both authors, notably Corbin (Strauss and Corbin, 1990, 1998). And over the years their published views have diverged considerably. Glaser has persistently advocated a more open, flexible approach in which the theory emerges from the data, almost without human intervention. He is hostile to the elaboration of analysis procedures and wrote a critical book where he claimed that the fractured, technical approach being adopted by Strauss was tantamount to a 'whole new method' which forced data into categories. This made the process too rigid and uncompromising (Glaser, 1992).

Strauss and Corbin (1990, 1998) have moved in the direction of increased prescription and elaboration. Their strategy for sampling data operates at three levels (Strauss and Corbin, 1998). This is shown in Figure 5.9 below.

It is important to note that the figure below contains both guidance on sampling and analyis. This is a central idea of grounded theory – that the sampling of data runs in parallel to, and is directly influenced by, the analysis of existing data. The fundamental logic of theoretical sampling is that data needs to be collected from areas which are most likely to throw light on the central questions of the study, and this is present in each of the three main stages.

One of the problems with using structured forms of analysis for grounded theory is that the research may get drawn down into detailed analysis and find it very hard to identify themes and story lines at higher levels of abstraction. For this reason some researchers follow Glaser (1992) in rejecting the detailed analytic procedures proposed by Strauss and Corbin (1990); moreover Glaser is much more insistent than Strauss and Corbin that researchers should avoid contact with prior literature and research relevant to the case in question. The following example from Richard and a colleague, Ardha Danielli, follows some, but not all of the advice from the above protagonists. First, they used a pre-determined sample framework (and hence did not use theoretical sampling); second, they did not use the system of open, axial and selective coding in a systematic way; and third, they focused on identifying a clear story line using information from outside their own study (which goes against the advice of Glaser).

Their study was into the use of a local park, and information was collected from ten different groups of park users. These included: a women and toddler group, representatives from two schools who used the park as a consequence of changes in the requirements of the national curriculum, an Asian women's group (the area was predominantly built up with a high ethnic population), a disabled group (who used the uncongested pathways to exercise and use their wheelchairs), a young Asian youth team (who used the bowling green to play football!) as well as others. Interviews were transcribed and analysed using the grounded theory approach described. What was striking as a category from the data collected from each group, was the way *fear* emerged as one of the main

Coding practice	Theoretical sampling strategy
Open	*Open sampling* – relatively indiscriminate sampling of people, places and situations that will provide the best opportunities for collecting relevant data
Axial	*Variational and relational sampling* – focused sampling of people, places and situations that will provide opportunities to gather data about the properties and dimensions of the categories as well as how the categories are related to each other. Data gathering in terms of coding paradigm is also clearly implicated here
Selective	*Discriminate sampling* – very focused and deliberate sampling of people, places and situations that will fill in and refine the story line of the core categories and the proposed relationships between categories

FIGURE 5.9 Data sampling process recommended by Strauss and Corbin (1998)

constructs for each. This is what Strauss and Corbin would describe as an *axial code*.

But further (*discriminant*) sampling of the data in the transcripts showed the manifestation of fear was quite different in each group. For the women and toddler groups, it was fear of large groups of Asian boys playing football on the bowling green. For the Asian boys, it was fear of being intimidated by white youths if they went to the Sports Hall in the town centre. For the Asian women's groups, it was a fear of spirits which they thought inhabited parts of the park, particularly those parts which were poorly lit, where the trees hung over the walkways.

Through further discriminant sampling it was possible to connect this category to other categories such as *absence*. Over the years for a variety of reasons there had been a gradual withdrawal of park staff, the community charge had put pressure on the level of service the Council was able to provide, which curtailed the time park staff could spend in the park, and into this space left in the park, anti-social elements and behaviour had begun to develop.

Understanding the context and interrelationships between variables in this way is extremely important for qualitative researchers and hence Richard and Ardha decided to go beyond the specific case under examination to show the context within which it was located. So, for example, when explaining and presenting the results of the above park study and the experiences of individuals in relation to the park, Richard and Ardha placed the concept of a Northern Town Park in the context of its role in civic society in late nineteenth and early twentieth century Britain.

The story is one of a six-day working week for many manual workers when religion still played a significant part in people's lives and, when going to church on Sunday was a time when the family could be together and when 'Sunday best' clothes were worn. One of the places where individuals could promenade was in the park. Cars were few and far between and other forms of transport limited and expensive, so parks were local places where people could meet and enjoy themselves and congregate. The increase in affluence and the decline of religion, the changing hours of work and now Sunday shopping have all been contextual factors to the traditional uses of town parks and a reason for their decline and the problem needs to be understood in this context.

One final lesson from this particular study is perhaps apocryphal and relates to what happened when the findings were presented to the Council. The leader of the Council sub-committee thanked Richard for his presentation but questioned him as to the validity of the study as there were no large samples or statistics. Later during coffee, park warden staff approached him to say that the report revealed something very close to their experiences on a day-to-day basis.

THE USE OF COMPUTERS WITH QUALITATIVE DATA

Computers have now established themselves as key aids in qualitative data handling and analysis. At the simplest level one can use word-processing packages to store transcripts and data and to conduct simple searches for concepts. Spreadsheets and tabulations can also aid the thematic analysis of data along the lines suggested by Miles and Huberman (1984/1994). But the major development over the last decade has been the availability of qualitative analysis software packages (QASPs). Most qualitative research ends with the researcher attempting to make sense of a mass of data that is so complicated that it defies the challenge to deliver it into a short research report. When this happens, it may be that computers and QASPs can be used to facilitate the analysis process to make this mountain of seemingly shapeless data more manageable.

Seale (2000) outlines several advantages of QASPs, including their contribution to speed, rigour and team research. The *speed* of these packages when sorting or searching data is most obvious, since it is now possible to search through hundreds of pages of transcripts in a moment, and a particular advantage is in identifying patterns within, or between, data sets. *Rigour* is important because qualitative researchers are easily accused of selecting data and quotes which support their case and neglecting all counter-indicators. QASPs can enable rapid counting of the times things occur, as well as the search for negative instances by examining the whole corpus of data. When put under pressure the qualitative researcher can provide precise figures to substantiate their qualitative research. This feature might have enabled Richard and Ardha to counter the objections of the Council sub-committee leader in the example above.

When several people are conducting interviews in the same study it can be very hard to share and compare data. The ability to transmit transcripts and memos electronically makes it much easier to share data, but QASPs can also enable those not involved with data collection to become fully involved in the analytic phases. This facility would have greatly helped the *team research* in Mark's China/UK decision making project where the full-time research staff controlled the primary data and principal investigators found it increasingly difficult to contribute to analysis and interpretation.

Currently there are three packages which dominate the market: *Ethnograph*, NUD*IST and *Atlas-ti*. *Ethnograph* (http://www.QualisResearch.com) was developed in the 1980s and was used very extensively by qualitative researchers. As with other QASP software it requires that data be entered from a word processor, and once imported all the lines are numbered. The researcher can then highlight and assign codes to portions of text. The meaning of the codes recorded in memoranda enable the development of the conceptual framework to be logged, and there are then flexible procedures for searching for codes and concepts within various segments of the data.

NUD*IST (http://www.qsr.com.au) was developed initially for the Apple Macintosh, and then adapted for use on PCs. It has overtaken *Ethnograph* in popularity, partly because it has been promoted energetically by Sage, but also because it contains some additional analytic features. One of these is the facility to store analytic memos produced by the researcher while interacting with the data, and for these memos to be searched along with the rest of the data in the file (a process known as 'system closure'). Another feature is the ability to provide a visual display of the coding system in the form of a hierarchical tree stucture. On the downside NUD*IST is more difficult to learn and some of the procedures, such as printing out the results of a search, are more complex than in *Ethnograph*.

Atlas-ti (http://www.atlasti.de) adds further sophistication, and is especially oriented to the development of grounded theory. In particular it has the capacity to create conceptual diagrams which show the relationship between emergent concepts, and which can also be linked to the original instances in the data, thus facilitating the selection of appropriate quotes that support the theoretical argument. Once again it is more complex than the other programmes to use, so researchers will have to decide whether the sophistication of their required analysis justifies the additional effort needed to master the package.

Choosing the particular software package that will suit the needs of each research project is a difficult one, especially as most are commercial products, and liable to have their benefits oversold. Most QASPs offer researchers the facility to get to grips with very large data sets, whether interviews or ethnographic field notes. If however the data set is relatively small (say, fewer than 20 interviews) then it may be that the investment of time, money and energy will not be justified. These relatively small data sets may still be best understood and analysed through the older methods of multi-coloured highlighting pens and close reading on screen or paper.

In conclusion we feel it is important to emphasize four general points about the use of computers for analysing qualitative data. First, they always depend on the judgement of the researcher, and cannot substitute for this. Second, packages and programs need to be chosen for, and be appropriate to, the tasks required. Third, it may often be much easier to analyse qualitative data by hand; and finally, beware of the possibility that the availability of computer analysis may lead to an emphasis on counting the frequency of categories, at the expense of understanding the *quality* of ideas and experiences.

CONCLUSION

In this chapter we have attempted to provide an overview of some of the main ways of capturing qualitative data and making sense of it. A commitment to qualitative research is likely to derive from the researcher's view about which features of the world are significant and relevant to her enterprise. The key question is whether the quality of experience is more important than the frequency of opinions and events.

Along the road of qualitative research there are also many dilemmas. There is the problem of gaining public access to private experiences, and the difficulty of deciding how and when to impose any interpretive frameworks on this. There is the question of how accurate is one's information, and how accurate it needs to be, or can be. And there is the continual tension underneath the research process between creating meanings and counting frequencies. It is in the next chapter that we consider some of the methods and issues associated with the latter problem.

6 Quantitative Methods

In this chapter we review some of the more important quantitative techniques of data collection and analysis. Although the emphasis of the book has been on the use of qualitative methods, it seems important to provide some coverage of quantitative methods both to illustrate the possibilities and problems of these methods, and to show the contrast with qualitative methods.

As we have explained in the previous chapter the distinction between quantitative and qualitative techniques is not always clear. Some techniques, such as interviews, can be used to gather data in either a quantitative or a qualitative way; similarly, a single piece of data, such as an interview transcript, can be analysed in either way. But there are a number of other techniques, such as psychological tests, or activity sampling, which tend to be used predominantly in quantitative ways. One important feature of quantitative techniques is that the process of data collection becomes distinct from analysis. Hence the chapter is organized into two main sections according to this distinction.

In the section on data collection we concentrate primarily on the design of questionnaires, and on survey methods which make extensive use of questionnaires. In the second section we will look at different ways of summarizing different forms of quantitative data – and making some sense of it. We conclude with some thoughts on the possibilities of using different kinds of methods within the same study.

DATA COLLECTION

We distinguish four main ways of gathering quantitative data: interviews, questionnaires, tests/measures and observation. Information can also be gathered from archives and data banks, although this seems more straightforward because the data are already in existence and do not need to be 'created' by the researcher in the same way as the responses to an interview are created. The emphasis will be placed on questionnaires because most of the general issues of quantitative techniques can be illustrated with them, but we start with some brief comments on each of the other techniques.

Interviews are often used in market research or opinion polls to gather quantitative data. In this case the interviewer will have a series of precisely worded questions (i.e. 'When did you last travel on a train?'), and will expect to receive either a factual answer ('Last Thursday'), or a less precise answer ('Oh, I think it must have been a few months ago'). Where the answer is likely to be imprecise, as is often the case with matters of opinion, the interviewer will be furnished with four or five alternative answers, into which she, or the interviewee, is expected to fit the response. Each alternative response will have been given a numerical code, so that the whole interview can be recorded as a series of numbers. It is possible to carry out these interviews either face-to-face or over the telephone.

Although most people are prepared to answer three or four questions without prior warning, organizational interviews that will last any longer need to be legitimized by someone like a departmental manager, and arranged in advance. Even if the interview is highly structured it should still be remembered that the interaction is a social process. During the interview the respondent will be sizing up the interviewer, and responses may well be affected by the inferences drawn. Factors such as gender, social class, age and apparent motives are likely to have an influence on the data provided. Accuracy can be increased if the interviewer avoids stating her own views, phrases questions impartially, and appears equally accepting of any answer (Moser and Kalton, 1971). The only problem with this is that the interviewee may feel the interaction is 'phoney', and therefore become less prepared to co-operate.

Tests and measures can be used to find out how, or what, the individual thinks. In most cases they take the form of a series of written questions (50–100) with Yes/No answers. The pattern of answers given by an individual can be compared with the patterns of answers given by past respondents to see whether she is normal or abnormal in certain respects. The term 'abnormal' is, of course, being used in a statistical sense here to indicate that a particular response is unusual, it contains no implications of whether the response is right or wrong.

Personality tests, such as Eysenck's EPI or Cattell's 16-PF, are claimed to be 'objective' in several senses (Cattell and Warburton, 1967; Eysenck and Eysenck, 1973). They have no implications for which answers are right or wrong; the scores produced by an individual on different occasions are fairly constant; it is very difficult for the respondent to fake a particular result; and the person who administers the test is assumed to have minimal influence on the results. Thus, for the psychologist they have the attraction of providing measures of human characteristics with an accuracy that approximates measures in the natural sciences. Tests are used very extensively within organizations, although normally where a power differential exists: for example, by the recruitment manager on the job applicant, by the management development manager on the ambitious junior manager, or by the therapist on the patient.

In educational settings tests may also be used in a self-diagnostic sense to help the individual identify his own 'learning style' (Honey and Mumford, 1982) or natural 'team role' (Belbin, 1993). These tests are less elaborate and 'objective' than the ones mentioned above, but they have the advantage of being more open to the respondent and they do not rely totally on the expert to unravel their mysteries. The other forms of test that are used very frequently in educational settings are *attainment* and *intelligence* tests, which measure attributes like reading performance, mathematical ability, aptitude for conducting graduate management studies (GMAT), and so on. These tend to be used diagnostically, or to aid the decision-making of teachers.

Although *observation* is most often used as a qualitative technique, it can also be standardized and systematized in a highly quantitative way. This is the technique of Activity Sampling, which is extensively used in work study and operations management (Currie, 1959). Instant observations are made at regular intervals of processes or individuals at work. The nature of activity or process is classified and recorded at each observation time, and over a period of time the frequency of each category is calculated as a percentage of all the activities observed.

This approach to observation is very useful in understanding how individuals spend their time, in reviewing the allocation of resources, or in assessing the frequency of delays. The advantages of the method are that observations can be made by relatively untrained observers, observations can be carried out simultaneously or over a long time period, and in order to increase accuracy one simply needs to increase the number of observations. On the other hand care needs to be taken in the allocation of observation times to ensure that results are not unduly dominated by unrepresentative periods of the day. For this reason it is often worth conducting a preliminary study so that one can be confident that the observation programme is feasible and unlikely to produce bias.

Finally there are *written records and indices*. House journals, internal reports, memoranda, Chairman's statements, and newspaper articles have always provided good material for the qualitative researcher. But the development of public databases, such as DATASTREAM, now provides instant access to quantitative indicators of corporate performance. The main limitation of this kind of data is that it is constructed at a 'macro' level, regarding each company as a single entity. Researchers who are more interested in internal quantitative indicators will need to look for management control data, which may be easy to come by if one is already an employee of the organization.

Questionnaires

Questionnaires are very widely used in large scale investigations of political opinions and consumer preferences. Although they may seem simple to use and analyse, their design is by no means simple. There are a number of sources which provide good guidance on this. The classic books by Oppenheim (1966) and Moser and Kalton (1971) still provide very good guidance, even if their examples are looking a bit dated; more recent, and very practical, guidance is provided in Hussey and Hussey (1997). The main decisions to be made in questionnaire design relate to the type of questions to be included and the overall format of the questionnaire.

Question types First, we distinguish between questions of fact and questions of opinion. For example biographical details such as age, level of education or length of service are reasonably factual: the respondent may still choose to give incorrect answers, but there still exists, in most cases, a correct answer. With questions of opinion there can be no assumption about underlying correct answers; indeed, they are useful precisely because people will respond to them in different ways. Second, there is the distinction between open and closed questions. If for example one wished to find out how a manager felt about her company as an employer, an open question might ask: 'In what respects is this company a good employer?' – to which the answer would be a written statement, perhaps a couple of lines long. A closed question with the same focus might be: 'Do you consider this company to be a good employer?' – and the response would be limited to circling either a Yes or a No.

It is also possible to construct open questions which provide some structure to the answers: 'List, in order, the three things you like most about this company as an employer'. And closed questions can be constructed to allow more discrimination than a straight Yes/No choice. One of the most common forms is known as a Likert scale:

This company is a good employer:	Agree strongly	1
	Agree	2
	Undecided	3
	Disagree	4
	Disagree strongly	5

The respondent will be asked to ring one of the five answer categories indicating the strength of agreement or disagreement with the initial statement. Another form of closed question which still requires the exercise of judgement is the ranking exercise, where the respondent is asked to indicate the order of importance of a list of attributes or statements. Given the complexity of ranking long lists of items it is normally advisable to restrict the number of items to a maximum of six.

The strength of closed questions is that they are quick to complete and analyse; the weakness is that the data obtained may be very superficial. Open questions allow the possibility of asking deeper questions and obtaining unanticipated perspectives on an issue, but the corresponding weakness is that completion and analysis can be difficult and time-consuming. There are a number of general principles to consider when drafting items for a questionnaire. These are:

- make sure that the question is clear;
- avoid any jargon or specialist language;
- avoid negatives (e.g. *Q*: Do you dislike your work? *A*: Yes/No);
- avoid personal questions;
- don't ask two questions in one item;
- avoid leading questions which suggest indirectly what the right answer might be.

Questionnaire layout It is important that questionnaires are well produced, and that they seem easy to complete. Sometimes, especially with open questions, the respondent may get so interested that he will willingly devote a lot of time to it. But the principle remains the same: the benefits of completing the questionnaire should outweigh the costs measured by time or inconvenience. Unfortunately managers seem to be increasingly busy nowadays, so their time is becoming more and more valuable.

Although the formatting and layout of questionnaires may be considered something of an art, there are still some widely accepted principles of good practice. These include:

- provide a short covering letter explaining the purpose of the research and why/how the respondent was selected;
- start the questionnaire with brief instructions about how to complete it;
- vary the type of question occasionally, but keep similar types of question together in bunches; and
- start with simpler factual questions, moving on later to items of opinion or values.

In addition, it is worth considering photo-reducing the questionnaire so it does not appear too daunting to the respondent, and differentiating between instructions and questions by varying the typeface between italic and Roman script.

Sometimes it is possible to borrow items and portions of questionnaires from other sources, especially when a lot of prior questionnaire-based research exists into concepts such as motivation or organizational climate. But however good the design, or prior testing of questions, it is always advisable to pilot the questionnaire on a small number of people before using it for real. This enables one to check that the items are easily understood and that there are no obvious problems to do with length, sequencing of questions, sensitive items, etc. It is also most important at this stage to see whether it is possible to analyse the data produced by the questionnaire . . . and whether the results appear to make any sense.

Reliability and validity We discussed in Chapter 3 the importance attached to ensuring validity and reliability when gathering quantitative data. *Validity* is a question of how far we can be sure that a test or instrument measures the attribute that it is supposed to measure. This is not too easy to ascertain, because if one already had a better way of measuring the attribute, there would be no need for a new instrument. In this context, George Kelly defined validity as, 'The capacity of a test to tell us what we already know' (Bannister and Mair, 1968: 177).

Nevertheless there are various ways of estimating validity (Patchen, 1965):

Face validity:	whether the instrument or its items are plausible;
Convergent validity:	confirmation by comparing the instrument with other independent measurement procedures;
Validation by known groups:	comparing groups otherwise known to differ on the factor in question.

Reliability is primarily a matter of stability: if an instrument is administered to the same individual on two different occasions the question is, will it yield the same result? The main problem with testing this in practice is that no one can be sure that the individual, and other factors, have not changed between the two occasions. Hence it is more common to examine 'equivalence reliability', which is the extent to which different items intended to measure the same thing correlate with each other.

Ideally, tests for validity and reliability should be made at the pilot stage of an investigation, before the main phase of data collection. Responses to items are correlated with each other along the lines indicated above to provide reliability coefficients and indications of the accuracy of the results that might be produced. We discuss correlations later in this chapter, but can note here that for exploratory research reliability coefficients in the order of 0.6 are acceptable, but psychological tests designed for public use would require coefficients of around 0.9.

Surveys

Questionnaires and interviews are used extensively in surveys. Occasionally tests and observations are included, but they are more frequently used to aid decisions about individuals, or as an element of experiments. We have discussed these briefly in Chapter 3, and propose to focus here on survey methods, particularly when they rely on questionnaires or structured interviews.

The main purpose of a survey is to obtain information from, or about, a defined set of people, or population. This population might be defined to include: all the people in one country; all women aged between 30 and 40 who live in Paris; all managers of Grade 7 or above who work for the Mega Corporation; or all supervisors in a company who have attended course Y during the last 3 years. When the population is small (perhaps less than 500) it is customary to send the questionnaire to all members. This 100 per cent sample is known as a census. In the case of structured interviews the size of sample is limited by the time available to interviewers, and with qualitative questionnaires it is limited by the feasibility of coding and analysis. But with quantitative questionnaires the sky is the limit given some help from the postal system or the Internet, the dexterity of data processing staff, or the availability of optical character recognition equipment.

However, it is not always necessary to contact everyone in a population in order to know what they think, and this is where sampling methods come in. The main aim of sampling is to construct a subset of the population, which is fully representative in the main areas of interest. It is then possible to infer statistically the likelihood that a pattern observed in the sample will also be replicated in the population.

The simplest form of sample is the random sample. Here every 'unit' of the population has an equal chance of being selected for the sample, and this can be done by using a table of random numbers, by picking out every fifth name on a list of employees, by taking the first name on every right hand page of the telephone directory, or whatever. If some key features of the population are already known it is possible to take some short cuts. For example, one might wish to compare the attitudes of supervisors and middle managers towards their company. If there are 1000 middle managers and 5000 supervisors one might choose to sample 20 per cent of the middle managers and 10 per cent of the supervisors. This would give respective sub-sample sizes of 200 and 500 individuals, both of which are reasonable numbers (we give further guidance on sample sizes below). This would form a *stratified sample*, and individuals would be selected at random within each of these strata. If wished, further strata could be included in the sample, such as departments or gender, provided they contain mutually exclusive categories; but if the process of stratification is continued too far one can end up with tiny groups that may not be representative of anything.

Two other forms of sampling which produce less representative pictures than the above methods are quota and cluster samples. With a *quota sample* there is no attempt to randomize selection. For example the instruction might be to: 'Interview the first 20 people wearing baseball caps who enter the station after 6.00 pm'. Interviews continue until the quota has been filled, then they stop. The method can easily introduce bias into the sample if, continuing the above example, all the people entering the station between 6.00 and 7.00 pm were pizza delivery men, and those entering the station after 7.00 pm were women returning from keep-fit classes. *Cluster sampling* has similar limitations because it involves taking all members of a unit, say departments 3 and 6 in a retail store containing 10 departments. The main advantage of both these methods is that they are comparatively cheap. For those wishing to look further at issues of sampling, Sapsford and Jupp (1996) provide a good overview of principles and methods.

Sample Size and Accuracy

The question everybody asks is: 'How big a sample do I need?'. The good news is that there is an answer to this question; the bad news is that the answer depends on already knowing a lot about the population to be investigated, and it may also vary with the question asked. The formula to use is:

$$n = \frac{P(100 - P)}{E^2}$$

where n is the sample size required, P is the per cent occurrence of the state or condition, and E is the maximum error required.

For example if one item in a questionnaire asked employees in a call centre whether they were satisfied, and it provided a Yes/No answer, we could use the formula to determine how many responses would be required to produce a standard error[1] of, say, no more than 5 per cent. The one snag is that we would still have to estimate the likelihood that employees would answer Yes or

No. If we guessed, perhaps as a result of a quick pilot study, that 60 per cent would say yes, we could now use the formula as follows:

$$n = \frac{60(100 - 60)}{25} = 96$$

And that would be the minimum sample required to provide 95 per cent accuracy for that one question.

With a questionnaire containing many such items the calculation would need to be carried out several times to get a feel for the range of sample sizes indicated. But as a quick rule of thumb, provided the distributions of responses to each question are fairly well balanced, then:

$$n \cong \frac{2500}{E^2}$$

Three further factors can be considered which have different effects on the required sample size. First, if the population is not much greater than n, the sample size does not have to be so large in order to provide an accurate estimate of features of the population. The formula for reducing n (known as the *finite population correction*) is:

$$n' = \frac{n}{1 + (n/N)}$$

Where n is the sample size indicated above, N is the total population size, and n′ is the reduced sample required. Thus, if the population was five times n (i.e. 480), then:

$$n' = \frac{96}{1 + 1/5} = 80$$

Now the downside. The above discussion has assumed that the full sample size will be available for analysis. If, however, this is a questionnaire distributed by internal mail to members of a company it could be unreasonable to expect a response rate of more than 50 per cent. Thus in order to ensure that an adequate number of questionnaires are returned for analysis, the number dispatched would need to be doubled (to 160), at least.

Third, we have assumed in our calculations that the selection of sample members has been truly random, and that all are equally likely to respond, or non-respond. But because of some of the factors discussed in the previous section it is quite likely that the sample is not truly representative of the population. Equally there may be considerable bias produced by non-response. If, the survey is about job satisfaction it may well be that the least satisfied people will not respond, thus biasing the overall response towards a more positive picture. There are no statistical solutions to this problem other than through increasing the overall sample to provide a greater margin of safety, or by conducting an additional survey of those who don't respond. Of course, the latter will only be possible if all questionnaires are identifiable – and identification could produce yet another source of bias.

DATA ANALYSIS

Types of Quantitative Data

Before attempting any form of quantitative analysis it is important to be clear about the kind of data involved. There are three main kinds that are encountered in management research: nominal, ordinal and interval.

Nominal data implies no more than a labelling of different categories. The gender classifications, male/female, or occupational classifications such as lawyer, artist, engineer, teacher, etc. would provide nominal data; there is no obvious ordering of these categories. But if we used classifications of social class, or responses to a questionnaire item which offered a range of answers (i.e. strongly agree, agree, neither agree nor disagree, disagree, strongly disagree), it would be possible to place all of the classifications in order. Consequently this would be known as *ordinal data*. Although it is possible to say that with social class classifications that Class 1 is above Class 2, and so on, it is hard to claim that the difference between Class 1 and Class 2, however defined, is the same as the difference between Class 3 and Class 4. A similar point applies with the questionnaire responses: one cannot be sure that the difference between 'agree' and 'strongly agree' is the same as the difference between 'neither agree nor disagree' and 'agree'. It is only when looking at classifications such as age, weight or salary that we can be confident that the interval between, say, 25 years and 30 years is the same as the interval between 47 years and 52 years. This is what is known as *interval data*.

Descriptive Statistics

The distinction between types of data is most important when statistics are used to summarize features of the sample. With interval data it is possible to use 'parametric' statistics such as measures of mean, standard deviation and variance to describe key features of the data. When the data is merely ordinal it is usually necessary to use 'non-parametric' statistics, which do not assume equal intervals between successive points on a scale. The simplest of these are frequency counts, and indicators of averages such as medians and modes. The *mean* is obtained arithmetically by adding up all the scores in a sample and dividing by the total number in the sample; the *median* is the middle number, and the *mode* is the most frequent number. For example, if the ages of a group of students in a class are:

21, 21, 21, 21, 22, 23, 24, 24, 26, 26, 28
the mean is 257/11 = 23.4 years,
the median is 23 years and
the mode is 21 years.

Here the mean is probably the most useful description of the average age in this group, although there are occasions (say, if one member of the group had been aged 74) where the arithmetic mean might be more misleading, and the median would provide a better indication of the average age.

If, however one wished to summarize the distribution of social class in the group and the eleven students were classified as follows on an A to D system:

B B A D C C A B B C B

this would have to be summarized as a frequency count:

Class	*Frequency*
A	2
B	5
C	3
D	1

or as a histogram:

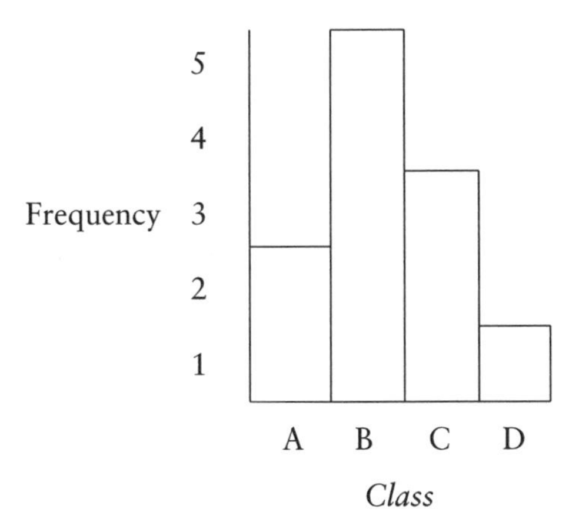

Clearly the most frequent class (mode) is Class B, and the middle case (median) is in Class B.

However it is often tempting to go further by treating ordinal data as if they were interval data and hence use parametric statistics on them. Thus the four social classes above might have been expressed as Classes 1 to 4, and one could then produce an arithmetic mean for the group as 25/11 = 2.27. Exactly what is meant by Class 2.27 is another matter; but this procedure is often used to summarize the results of Likert scales (see p 133, above). This is, strictly speaking incorrect; but with a large sample and a continuous dimension such as 'strongly agree' to 'strongly disagree', the result is often both accurate and useful.

Other statistics that are useful for describing parametric data are the standard deviation and variance. The standard deviation (s) of a variable is given by the formula:

$$S^2 = \frac{\Sigma(x_i - x)^2}{n - 1}$$

Where x_i is the score for the ith person, x is the arithmetic mean for that variable, and n is the number in the sample. This is fairly easy to work out manually for a small sample, although scientific calculators and statistical packages provide short cuts. In the case of the above data about ages of students the calculation runs:

$$s^2 = \frac{(23.4 - 21)^2}{(11 - 1)} + \frac{(23.4 - 21)^2}{(11 - 1)} + \ldots\ldots + \frac{(23.4 - 28)^2}{(11 - 1)}$$

$$= \frac{5.76}{10} + \frac{5.76}{10} + \ldots\ldots \frac{21.6}{10}$$

$$= \frac{60.56}{10} = 6.056$$

Hence $s = \sqrt{6.056} = 2.46$

This indicates the extent to which the scores on the variable are bunched together; the higher the standard deviation, the more dispersed they are. The other term, variance, is simply the square of the standard deviation, which brings us back to 6.05 in this case.

Measures of Similarity and Difference

Although simple descriptive statistics are a useful preliminary, it is often more interesting for research purposes to show that one group of people, or objects, are similar to, or different from, another group. This is particularly so where, in the more positivist forms of research, one wishes to establish the causes and effects of different factors. For example one might want to know whether the presence, or absence, of a new performance management system would have any effect on the morale or productivity of employees in a health trust.

There are many statistical techniques, both parametric and non-parametric, for demonstrating similarities and differences in data. These are available on most statistical packages (see below), and technical details are covered fully in the accompanying manuals. Two classic books on this topic are Maxwell

(1970), mainly on parametric statistics, and Siegal (1956), which provides comprehensive treatment on non-parametric statistics. In this section we mention briefly some of the more useful tests. In addition Bryman and Cramer (1997) have produced an excellent book which covers both parametric and non-parametric statistics in relation to their application within SPSS.

First, *similarity* is most commonly demonstrated using correlation statistics. This requires variables to be matched, item by item, as would be the case, if, say, the relationship between salary and physical height was being investigated across a sample of 50 managers. For each manager there would be two scores, height and salary, and the statistic would measure how far high scores on one were associated with high or low scores on the other. The *product moment correlation coefficient* is most commonly used with parametric data. With non-parametric data there are a number of tests such as Kendall Tau or Spearman Rho (Siegal, 1956) which are based on the rank order of scores rather than the absolute numeric scores themselves. Correlation coefficients vary between –1 and +1, which indicate total negative and positive relationships respectively, and the mid-point, zero, which indicates no relationship whatever. It is important to note, however, that correlations only demonstrate relationships between variables, and they do not necessarily indicate any causality in the relationship.

This is also the case when assessing relationships between several variables at the same time. For example, absenteeism may be thought to be affected by a number of factors such as age, work location, family status, gender, seniority, and so on. The technique used to assess the degree of such linkage is known as a *regression*. The simple linear regression uses two variables and attempts to identify the relationship between an independent variable (X, called the predictor) and a dependent variable (Y). This can be represented visually as the attempt to draw the best straight line through a number of points plotted onto a graph (see Figure 6.1).

Mathematically it is represented by a formula of the kind:

$$Y = a + bX + e$$

where a and b are constants, and e is the error component, or residual. The residual is based on the mean distance between the line and each point, and it is important since it indicates the strength of association between X and Y. If the points on the scattergram are spread widely, then the residual will be high

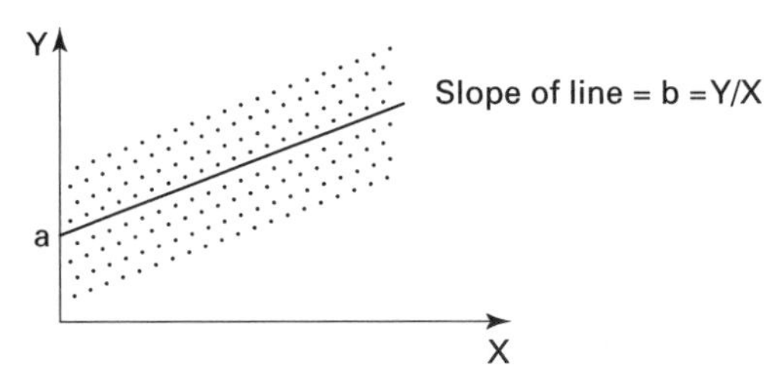

FIGURE 6.1 Linear regression line and regression coefficient

and hence the correlation between the two variables will be low. If the points cluster closely along the line then the residual will be low and the correlation between X and Y will be high.

The strength of regression techniques is that they can include a number of predictor variables into the equation. Thus absenteeism (Y) might be considered to be affected by age (X_1), seniority (X_2) and individual health records (X_3). The regression programme would first seek out the predictor with the strongest association to absenteeism, and would then include the next strongest predictor, and so on. At each stage the residual will decrease as more of the variations in Y become accounted for by the collective effect of $X_{1, 2, 3}$. This process is known as a Stepwise Multiple Regression.

Tests of *difference* can either be applied to attributes of individuals/objects, or to groups as a whole. If one wished to assess whether male managers in a company have higher salaries than female managers at equivalent levels, one measure would be an Analysis of Variance (ANOVA). This test assesses whether the dispersion (variance) in salaries for the male and female groups together is large in comparison with the variance within each separate group. A large common variance, combined with low variance in the separate groups would indicate that each group was tightly bunched, but that the two do not overlap significantly. Hence that the difference may be important.

Figure 6.2 shows the separate distributions of salaries for men and women in an organization, and the dotted line in the middle shows the effect of adding the two distributions together. Clearly the two separate distributions bunch more tightly than the combined distribution – which might then be presented as data suggestive of possible gender discrimination in that organization.

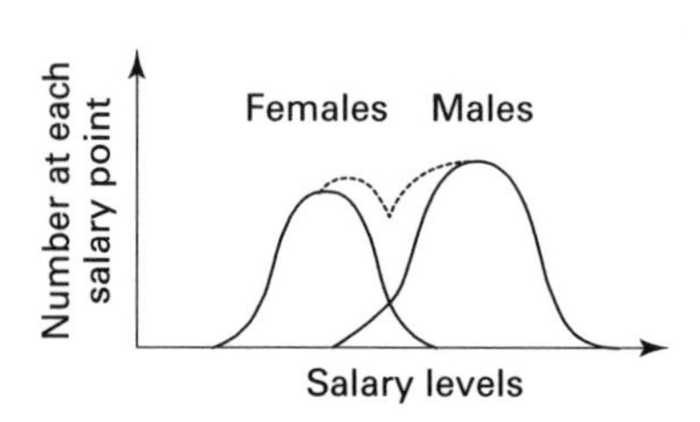

FIGURE 6.2 Distribution of female and male salaries for ANOVA

When the effect of a single factor is studied, we have one-factor ANOVA. The same technique can be extended to determine the effect of two or more factors acting simultaneously. Kvanli et al. (1996: 397) state the following three assumptions behind the ANOVA analysis:

1. The observations must be obtained randomly and independently from each of the populations. The value of the observations has no effect on any other observations within the same sample or within other samples.
2. The observations from each population follow (approximately) a normal distribution.

3 The normal populations all have a common variance, and it is expected that the values in each sample will vary about the same amount. The ANOVA will be much less sensitive to violations of this assumption when samples of equal size from each population are obtained.

Another useful way of examining differences between groups, especially when the factor under investigation can be reduced to a few nominal categories, is the *chi-square* (χ^2) test. This can be done manually in most cases so we shall give a brief example of the calculation here. However, it is one of the many standard statistical routines available within the widely used SPSS (Bryman and Cramer, 1997).

First it is necessary to draw the data up into a contingency table where each box contains the number of cases falling into that category. This, for the above example of gender and salary could look as in Table 6.1:

TABLE 6.1 *Contingency table for salary and gender*

	Salary		
	Under £30k	**Over £30k**	**Totals**
Male	18	15	33
Female	13	4	17
Totals	31	19	50

The formula for the chi-square test is:

$$\chi^2 = \frac{\Sigma(O - E)^2}{E}$$

where O is the observed (actual) number of cases falling into that category, and E is the expected number of cases falling into that category.

E is calculated for each category as the product of the column and row subtotals divided by the full total. Thus for ‘males, under £30k’ the expected frequency would be:

$$\frac{33 \times 31}{50} = 20.46$$

The expected frequency for ‘males, over £30k’ is 12.54, and for the two female groups, respectively 10.54 and 6.46.

The formula for chi-square therefore gives:

$$x^2 = \frac{(18 - 20.46)^2}{20.46} + \frac{(15 - 12.54)^2}{12.54} + \frac{(13 - 10.54)^2}{10.54} + \frac{(4 - 6.46)^2}{6.46}$$

$$= 0.30 + 0.48 + 0.57 + 0.94 = 2.29$$

The value of χ^2 required for significance at the 0.05 level with a 2×2 contingency table is 3.84, which suggests that the value obtained above does not reach this level of significance.

The chi-square test can be used with much larger contingency tables than the one above although the value of χ^2 required to reach statistical significance increases with the number of cells in the matrix. There are also limitations in the use of the chi-square test: no more than 20 per cent of cells should have expected frequencies of less than 5 and none of them should contain expected frequencies less than one. People wishing to use the chi-square test in practice are therefore encouraged to consult either Maxwell (1970) or Siegal (1956) for further details of use and limitations. Both of these books contain appendices which give the required value of χ^2 for different levels of significance under various conditions.

Levels of Significance

In the preceding section we introduced the term 'significance', and earlier in the chapter we discussed the idea of error and accuracy. There are both technical and commonsense versions of these terms, which are somewhat different. The idea of significance comes from sampling theory. It indicates the probability that, if a sample of the given size was drawn *at random* from a large population, an outcome of that level (size of correlation, χ^2 etc.) would have been obtained. Conversely the accuracy or confidence level indicates the likelihood, as a percentage, that the observed result could *not* have arisen by chance. When conducting a survey with a genuine sample drawn from a population the confidence level indicates the likelihood that the true attributes of the population lie close to those identified in the sample. When used in this way, the statistics are sometimes known as *inferential statistics*.

However, in many cases significance tests are used on data where there is no population, as such, from which sampling takes place. The test is thus used by the researcher to indicate which outcomes might be important or meaningful. However any results that show relationships should be examined carefully before claiming causality, because there are many ways that spurious associations can be produced. And it is worth remembering that statistical significance does not necessarily imply practical significance or causality, it merely indicates that there is a strong pattern between the variables under consideration. Maxwell (1970) gives a number of examples of spurious correlations, and Huff (1973) gives a delightful account of how statistics can be used to mislead people.

Statistical Packages

Although statistical analysis by hand may give the researcher a 'feel' for the data under consideration, the ubiquity of powerful computers means that most quantitative analysis is now done with computer packages. The most widely used package for analysing social data is SPSS. This used to stand for *Statistical Package for Social Sciences*, but given the enormous increase in breadth of the user base over recent years it has been re-branded as *Statistical Products and Service Solutions* (McCormack and Hill, 1997).

It offers a full range of contemporary statistical methods, plus good editing and labelling facilities. It has an interactive system of menus and an excellent online help system. It also has the capability of being able to produce output in both report and table formats which is very useful for management researchers, and one of the most reassuring aspects of SPSS is the ease with which it handles missing data. The recent editions operate through Microsoft Windows operating system, which makes it more user-friendly compared to earlier versions. Both Apple Macintosh and Microsoft Windows versions are based on similar principles.

Other packages that are used in management research include SAS/ETS, Microfit and MINITAB. SAS/ETS stands for Statistical Analysis System/Economic Time Series and is used mainly for forecasting, financial reports, economic analysis, economic and financial modelling, time series analysis and manipulation of time series data. One of the advantages of the SAS system is that it uses SAS/ACCESS files to read data directly from the most widely used database management systems and other interface products. Similar to SPSS it can also handle missing values effectively.

Microfit is perhaps the most popular package for econometric analysis of time series data. It provides powerful facilities for estimating and testing equations, forecasting, data processing, file management and graphic display. It is comparatively easy to use and operates through Microsoft Windows and DOS operating environments. A very helpful manual for this package is written by its creators, Pesaran and Pesaran (1997). Further information on packages for econometric packages can be found in Körösi et al. (1992: 290–9)

MINITAB as a program is friendly, fully interactive and easy to use. It is because of these features that it is often used for teaching statistics and, as a consequence, students can learn to use the software quickly. For a text on the use of MINITAB see Ryan et al. (1985). The disadvantages are its limitations in the area of editing and labelling, which are quite important for survey work. It is also rarely used in companies nowadays, and consequently its popularity in educational settings is also starting to fade.

There is also a great range of other packages available for the PC which include Statgraphics, Stata and Statpac Gold. And as we have noted above computer software is increasingly used in qualitative data analysis, with packages such as *Ethnograph*, NUD*IST and *Atlas-ti* being among the most popular. In France, STAT/ITCF and SPHINX are widely used. SPHINX is interesting as it incorporates a 'toolbox' and 'expert system' that assists students not only in designing their questionnaire, but also in determining the sample size they will need in order to draw significant conclusions from their data. This type of facility helps students to focus on the statistical aspects of data analysis.

MIXING METHODS

Up to this point the discussion in Chapters 5 and 6 has been primarily about the use, and choice, of individual methods of data collection and analysis. However, there are good reasons for using several different methods in the same study. Abrahamson (1983) points out that this approach prevents the research becoming method bound: the strength of almost every measure is flawed in some way or other, and therefore research designs and strategies can be offset by counter-balancing strengths from one to another.

The use of multiple, but independent, measures is known as *triangulation*, a term borrowed from navigation and surveying where a minimum of three reference points are taken to check an object's location (Smith, 1975). Within social and managerial research there are four distinct categories involving theoretical, data, investigator and methodological triangulation.

Theoretical triangulation involves borrowing models from one discipline and using them to explain situations in another discipline. This can frequently reveal insights into data which had previously appeared not to have much importance. *Data triangulation* refers to research where data is collected over different time frames or from different sources. Many cross-sectional designs adopt this type of research. *Triangulation by investigators* is where different people collect data on the same situation and data, and the results are then compared. This is one of the advantages of a multi-disciplinary research team as it provides the opportunity for researchers to examine the same situation and to compare, develop and refine themes using insights gained from different perspectives.

Finally there is *methodological triangulation*. Todd (1979) adopted this, using both quantitative as well as qualitative methods of data collection. These were extremely diverse and included questionnaires, interviews, telephone surveys and field studies. He points out that triangulation is not an end in itself, but an imaginative way of maximizing the amount of data collected.

This returns us to the discussion in Chapter 3 about the advisability of combining quantitative and qualitative methods. At the philosophical level there is definitely a problem: the positivist perspective which seeks for a single, objective and stable truth is not compatible with the social constructionist view of reality being flexible, fluid and continually re-negotiated. Quantitative methods can be used to study both 'hard facts' and human perceptions; likewise qualitative methods can be used and analysed in either objectivist or constructionist ways. Our advice to the researcher is to use different methods from within the same paradigm whenever possible, and also to move across paradigms occasionally, but with care.

NOTE

1 The terms (standard) error and accuracy are used here according to their statistical meanings. Technically the standard error is the standard deviation of estimates of the

population mean produced by random samples of the size indicated. In practice this implies that on approximately 95 per cent of occasions the estimate of a mean provided by the sample (say, the average age of employees) will be within two standard errors of the true population mean. Both error and accuracy are expressed in percentage terms, and both add up to 100 per cent. (See Maxwell, 1970: 52–59 for further discussion of this point.)

7 Finishing and Capitalizing on Research

Woody Allen, the American comedian and author, has remarked that 90 per cent of the success in writing lies is getting started and finished on time, and the bit in the middle is easy. It seems that this principle applies to the whole process of research, just as much as to the writing phase. Most people thoroughly enjoy gathering data and doing field-work; and there is often a strong temptation to continue collecting data for too long because of a basic anxiety that the data will eventually turn out to be inadequate.

This leads to two issues that are considered in this chapter. First, there are the problems of writing, and we consider different styles and strategies that may be adopted to overcome these. Second, there is the general anxiety about whether enough work has been done to ensure satisfactory completion of the research project. We therefore review some of the criteria that are likely to be employed in evaluating different forms of research, and hope this will help the researcher to judge when enough is enough. The chapter concludes with some thoughts about capitalizing from the research through publications and other forms of dissemination.

WRITING UP RESEARCH

The problems of writing vary somewhat according to the style of research that has been adopted. When quantitative methods and a positivist approach are adopted, there are fairly clear conventions regarding the structure of the report. Each section is self-contained and can be written independently as one proceeds. With qualitative methods the stages are less distinct, and although interim notes should have been produced throughout the course of the research, it is often necessary to rewrite the whole thing at the end.

Whatever style is adopted, one is repeatedly confronted with the blank page: this is exhilarating for some people, and intimidating for others. Many different strategies can be adopted to overcome writing blocks. Some people start writing anything in order to get started, and they only begin to work out what they are trying to say once they have written a couple of paragraphs of non-sense. Others cannot put pen to paper, or fingers to keyboard, until they have worked out precisely what they wanted to say. Steinbeck (1970) adopted an interesting strategy when writing *East of Eden* which is midway between these two positions. He always began his daily sessions by writing a letter to his editor about what he planned to say that day. The letters were written on the left hand pages of a large note book (and not sent); on the right hand pages he wrote the text of the book. He found this a useful way of starting his thought processes, and overcoming his own writing block.

Becker (1986) takes a slightly different line on how to overcome the barriers to effective writing. He feels that one of the reasons why writing is so difficult is the fear of exposing oneself in public to possible humiliation and ridicule (a thought that occasionally crossed our minds when we first wrote this book). To overcome this he suggests a six stage strategy: write with authority; use a direct style of English; be prepared to carry out editing at several stages; be professional and make writing a normal everyday occurrence; confront yourself with the risks of writing by inviting others to read preliminary drafts; and keep to deadlines however difficult it may seem.

Another strategy which we have adopted is to develop a 'mind map'. In Figure 7.1 we reproduce our mind map on the context of research, which was used when working out some of the material in Chapter 4. Many inexperienced researchers worry about how they will communicate their ideas in a formal written format to a critical audience. But they would do well not to emulate the obscure and stilted language which often creeps into academic reports and which has been rightly criticized by Mills (1959: 218) as follows:

> Lack of intelligibility [in scholarly writing] I believe, usually has little or nothing at all to do with the profundity of thought. It has almost entirely to do with certain confusions of the academic writer about his own status.

To increase the chances of the reader understanding what has been written, simplicity should be the main aim. This can be produced not only by avoiding jargon and complicated sentence construction, but also by using an active rather than passive style of writing. In other words, use concrete examples wherever possible instead of abstract concepts. Amplify ideas by adopting easily understood examples on all possible occasions. Use metaphors to give greater depth to the meaning and interpretation of ideas and theories.

Presenting Qualitative Research

One of the most difficult problems to overcome in dealing with qualitative data is how to communicate, in a systematic and honest manner, research findings to a readership who may not be very familiar with the detailed context of the research. Journalists are paid to interpret situations in a manner which is of interest to their readers, and this often requires editing out issues that they believe will not be of interest. Researchers will also need to edit their findings, but there is a difference here. One never finds out what the journalist has excluded, but the researcher has a duty to demonstrate not only what the line

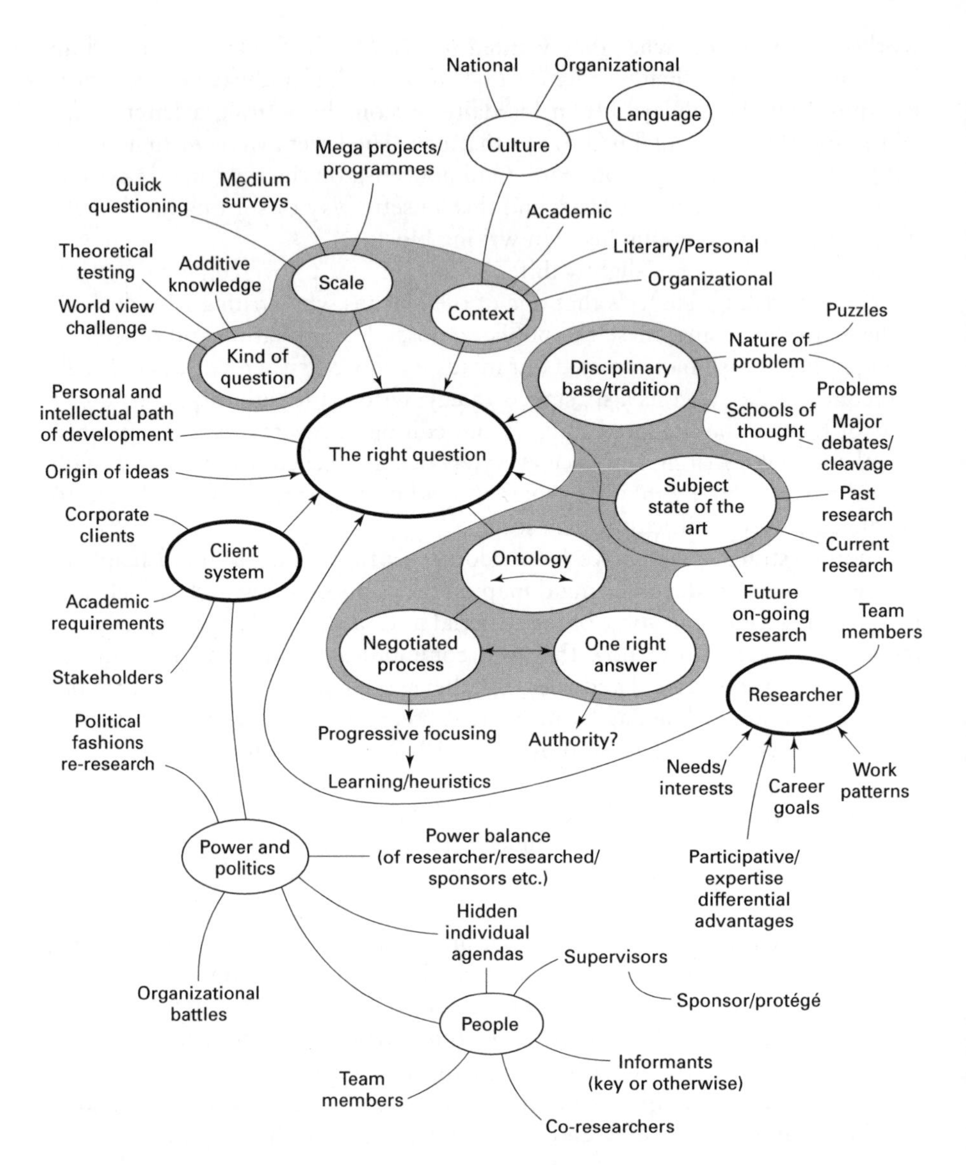

FIGURE 7.1 Mind map of the context of research – getting the right question: a mind map developed for this book

of argument is, but also to indicate what information supports and opposes this argument.

Fineman and Mangham (1983), in a persuasive article on qualitative data, suggest that in their experience it has been the 'soft' qualitative parts that have saved many of the research studies of the day, not the 'hard' quantitative parts. Whereas qualitative data can be both rich and deep, quantitative data which is obtained at a distance from everyday activities may have ceased to live. What Fineman and Manghan suggest qualitative researchers need to do therefore is to convey the richness of their experience. For example, consider this short extract from research by Nichols (1980) drawn from a miner's diary, discussing the influence of a monetary incentive scheme on his willingness to work at higher levels of performance.

> All the time we were packing unnecessarily, the coal was going, so no time could be booked, plus the fact that me and my two were working on dangerous uncovered ground. I was seriously injured a few years ago and this was in the back of my mind. I was off work on crutches for 8 months and all the bonus in the world is not worth being injured for again.

Left in this way the passage is understandable to all. But qualitative researchers need to take it further by developing theoretical themes and highlighting patterns grounded in the data in a way that can be recognized by an external body. This element of presenting findings for others to criticize is an important feature of all types of research. To be regarded as valid, research needs to have been placed in the public domain so it can be debated and defended.

Golden-Biddle and Locke (1997) discuss different strategies for combining data and theory. They distinguish between 'showing' the data/evidence and 'telling' what it means. Although some authors might be tempted to show large amounts of data, there is a limit to how far it will hold the attention of the reader without being put into the context of the wider narrative. Consequently one of the preferred strategies is to start with a theoretical point, then illustrate it with a quote, and then explain further what it all means (tell-show-tell).

Others ways of increasing the validity of qualitative research are:

- Include the voice of the narrator/storyteller in the write-up.
- Feed conclusions back to the subjects (co-researchers) for verification.
- Spell out the nature of the relationships, and the settings in which the observations and discussions took place; also state the degree of collaboration that took place.
- Ensure that honesty and values take a high place on the agenda of any research work undertaken. Honesty about the limitations of the research will increase confidence in the positive results that are presented.
- Spell out the standpoint that the researcher is taking. Reference frames from past experiences are bound to bias the researcher in one way or another, and they are bound to creep into qualitative research. These should not be ignored but declared, and, where appropriate, explained.

Presenting Quantitative Research

As we have suggested above there are more definite conventions when presenting quantitative research: in order to reflect the assumed objectivity of the researcher the writing style tends to more formal and distanced. Whereas the qualitative researcher should write in the first person whenever possible, this practice is still frowned upon by quantitative researchers.

There is also a standard format to the research report which goes along the following lines (Nisbet and Entwistle, 1984):

1 Outline of the research
2 Review of previous work
3 Statement of scope, aims and hypotheses
4 Description of procedures, samples and methods used
5 Statement of results
6 Discussion
7 Summary and conclusions
8 List of references

The report can be enlivened by graphical presentation of descriptive statistics, often in glorious technicolour. Unfortunately some researchers seem to become fascinated by the potential of colour graphics, and forget about the messages they are intended to convey. Beware – large numbers of beautiful pie charts and histograms in a project report are often a sign that limited thought has been given to the conclusions.

Some Practical Tips

We have emphasized the importance of getting started, anyhow, and the need to adopt different strategies according to the individual's preferences. One of the key points in writing is to adopt a medium which causes the least obstruction between one's head and the paper or screen. Mark generally writes direct onto his laptop, occasionally it is easier to put thoughts down on paper, and sometimes it all tumbles out onto an audio tape. The same session may start in one mode, switch to another, and then another. Having a good place to write also helps. Many academics claim to have written their key books while on sabbatical in Tuscany or the South of France. To provide the right frame of mind it is important to establish the association between a place and the ability to work. Other aspects of ritual may also be important: a room, the time of day, the correct type of paper, or a favourite pen.

Finally, when writing it is most important not to feel constrained by what has been written. It is often necessary to write several drafts before getting a document right. Each draft should be discarded not with regret, but as part of development and improvement. Ideally successive drafts should get shorter, rather than longer. Those wishing to read more about the arts of writing could consult some of the following works which we have found helpful: Barzun and Graff (1977), Becker (1986) or Huff (1999).

EVALUATING CONTRIBUTIONS

Part of the problems in finishing research is in knowing when one has done sufficient to meet the success criteria that are likely to be applied. These vary considerably from one piece to another. We discuss here the criteria that may be applied in evaluating four common forms of research activity.

Dissertations for Batchelors and Masters courses are the commonest forms of research project in the management field. In most cases these will include some theoretical ideas, based on literature and some form of data collected by the researcher. The general quality of the dissertation will depend on how well the overall theme/argument is maintained and the extent to which theory and data can be synthesized. It is not sufficient to provide either a good description of others' work or a good account of data gathered; it is important to go beyond what is immediately presented by providing some form of critical reflection. Bloom's taxonomy of educational objectives (Bloom and Krathwohl, 1956) provides a useful framework for thinking about the academic quality of a piece of work. There are six levels of hierarchy, as follows:

6 Evaluation
5 Synthesis
4 Analysis
3 Application
2 Comprehension
1 Knowledge

There is some uncertainty at the moment about whether it is more important for management dissertations to demonstrate evidence of application or analysis. This derives from a long-standing debate in the UK about whether management education should be a practical or an academic training (Whitley et al., 1981), and the more recent debate between Mode 1 and Mode 2 forms of research (Tranfield and Starkey, 1998). The rise of the MBA puts greater emphasis on practical relevance (see comments below on consultancy projects); while many in the scholarly community and the research councils are placing greater stress on the analytic and evaluative elements of the dissertation. Whatever one's view on this, one should be aware that most degrees are awarded by academics and it is therefore prudent to include some elements of analysis and synthesis in the work submitted.

Doctoral theses are similar to Masters' dissertations in that they require a synthesis of ideas and data. But they must also provide critical evaluation of relevant work, and demonstrate some kind of original *contribution* to the field. This contribution can be provided in three main forms: as new knowledge about the world of management (substantive contribution), as new theories and ideas (theoretical contribution), or as new methods of investigation (methodological contribution). In each case the contribution needs to be stated explicitly in the conclusions, and one would expect there to be a clear linkage back to the early part of the thesis where the existing theories and methods were reviewed and evaluated. Ideally the thesis should contain some element of each, although one form may be dominant.

An element of consistency is important in a thesis; it should contain one, or more, clear arguments which are supported by evidence presented in the document. Within the positivist tradition one might follow the dictionary definition of the word *thesis* as 'a proposition to be defended or proved' (Thompson, 1996), alternatively, within the constructionist tradition it might be best to see this as a story line. The title of a thesis is also very important because it gives a hint to the degree of clarity and focus that is likely to ensue in the rest of the document. Sometimes the 'right' title doesn't emerge until the very end, but it is still very important to have used provisional titles throughout – each of which becomes superseded as clarity improves. Beyond that, the degree of emphasis on, say, the accuracy of methodology or the creativity of ideas produced depends on the philosophical base underlying the research. Since the final evaluation may be conducted by independent external examiners (though practice in this respect varies surprisingly widely across Europe and North America), it is most important that the examiners are sympathetic to the worldview, or paradigm, of the researcher. This is not a matter of 'rigging' the result, but of ensuring that one gets a fair hearing.

Research projects supported by academic research councils invoke slightly different criteria. While the conduct of the research must be carried out with the same rigour as a doctoral degree (and be available for public scrutiny), the project will also be conducted within the framework of the proposal for which funds were awarded. Reports to research councils are normally evaluated by a process similar to that for the initial proposal. Thus they will be sent out to external referees who are chosen because they have expertise close to the area of research and may well have been cited in the original proposal. There is an interesting practical point here: it is unwise to be sharply critical of the work of others when writing proposals or reports (preferred terms are 'review/build on/extend the work of . . .'), since the objects of your attacks might well be sitting in judgement on your report!

There are three points to note here, perhaps in descending order of importance. First, the project report must demonstrate that the research has achieved the objectives defined in the original proposal, and that any hypotheses have been tested, whether results are positive, negative or ambiguous. Second, it is important to show that the amount of data collected, and the overall effort put into the project, were as originally specified. Any departure from the original objectives must be clearly explained and justified. And third it is worth showing that the outcomes from the project justify the financial expenditure incurred.

Consultancy projects normally involve work funded by clients and there is often a strong emphasis on application or action research. In these cases there is usually some flexibility with regard to the achievement of objectives which can sometimes be re-negotiated with the client. The crucial elements are clarity and brevity of the conclusions and recommendations. Explanation of methods and theoretical implications requires very limited treatment: much of this will be taken for granted by the client. Consultancy reports are often used by clients, and other managers, as a justification for change or for getting their own way. As such, it is most important in these cases to be sensitive to the political aspects of research discussed in Chapter 4.

However, client projects are being incorporated into MBAs and other degree schemes. In some cases they will be funded at modest levels; in other cases the client will simply make time and resources available to the student(s) involved. Either way, the researchers will now have two distinct sets of expectations, because the requirements of the industrial client and academic assessors may be quite different. This potential tension can be resolved in three main ways: (a) produce a report for the client which has sufficient elements of reflection and critical thought to pass academic muster; (b) write a distinct consultancy report which can be sandwiched within a more academic commentary that reflects on choices made, evaluates experiences, and develops any theoretical insights that might be relevant; or (c) produce two completely separate documents tailored to the distinct needs of the client and the academic assessors. The latter of these strategies is perhaps least desirable since it accepts the separation between the worlds of theory and practice. Nowadays the first two, more integrative, strategies are becoming more feasible since a growing proportion of 'clients' are former students of business and management courses, and they therefore have a greater understanding of the mutual contribution of theory and practice.

GETTING PUBLISHED AND BECOMING FAMOUS

In Chapter 2 we used the story of Fleming's discovery of penicillin to illustrate some of the factors that underlie scientific discoveries. There is a sequel to that story which relates to capitalizing on research.

Fleming discovered penicillin in 1923, but after undertaking only one experiment when he injected penicillin into a mouse and found that it disappeared from the blood stream within 30 minutes, he concluded that it would have little therapeutic application. Ten years later, Howard Florey and Ernest Chain, working with a team at Oxford, uncovered Fleming's description of penicillin following a systematic review of the literature (Macfarlane, 1985). Although the paper ignored previous literature on bacteriological inhibition and was vague about the chemical properties, it did note that the therapeutic potential might be worthy of further investigation. Florey and Chain concentrated on penicillin and eventually produced sufficient quantities to be able to demonstrate its life-saving properties. The results were published in a leading article in *The Times*. Following this, Sir Almroth Wright, the head of Fleming's department, saw an opportunity to increase charitable contributions to St Mary's, and wrote a letter to the editor claiming credit for penicillin for Fleming.

The upshot was that Fleming was given the major credit in the form of 25 honorary degrees, 15 civic freedoms and 1140 major honours, despite the fact that he had conducted no further research during the 11 years following his experiment with the mouse. The lesson from this story is that credit for research should not be taken for granted; it depends very much on how much the researcher is able to exploit his or her work through contacts, publications and other forms of dissemination.

The best route depends somewhat on the kind of research undertaken. With Masters' projects the pay-off might be quite direct, since they are often used as a demonstration of practical competence or relevant experience by those who are looking for jobs. Even consultancy projects can be written up in journals aimed at practitioners. If the journal has a large circulation, like *Management Today*, *Training and Development* or *People Management*, publication of past projects will lead to an enhanced reputation, if not directly to further consultancy opportunities. The best way of getting into practitioner journals is to note carefully the house style, and remember that the article will need to appeal to a fairly broad readership. Straight description of the project is unacceptable; articles need to be able to raise issues and answer questions that readers are likely to find interesting – the project results can then be incorporated to illustrate wider issues.

In the case of the leading 'practitioner' journals in the USA (such as *Harvard Business Review*, *Sloan Management Review* or *California Management Review*), the majority of papers are written by established academics who are seeking a wider audience for pieces of more scholarly research. Normally they will start by identifying a practical issue before demonstrating how the results of their study can promote further understanding of the practical issue. Alternatively these journals are often keen to publish the results of broad surveys of practitioner experiences with new issues, such as the survey by Ruggles (1998) of the experiences of 431 US and European firms in adopting knowledge management initiatives.

With academic research projects and theses the natural outlets are refereed journals, and these are very important for people seeking to make academic careers. In most cases academic journals look for articles with a narrow focus and well-supported argument; economy of style and expression are less important than with practitioner journals. However, it is important to be aware of the wide range in the reputation of journals. Individual academics, journals and publishers frequently publish rankings of journals, but these invariably contain some degree of selectivity or 'spin' which serves the interest of particular communities or institutions. So, beware of one-off, or self-referential ranking systems. The most widely respected ranking system for academic journals is provided by the Social Science Citation Index (SSCI). It is objective in the sense that it is based on bibliographic criteria for selection and evaluation – the Impact Rating, which is roughly, the frequency with which papers published in one journal are cited by papers published in other journals. Each year a rating of all SSCI journals is published, plus rankings within each sub-area of the social sciences.

Only a small portion of management journals are included in the SSCI, so inclusion is generally regarded as evidence that the journal has an international reputation. In most fields there will be a small group of journals, which always appear at the top of the ratings (impact factor over 2.0); in Management the top journals are *Administrative Science Quarterly*, *Academy of Management Journal* and *Academy of Management Review*. There are usually a further 10 journals with ratings between 1.0 and 2.0 which are regarded very highly, and a further 50 or so with ratings between 0.2 and 1.0. Anything below 0.2 is in danger of being removed from the Index. Naturally the top journals are highly competitive, and academics have to judge how high to aim in relation to the strength of their papers. Papers significantly below the threshold of accepability will be rejected out of hand; those falling just below may be offered rewrites – which means they are in with a chance!

In theory, publication decisions depend on the comments of anonymous referees who are unaware of the author's identity. In practice the editor(s) often have to make decisions amid conflicting advice from referees, and anonymity is not always maintained because referees who are very expert in a particular field may well be able to identify the contributions of different authors. The editors of most refereed journals try to be as fair as possible, without showing undue bias towards friends and colleagues. But, all things being equal, it still seems to help if one is known to the editor.

That is why it is important for the aspiring academic to go to conferences in order to develop the kind of networks that we discussed in Chapter 4. It is also worth offering to present research findings and ideas at these conferences and other seminars. At best one might be spotted by an editor or academic dean as a new and rising talent. At the very least one is likely to get some critical feedback on the paper which can be used to strengthen its claim to future publication.

Finally there is the possibility of publishing a book. Not many management theses, as such, find their way into book form. This is because a good thesis is likely to be far too narrow and focused to be of interest to more than a handful of readers. A few publishers are still prepared to accept academic work; but decisions are increasingly driven by commercial considerations, and books are not likely to be accepted unless a sizeable market can be clearly defined for the topic.

Peters and Waterman (1982) are reputed to have received royalties of $1.8 million in the first year of their book's publication, and Mintzberg (1973) did well out of his book (unusually, based on his PhD thesis). But these are the exception: for most people the direct financial rewards are not great. Fortune is most likely to follow the fame of being a published author, and academic careers depend on both the reputation of the publisher and the quality of the reviews that ensue. The nice thing about books is that it is usually possible to develop ideas over a period of time with the help of the publisher. Once again contacts with publishers are most easily established at conferences, where more of the relevant firms are represented.

As with all forms of publishing it is important to believe that one has something worth saying. Taking it further, we see publication and dissemination of ideas not merely as a means to the researcher's own ends, but as an obligation that each researcher has to the wider community. We hope that this book will have provided some of the armoury both to complete worthwhile research, and to use it.

Appendix I: Searching the Literature

This appendix considers how researchers can discover what is already known about a field of study, from published texts, electronic sources and from other communities of practice and official bodies. As we have seen in previous chapters, researchers need to be in touch with the literatures from a range of perspectives and sources, whether these be internal or external sources, public sources or private sources.

Reviewing the literature is a research activity all in itself. It is not unusual to see articles that publish reviews of the literature in a particular field. These invariably focus on research questions which have been raised and highlight the main influential conceptual or empirical studies conducted in the area. The first part of the appendix reiterates the importance placed in any research study of being familiar with the literature. Researchers need, we suggest, to follow the development of the field on a regular basis. One student of Richard's described his weekly scan of the shelves and reviews of the content pages of the journals rather like circuit training on a weekly basis.

The second part outlines how to undertake a bibliographical search; even if the process doesn't become obsessive, as in the case of the individual mentioned above, researchers will need to work with other material on their topic. Finally, the third part discusses how material can be collected, recorded and organized.

DOING A LITERATURE REVIEW

There are numerous ways in which a literature review can be done. Perhaps the most obvious is to begin from the library but it is also possible to use articles or books which directly relate to the literature in your field of study. JAI, for example, publishes a series of editions on research in various disciplines. These are updated regularly as new material is published. It is also important to take note of seminal works in the area. For example, Mark published a review of the field of organizational learning from the perspective of six different disciplines (Easterby-Smith, 1997) which many people have subsequently used as a starting point for more specific investigations.

Another way of getting started is to begin with the relevant historical articles.

Some publications offer a systematic précis of the literature. For example, the *Journal of Marketing* offers such a précis. Over several pages it covers all types of significant articles and publications in all aspects of marketing (e.g. distribution, publicity, sales, strategy, etc.) for that volume year.

It is also an excellent strategy for students to seek out research networks so that they can become part of a wider research community. These can be very fruitful ways of getting to know like-minded colleagues not just in their own country but all over the world, all who work in a similar sphere or on a similar topic. These are to be found at conferences or similar academic associations. For doctoral candidates this kind of networking is vital because it enables them to locate themselves within the wider field. Doctoral streams are organized by most of the big US, UK and European conferences. For example, the Academy of Management, the British Academy of Management, the British Academy of Marketing and the American and European Academies of Management EDEN (European Doctoral Network) and EIASM (European Institute for Advanced Studies in Management). All these groups encourage doctoral candidates to meet and submit their current research for discussion and debate.

The American and British Academies of Management are also organized around disciplinary and cross-disciplinary groups, known respectively as Divisions and Special Interest Groups. In addition to organizing academic tracks within the major conferences they also hold seminars and workshops, and they are always keen to welcome new blood. Perhaps it is also worth noting here that researchers often publish their most recent work as working papers, published through their own universities or through symposia. It is important to know which groups are active and how to get hold of their most recent working papers (which are increasingly available through conference and institutional websites).

SOURCES

The library represents the obvious source for obtaining published material. Behind the library shelves are some very highly trained information scientists who have the job of keeping on top of an ever increasing quantity of information whether it's in Britain, France or the USA. In Great Britain alone there are 10,000 publishing outlets, 125,000 items in print in the area of social sciences, 8000 journals and 5 million entries in the British Library. The single most important aspect of using a library is to establish a rapport with one or a number of these professionals and once the contact has been established, never neglect it. The ability to do this effectively means that researchers have a go-between in someone who can communicate with the library system on their behalf. This is particularly important, since research can require a high level of specialized information and skills and abilities in library use.

We assume that most of the readers of this book will have some general familiarity with the arrangements of libraries – particularly the three main parts of the catalogue, that is, the *author* catalogue (this classifies all the works of any given author alphabetically), the *subject* index and the *classified* catalogue (which shows the various knowledge domains held by the library). For those who are not familiar with them, most libraries these days have online computer catalogues with good search facilities. Guides are usually available which include how they can be operated and for this kind of information, all the researcher needs to do is ask at the desk.

At present, although with new technology things are continually changing, there are two main types of delivery for bibliographic information, print and electronic. The latter includes both CD-ROM and online resources. When beginning any 'search' it is useful to weigh the advantages and disadvantages of the support likely to be available. Issues that researchers ought to consider are: availability, cost and time to gain access. There are two main ways of tackling a literature research, either the researcher needs a wide overall review of the literature in a specific field, or she will know exactly the articles that she wants and simply need to retrieve them. To distinguish between these two aims, we use Selvin and Stuart's (1966) terminology to call the former 'trawling' and the second 'fishing'.

SUBJECT SEARCHES

Before going to the library on a trawl, time can be saved by being selective in what you are after. More specifically, you need to think about the keywords which you would use to identify your field of study. It is useful to remember that unduly broad keywords will produce too many references (often thousands), whereas a narrow choice may produce no references.

What researchers often find is that the keywords they choose and find useful do not necessarily coincide with those chosen by the library. An example might be 'Gas Distribution'. In Britain, this might refer to North Sea Gas, and in an American database this would refer to gasoline, or petrol. If the former, are you looking at its distribution by piping from a field to shore or the conveyance of gas under pressure by lorry? In addition, the subject heading 'Gas Distribution' may just as easily draw on works from an area outside industry, such as physical geography or civil engineering.

The point we are making here is that terminology is very important because in order to find out what you want from the mass of information in the library, you need to identify your interests clearly. A subject search then demands as a precondition some good keywords. Don't think though that you have to find an exact match with those words used in the library to name a subject – any classification system provides for alternative 'names' – your part is to be aware of the most likely alternatives. Try writing a list of the different ways your subject area might be described.

Three of the pitfalls you might encounter in conducting this sort of research need to be borne in mind:

1 Don't be afraid to change your concept of what you're looking for. For

example, returning to our search under 'Gas Distribution', the wrong keywords can give some crazy titles, e.g. 'The Cellular Structure of Air Balloons in the 21st Century'. Keywords clearly work better in some fields than others, but mistaken terminology can sometimes help to refine your objectives. If your search reveals many works on the economics of tanker delivery or the civil engineering aspects of pipelining, then your conception of what's included in your subject expands. If no matches can be found, then other keywords, sometimes broader, will need to be used. If on the other hand the research is too wide, more specific keywords will need to be used.
2. Equally, don't be misled into thinking that an excessively detailed analysis of the subject area shortcuts research – that is, it is rare to find someone who has already undertaken the same type of study as the one you plan yourself (and published the results). Research, as we have discussed before, is not exclusively about refining what has been said by others, it is also in part an act of synthesis. Detailed analysis of your subject will provide the keywords for you to commence your search, but it won't do it for you!
3. One cannot expect to find a single document that answers the essential points you are searching for. For example, a complex group of keywords such as *consumer, culture, scale, measure, psychometric* will not automatically lead you to some specialized articles in the marketing literature dealing with problems of cross-cultural equivalence of the scales of measures used in commercial consumer marketing research. It is even less likely to lead to a specific book on the subject! Consequently when entering a library, even a well organized one, the researcher must be ready to consult a selection of materials.

Management comprises a wide range of subjects and is continually expanding as a discipline and body of knowledge. Fortunately there are a number of bibliographical publications and document services, which can assist in searches. These fall into five broad groupings:

1. Books.
2. Periodicals.
3. Theses, dissertations and research-in-progress.
4. Government publications and official statistics.
5. Reference works, general guides to the literature and guides to the literature in particular subject areas (compendium catalogues).

Each of these will be dealt with in detail below. Also bear in mind that the extent of your search will relate to the number of years you wish to cover, and the subject headings used in the bibliographies and abstracting indexes. If you fail to locate anything at this stage, broader headings can be used and if the material needs to be more specific to reduce the volume, a thesaurus of management indexing terms and one of a number of dictionaries on management might be useful.

Books

Most libraries classify books in themes by subject according to one of the major published classification schemes (most usually the Dewey Decimal System or the Library of Congress classification) often with some modification to suit local requirements. Browsing amongst books in your chosen subject can be a useful way of providing an overview but it is always likely to be a partial one. If all aspects of the literature were grouped in a single place, searching would be a simple undertaking, but the subjects might be scattered across economics, industrial sociology and psychology. The logic of this stems from the general structure of knowledge, which is far from being immediately obvious. Sometimes it can be difficult to know where to classify a book – for example, where would you expect to find a book on the consequences to UK business of entry into the Euro? The catalogue is, therefore, the best place to start a search for books. If the subject is a fairly specific one, it could be the case that there are no books on the topic and there may be a need to look under a wider heading in the subject index. Here you are likely to find several, and if there is a bibliography it will refer to other works, making reference to books and papers in journals. This should point the way to other potentially useful items.

The subject index and catalogue can also reveal any bibliographies that exist in the library's stock. If it is obvious at this stage that there are other published bibliographies in existence which are relevant to the research then the next step is to consult one of the guides that list bibliographies. The *Bibliographic Index* is a list both of separately published bibliographies and of those occurring in books and articles. By examining this, it should be possible to find references to promising bibliographies including books that are in the stock of the library.

The output of published material has become so great that it is unlikely that any library, however large, will be able to meet all of a researcher's needs from its own resources, so once the stock of books available in the local library has been reviewed, the researcher may want to take things further and see what else has been written. To do this, the appropriate national bibliographies need to be consulted – these list the book output of individual countries. COPAC provides access to the merged online catalogues of 20 of the largest university research libraries in the UK and Ireland: http://copac.ac.uk/copac. The British Library Public Catalogue (BLPC) offers free online access to over 16 million book and periodical records of items in the British Library Collection, and includes a document ordering link: http://blpc.bl.uk. Similarly NISS provides access to online public access catalogues by region: http://www.niss.ac.uk/lis.opacs.html. Hytelnet (UK Mirror Site) http://www.cam.ac.uk/Hytelnet/sites1.html provides access to online public access catalogues by region across the globe, including the USA.

If the research has a European dimension, it will be useful to refer to other national bibliographies, such as *Livres-Hebdo* (France), *Deutsche Bibliographie* (Germany) or *Bibliografia Espanola* (Spain). A comprehensive list of links to world libraries is available at the following address: http://www.ifla.org/II/natlibs.htm. Naturally, when searching outside the English medium the researcher will need to know the foreign equivalents of the subject keywords being searched, and thus access to a translator or interpreter may also be necessary. For the non-linguist, there are information sources which refer to works that have been translated, such as the *Index Translationum* and the British Library's *British National Bibliography for Report Literature.*

Before concluding the section about books, it is worth mentioning the existence of catalogues from other libraries which can be a very useful source. The printed catalogues are, of course, restricted to the holdings of the library concerned, but are not limited to the output of any particular country. Very large libraries such as the British Library (http://blpc.bl.uk/) or the Library of Congress (http://catalog.loc.gov/) contain almost *all* publications in the English-language and a large percentage (although on the decline) of foreign-language publications. WorldCat (on the OCLC site at http://newfirstsearch.uk.oclc.org/), is a joint online catalogue which draws on the resources of about 2000 large American libraries and contains an enormous listing of books of all periods and all countries, but registration by your library is required, and a password is needed. In addition there are national/international catalogues like COPAC (http://copac.ac.uk/copac), *Bibliotheque Nationale* (France) (http://www.bnf.fr/), *Deutsche Bibliothek* (http://www.ddb.de/) and *Biblioteca Nacional* (Spain) (http://www.bne.es/esp/catfra.htm). An Internet gateway to Europe's national libraries is provided by Gabriel at http://www.bl.uk/gabriel. Specimens of more specific catalogues can be supplied by institutes such as the Institute of Chartered Accountants (http://www.icaew.ac.uk) and also by the Baker Library from the Harvard Business School, entitled *Core Collection – An Author, Title and Subject Guide.*

Periodicals

Perhaps the most important area is the stock of periodicals and journals. These hold the key to the most up-to-date research: they are the sources that researchers need to make sure they cite on proposals and they represent the means by which the most recent research is placed in the public domain. They also, because of the screening employed (through the refereeing process adopted by the highest ranked journals), represent quality. There are a number of ways in which articles might be found on relevant topics. For example, the researcher could simply leaf through some of the best-known business journals in order to spot how journals deal with particular topics or themes by using their annual indexes which produce a subject and author guides.

Many libraries also keep up-to-date summary catalogues which can be consulted on the spot, for example, the contents pages of everything new in a particular month. However, a far more effective way of locating articles is to use the appropriate abstracting and indexing services, since by doing this you can scan as many as several hundred journals at one time, whose contents have already been extracted and indexed (by subject, keyword and author) and precised (abstracts). Because such abstracting services not only provide references to journal articles but also abstracts of the subject matter, they can help you decide whether an article is worth following without having to see it.

Most business school and university libraries offer a wide range of abstracts and indexes which cover a range of management themes. The leading business database, ABI/Inform, abstracts and indexes from about 1000 management and business journals. The online version, ProQuest, contains the full text of about half the articles in the database. Other general services are *Emerald Reviews*, a searchable online database, which covers 400 of the world's top management journal titles and the American *Business Periodicals Index*, which is only an index but with very impressive coverage. The Business Periodicals Index is produced in print in paperback, on CD-ROM, and as an online resource. It is available in most university libraries in Europe and the USA.

Despite the diversity of material available on the web, perhaps the single most comprehensive and effective source for the researcher is the Web of Science (incorporating the ISI Citation Indexes). For management research, the Social Sciences Citation Index area of this service is often the most relevant. This database is updated on a weekly basis and provides access to over 1725 high quality academic journals, across 50 disciplines, from 1973 onwards. There are more than 2700 articles posted each week, with a total of more than 3 million articles available.

Another general service that is particularly useful for tracing up-to-date information is *The Research Index*; http://www.researchindex.co.uk. It is particularly useful for financial and economic and company information and it also scans the national press and some academic journals. Issued fortnightly, it gives accounts of what has been published one to three weeks previously – which is about as up-to-date as you can get with this type of service, although the FT-web page at http://www.ft.com is perhaps more immediate. In addition to the general abstracts and indexes there are several others which focus on specialized fields such as, for example, *Personnel Management Abstracts, International Abstracts in Operations Research*, *International Packaging Abstracts*, *Psychological Abstracts*, *Training Abstracts*, and many more. Others such as *Public Affairs Information Service Bulletin* (PAIS Bulletin) which is useful for everything connected with the international environment, and *Abstracts in New Technologies and Engineering,* although being on the boundary of management studies, can also be very useful.

One abstracting service that we have found particularly useful are the *DfEE Research Briefs* which are available online at http://www.dfee.gov.uk/research. The publication includes the reports from conferences and the notification of future conferences in the field of management. As already mentioned, these abstracts and indexes may be found in hard copy form, CD-ROM and online via the Internet which makes them accessible from any computer with an Internet browser, and many university libraries are now geared up to access them remotely from home.

Most abstracts and indices are published monthly, but there is usually a time delay of several months between the article's publication and its appearance. If early notice of material is essential then there are a number of current awareness services such as the British Library's alerting service ZETOC at http://zetoc.mimas.ac.uk which will deliver the contents pages of new journal issues to you by e-mail.

Theses, Dissertations and Research-in-Progress

For those undertaking higher degree research as well as those who are undertaking research generally, it is often important to know what theses have already been completed, if only to identify others working in the same field. There are several ways of knowing just what research is being conducted. In Britain theses are available through the *Index to Theses with Abstracts* accepted for Higher Degrees by the Universities of Great Britain and Ireland (with online access at http://www.theses.com). *Dissertation Abstracts* provides electronic access to international dissertation abstracts by library subscription, or free access to the most current two years of data on the web (http://wwwlib.umi.com/dissertations/). In France, there is a national register of current theses managed by the University de Paris-X, Nanterre. There is also DOGE, an abstract of the underground literature on management in France, mainly comprising research papers and theses.

Dissertation Abstracts offers one of the largest and up-to-date lists. It is divided into several parts: Humanities and Social Sciences (Section A); Physical Sciences and Engineering (Section B) and the European Abstracts (Section C). *Dissertation Abstracts* covers most theses produced in North America. Management is contained in Volume 8 of the index. A check needs to be made under the keywords; but if no titles of interest are listed, then the individual volumes will need to be checked. And remember that a negative result is not necessarily a waste of time since it helps to ensure that there is no duplication of research. The European countries have similar systems to the American *Dissertation Abstracts*, for example in Germany, the *Jahresverzeichnis der Deutchen Hochshulschriften* and in England, the Aslib *Index to Theses*.

It is harder to find out about research in progress and it is here that experienced researchers, who have built up contacts over the years have a considerable advantage. As we have indicated above, Membership of the American Academy of Management Divisions or a British Academy of Management Special Interest Group can give access to a vibrant network. However, the British Library's annual publication, *Current Research in Britain* (CRIB) is an important source, as is the Economic and Social Research Council's *Newsletter* which provides details of new and ongoing research, including that in the management field. It is available online at http://www.esrc.ac.uk. Other possible sources of information include websites of business schools and individual researchers. These are becoming increasingly valuable sources of information about current research activities and forthcoming conferences. Many researchers now provide direct access both to their publications and to working papers on the web.

Government Publication and Official Statistics

On a case by case basis, libraries choose to classify official publications either separately or include them within the general catalogue. In Britain, researchers should refer to the online database of United Kingdom Official publications at http://www.ukop.co.uk In hard copy there is the Stationery Office *Annual Catalogue*. There are many published introductions to government publications and official statistics, and many libraries produce their own guides to their stocks. For more comprehensive information on official statistics, the National Statistics *Guide to Official Statistics* is an invaluable source, also on the website http://www.statistics.gov.uk. Online resources of the British Publications Current Awareness Scheme are available at http://www.bopcas.com/ and information about earlier publications can be found in the British official publications collaborative reader information service (BOPCRIS) at http://www.bobcris.ac.uk. It should be said that the whole area of British Government Publications and, in particular, the maze of official statistics present problems to the uninitiated, so this is one of those occasions when the help of a friendly librarian will prove invaluable!

In the United States, details of government publications can be found online at http://www.access.gpo.gov. Some international organizations also offer important statistical information. The OECD, for example, provides information on the economic indicators for international trade and statistics on products (see OECD online at http://www.oecd.org/statistics). The IMF at http://www.imf.org sums up the main economic and financial data for all EU member states. Eurostat at http://europa.eu.int/comm/eurostat provides the key to European statistical information some of which is available for downloading by the academic community from r.cade at http://reads.dur.ac.uk. An online catalogue for The Stationery Office (formally the HMSO) can be found at http://www.thestationeryoffice.co.uk.

Reference Books, General and Specialized Bibliographic Guides

The final group of important publications are the general guides to the literature or subject areas. New researchers can use reference words, for example, to become aware of any organizations relevant to their interests, and these can be very fertile sources of information.

In the UK, publications such as A. J. Walford's *Guide to Reference Material* and *Current British Directories* or its European counterpart, the *Current European Directory* provide a guide to relevant reference resources which are available for a subject area. Further information on business resources can be found in guides such as M. Burke and H. Hall *Navigating Business Information Sources*, London: Library Association, 1998 or J. Haythornthwaite's *The Business Information Maze: An Essential Guide*, London: Aslib, 1990. Directories such as *Register* and *Who Owns Whom*, alongside lists like the *Major UK Companies Handbook* constitute a vital source of information on businesses. For those who need detailed financial information on a company, services such as DAFSA in France, and the Thomson Financial/Primark's Extel Service in Britain, supply data on most businesses quoted on the stock exchange as well as the main European companies. Data is also held for unit trusts. Services such as Datastream and Primark's Piranhaweb give direct access to financial data. In France, Diane supplies financial data on CD-ROM on 135,000 French businesses.

USING THE INTERNET IN MANAGEMENT RESEARCH

One method of undertaking research that has become much more of an everyday facet of both doing business and conducting management research is the Internet. From its beginnings in the late 1960s as a means of networking the US Defence Agency, through the introduction of the World Wide Web, to the current Internet information structure, the Internet has had a high impact on the ways in which information flows and where information resides. This is also felt on the way research is conducted.

Raymond Lee has outlined the potential uses of the Internet as an 'unobtrusive' way of gathering data for social research (Lee, 2000). He argues that the wide availability of personal computers now affect the researcher in a new way to acquire, store and manage data. The advantages are fourfold; first, access to 'unusual' groups has become easier, due to their increased visibility and the lessening of time and space constraints. Second, it is possible to trace patterns of social interaction and social trends through a record of Internet usage and perhaps through the tracing of Internet trends. Third, researching through the Internet may well provide a very reliable means of guaranteeing anonymity both to respondents and the researcher during research projects, which could be useful in researching sensitive topics. Fourth, the Internet may enable social researchers to trace social processes more easily than through face-to-face interaction.

The enormous information resource that is potentially available is, however, both a blessing and a curse. The sheer volume of information makes finding what you are looking for both more likely and more difficult. This is where search engines play their part. Lee (2000) has some suggestions when deciding which search engines to use, particularly the choice between the active and the passive. Active engines search (or crawl) through the Internet pages themselves, cataloguing by vocabulary used. Passive engines on the other hand, depend on the page owner forwarding a description to the search engine administrator. Each has inherent advantages and disadvantages: active searching may generate more contemporary links, and a larger number; passive engines may, however, generate hits that are more relevant to you.

Of course, as with any data collection, the best way of moving forward is to try out different approaches. In this way experience will help the user decide between alternatives. Richard's research colleagues most often use Alta Vista http://www.altavista.com They find that it generates the most relevant links, is the easiest for them to use, often the quickest, and has less intrusive advertising than many other search engines! Others include:

Webcrawler:	http://www.webcrawler.com
InfoSeek:	http://www.infoseek.com
Yahoo:	http://www.yahoo.com
Lycos:	http://www.lycos.com
Google:	http://www.google.com

Also, there are gateways or portals which point to quality information resources available on the Internet such as Business Information Services on the Internet: http://www.dis.strath.ac.uk/business/index.html and SOSIG (Social Sciences Information gateway) http://www.sosig.ac.uk/.

COLLECTING, CATALOGUING AND MAKING SENSE

Never read or review literature without making detailed systematic notes. To do this in a useful way requires pre-planning which means spending time working out how to evaluate the literature. Many new researchers fail to appreciate the lead-time associated with a thorough literature search. In doing so, they forget to build into their research plans a sufficiently adequate time budget. Even if one has an extremely helpful and competent librarian, there will inevitably be delays in obtaining secondary data.

Some academics make cutting remarks about researchers who quote material that they have not actually read (they have perhaps come across concepts in other articles). If the material is a quotation from a secondary source, for example an author cited by another author then it is best to track down the original reference because it may have been used out of context, or worse, misquoted. If this is not possible then it is important to make clear that your quotation is derived from the secondary source.

It might appear an obvious point to make, that all references should be recorded, but once books have been read and returned to the library shelves, or TV programmes have finished, it is extremely difficult and very time-consuming to find references unless the researcher has developed some kind of systematic cataloguing system. Some people prefer systematically writing on cards, or typing them into a file as the literature is being read, others use custom-built bibiographic databases such as Endnote. Whatever system you use, there is a need to build bibliographies from the start of a research project.

Having read critically and produced analytical summaries of the literature, it is necessary to synthesize your interpretation in a manner which demonstrates your familiarity and comprehension of the literature being reviewed. There are several ways in which this can be accomplished. One approach advocated by Buzan (1977) involves creating idea maps. A mind map of how part of this book was planned and organized is shown on page 150 but whatever place the researcher starts, he or she will need to be able to construct a literature review clearly and in a way that holds the interest of the reader. Further details on effective literature searching can be gained from Sarah Gash (2000) whose book offers a comprehensive study of the field.

Appendix II: Academic Societies in Management and Business

Academy of Management
Pace University
PO Box 3020
Briarcliff Manor
NY 10510-8020
USA
Email: aom@fsmail.pace.edu

Academy of International Business
AIB Executive Secretary
2404 Maile Way
University of Hawaii
CBA C-306
Honolulu
Hawaii 96822
USA
Email: aib@cba.hawaii.edu

Academy of Marketing
c/o Admad Jamal
Cardiff Business School
Aberconway Building
Colum Drive
Cardiff CF10 3EU
Wales
UK
Email: Jamala@cardiff.ac.uk
Website: www.stir.ac.uk/departments/management/marketing/academy

American Accounting Association
5717 Bessie Drive
Sarasota, FL 34233
USA
Tel: +1-941-921-741
Email: AAAhq@packet.net

American Economic Association
2014 Broadway
Suite 305
Nashville, TN 37203
USA
Tel: +1-615-322-2595
Email: eainfo@ctrvax.vanderbilt.edu

American Finance Association
Haas School of Business
University of California
Berkeley, CA 94729-1900
USA
Tel: +1-800-835-6770

American Marketing Association
311 South Wacker Drive
Suite 5800
Chicago, IL 60606
USA
Tel: +1-312-542-9000
Email: info@ama.org

British Academy of Management
Membership Services (BAM)
Blackwell Publishers
PO Box 1269
Oxford OX4 1JD
UK
Email: membershipservices@blackwellpublishers.co.uk

British Accounting Association
c/o Sheffield University Business School
9 Mappin Street
Sheffield S1 4DT
Email: BAA@shef.ac.uk

Chartered Institute of Marketing
Moor Hall
Cookham
Maidenhead
Berkshire SL6 9QH
UK
Tel: +44(0) 1628 427500
Email: membership@cim.co.uk

European Finance Association
c/o EIASM
Rue d'Egmont-straat 13
B-1000 Brussels
Belgium
Tel: +322-511-9116
Email: EFA@EIASM.BE

European Group for Organization Studies
c/o Ms Marianne Risberg
Copenhagen Business School
Department of Organization and Industrial Sociology
Solbjerg Plads 3
DK 2000, Fredericksberg
Denmark
Tel: +45-3815-2823
Email: egos.ioa@cbs.dk

INFORMS
901 Elkridge Landing Road
Suite 400, Linthicum
MD USA 21090-2909
Phone: (+1)(800)-4INFORMS
Fax: (+1)(410)684-2963

Operational Research Society
Seymour House
12 Edward Street
Birmingham, B1 2RX
UK
Tel: + 44 (0) 121 233 9300
Fax: + 44 (0) 121 233 0321

Royal Economic Society
c/o Kathy Crocker
University of York
Heslington
York YO1 5DD
UK
Website: http://www.res.org.uk

Appendix III: 2000 SSCI Journal Citation Report – Management

Ranking	Journal Title	Publisher	Impact Factor
1	Academy of Management Review	ACAD MANAGEMENT	3.912
2	Administrative Science Quarterly	ADMINISTRATIVE, SCI QUARTERLY	3.333
3	California Management Review	UNIV CALIF	2.877
4	Harvard Business Review	HARVARD BUSINESS SCHOOL PUBLISHING CORPORATION	2.561
5	Strategic Management Journal	JOHN WILEY & SONS LTD	2.531
6	Academy of Management Journal	ACAD MANAGEMENT	2.375
7	MIS Quarterly	SOC INFORM MANAGE-MIS RES CENT	2.064
8	SLOAN Management Review	SLOAN MANAGEMENT REVIEW ASSOC, MIT SLOAN SCHOOL MANAGEMENT	1.794
9	Human Resource Management	JOHN WILEY & SONS INC	1.268
10	Journal of Management	ELSIVIER SCIENCE INC	1.235
11	Organisational Behaviour and Human Decision Processes	ACADEMIC PRESS INC	1.200
12	Management Learning	SAGE PUBLICAITONS LTD	1.186
13	Research Policy	ELSEVIER SCIENCE BV	1.078
14	Organization Science	INST OPERATIONS RESEARCH MANAGEMENT SCIENCES	1.052
15	Journal of International Business Studies	JOURNAL INT BUSINESS STUDIES	1.012
16	Management Science	INS OPERATIONS RESEARCH MANAGEMENT SCIENCES	1.011
17	Journal of Product Innovation Management	ELSEVIER SCIENCE INC	1.000

Ranking	Journal Title	Publisher	Impact Factor
18	Organization	SAGE PUBLICATIONS LTD	0.963
19	Human Relations	SAGE PUBLICAITONS LTD	0.832
20	Leadership Quaterly	ELSEVIER SCIENCE INC	0.830
21	Organization Studies	WALTER DE GRUYTER & CO	0.818
22	Organizational Dynamics	ELSEVIER SCIENCE INC	0.800
23	Advances in Strategic Management: A Research Annual	JAI PRESS INC	0.739
24	R & D Management	BLACKWELL PUBL LTD	0.737
25	Information and Management	ELSEVIER SCIENCE BV	0.683
26	International Journal of Forecasting	ELSEVIER SCIENCE BV	0.677
27	Journal of Mangement Inquiry	SAGE PUBLICATIONS INC	0.649
28	Journal of the Operational Research Society	NATURE PUBLISHING GROUP	0.648
29	Journal of Management Studies	BLACKWELL PUBL LTD	0.646
30	Interfaces	INST OPERATIONS RESEARCH MANAGEMENT SCIENCES	0.629
31	Group & Organization Management	SAGE PUBLICATIONS INC	0.590
32	New Technology Work and Employment	BLACKWELL PUBL LTD	0.524
33	Decision Sciences	DECISION SCIENCES INST, GEORGIA STATE UNIV	0.473
34	System Dynamics Review	JOHN WILEY & SONS LTD	0.455
35	Omega – International Journal of Management Science	PERGAMON-ELSEVIER SCIENCE LTD	0.453
36	Industrial Marketing Management	ELSEVIER SCIENCE INC	0.420
37	International Journal of Operations & Production Management	MCB UNIV PRESS LTD	0.412

38	International Journal of Selection and Assessment	BLACKWELL PUBL LTD	0.395
39	Journal of Information Technology	ROUTLEDGE	0.382
40	Journal of Economics & Management Strategy	MIT PRESS	0.378
41	Journal of Forecasting	JOHN WILEY & SONS LTD	0.377
42	Tourism Management	ELSEVIER SCI LTD	0.328
43	IEEE Transactions on Engineering Management	IEEE TRANSACTIONS ON ELECTRONICS ENGINEERS INC	0.325
44	Negotiation Journal on the Process of Dispute Settlement	KLUWER ACADEMIC/PLENUM PUBL	0.317
45	Research-Technology Management	INDUSTRIAL RESEARCH INST INC	0.299
46	Group Decision and Negotiation	KLUWER ACADEMIC PUBL	0.294
47	Total Quality Management	ROUTLEDGE	0.269
48	Canadian Journal of Administrative Sciences-Revue Canadienne des Sciences de l'Administration	ADMINISTRATIVE SCIENCES ASSOC CANADA	0.264
49	Journal of Organizational Change Management	MCB UNIV PRESS LTD	0.250
50	Systems Research and Behavioral Science	JOHN WILEY & SONS	0.242
51	Review of Industrial Organization	KLUWER ACADEMIC PUBL	0.241
52	Service Industries Journal	FRANK CASS CO LTD	0.213
53	Long Range Planning	PERGAMON-ELSEVIER SCIENCE LTD	0.207
54	Journal of Organizational Behavior Management	HAWORTH PRESS INC	0.206
55	International Journal of Service Industry Management	MCB UNIV PRESS LTD	0.200
56	International Journal of Technology Management	INDERSCIENCE ENTERPRISES LTD	0.198
57	Systemic Practice and Action Research	KLUWER ACADEMIC/PLENUM PUBL	0.179
58	Journal of Small Business Management	INT COUNCIL SMALL BUSINESS	0.167
59	International Journal of Manpower	MCB UNIV PRESS LTD	0.116
60	Workforce	ACC COMMUNICATIONS INC	0.075

Bibliography

Abrahamson, M. (1983) *Social Research Methods*. Englewood Cliffs, NJ: Prentice Hall.

Agar, M.H. (1986) *Speaking of Ethnography*. Beverly Hills: Sage.

Ahmed, S. (1998) *Differences that Matter: Feminist Theory and Postmodernism*. Cambridge: Cambridge University Press.

Aiken, H.D. (1956) *The Age of Ideology*. New York: Mentor.

Alvesson, M. and Deetz, S. (2000) *Doing Critical Management Research*. London: Sage.

Alvesson, M. and Wilmott, H. (1992) *Critical Management Studies*. London: Sage.

Anderson, M.L. (1993) 'Studying across difference: race, class and gender in qualitative research', in J.H. Stanfield and R.M. Dennis (eds), *Race and Ethnicity in Research Methods*. London: Sage. pp. 39–52.

Andrews, K.M. and Delahaye, B.L. (2000) 'Influences on knowledge processes in organizational learning: the psychosocial filter', *Journal of Management Studies,* 37(6): 797–810.

Ansoff, I. (1986) 'The pathology of applied research in social science', in F. Heller (ed.), *The Use and Abuse of Social Science*. Beverly Hills: Sage.

Argyris, C. and Schon, D.A. (1978) *Organisational Learning*. Reading: Addison-Wesley.

Ashton, D.J.L. and Easterby-Smith, M. (1979) *Management Development in the Organisation*. London: Macmillan.

Austin, J.H. (1978) *Chase, Chance and Creativity*. New York: Columbia University Press.

Bainbridge, W.S. (1989) *Survey Research: A Computer Assisted Introduction*. Belmont, CA: Wasworth.

Baker, S. (1996) 'Consumer cognitions: mapping personal benefits relating to perfume purchase in the UK and Germany', 207th ESOMAR Seminar, *Capturing the Elusive Appeal of Fragrance: Techniques, Experiences, Challenges*. Amsterdam.

Baker, S. and Knox, S. (1995) 'Mapping consumer cognitions in Europe', in M. Bergadaa (ed.), *Marketing Today for the 21st Century*. Proceedings of 24th EMAC Conference, Cergy-Pontoisse, France. 1: 81–100.

Bannister, D. and Fransella, F. (1971) *Inquiring Man: The Theory of Personal Constructs*. Harmondsworth: Penguin.

Bannister, D. and Mair, J.M.M. (1968) *The Evaluation of Personal Constructs.* London: Academic Press.

Bartunek, J.M. and Louis, M.R. (1996) *Insider/Outsider Team Research.* Thousand Oaks: Sage.

Barwise, P., Marsh, P., Thomas, K. and Wensley, R. (1989) 'Intelligent elephants and part-time researchers', *Graduate Management Research,* Winter: 12–33.

Barzun, J. and Graff, H.F. (1977) *The Modern Researcher.* New York: Harcourt Brace.

Bateson, G. (1973) *Steps to an Ecology of Mind.* London: Paladin.

Becker, H.S. (1958) 'Problems of inference and proof of participation observation', *American Sociological Review,* 23: 632–60.

Becker, H. (1986) *Writing for Social Scientists.* Chicago: University of Chicago Press.

Belbin, R.M. (1981) *Management Teams: Why they Succeed or Fail.* London: Heinemann.

Belbin, R.M. (1993) *Team Roles at Work.* Oxford: Butterworth-Heinemann.

Bell, J., Bush, T., Fox, A., Goodley, J. and Goulding, S. (eds) (1984) *Conducting Small Scale Investigations in Education Management.* London: Harper and Row.

Berger, P.L. and Luckman, T. (1966) *The Social Construction of Reality.* London: Penguin.

Beynon, H. (1973) *Working for Ford.* Harmondsworth: Penguin.

Beynon, H. (1988) 'Regulating research: politics and decision making in industrial organisations', in A. Bryman (ed.), *Doing Research in Organisations.* London: Routledge.

Bhaskar, R. (1989) *Reclaiming Reality: A Critical Introduction to Contemporary Philosophy*. London: Verso

Billig, M. (1988) 'Review of: *Murderous Science: Elimination by Scientific Selection of Jews, Gypsies and Others. Germany 1933–1945*. B. Muller-Hill, Oxford: OUP' in *The Psychologist,* December: 475–6.

Bloom, B.S. and Krathwohl, D.R. (1956) *Taxonomy of Educational Objectives.* London: Longman.

Bockcock, R. (1974) *Ritual in Industrial Society.* London: Allen and Unwin.

Bogdan, R. and Taylor, S.J. (1975) *Introduction to Quantitative Research Methods: A Phenomenological Approach to the Social Sciences.* London: Wiley.

Boissevain, J. (1974) *Friends of Friends.* Oxford: Blackwell.

Boje, D.M. (1995) 'Stories of the story-telling organization: a postmodern analysis of Disney as "Tamara-land"', *Academy of Management Journal,* 38(4): 997–1035.

Boje, D.M. (2001) *Narrative Methods for Organizational and Communication Research*. London: Sage.

Bott, E. (1971) *The Family and Social Networks.* New York: The Free Press.

Bowey, A.M. and Thorpe, R. with Hellier, P. (1986) *Payment Systems and Productivity.* London: Macmillan.

Boxer, P. (1980) 'Reflective learning', in J. Beck and C. Cox (eds) *Advances in Management Education*. Chichester: Wiley.

Boyacigiller, N.A. and Adler, N.J. (1991) 'The parochial dinosaur: organizational science in a global context', *Academy of Management Review*, 16: 262–90.

Boyatzis, R.E. (1982) *The Competent Manager: A Model for Effective Performance*. New York: Wiley.

Brown, J.S. and Duguid, P. (1991) 'Organizational learning and communities of practice: towards a unified view of working, learning and innovation', *Organization Science*, 2(1): 40–57.

Bryman, A. and Cramer, D. (1997) *Quantitative Data Analysis with SPSS for Windows: A Guide for Social Scientists*. London: Routledge.

Bryn, S. (1966) *The Human Perspective in Sociology*. Englewood Cliffs, NJ: Prentice-Hall.

Buchanan, D. (1980) 'Gaining management skills through academic research work', *Personnel Management*, 12(4): 45–8.

Buchanan, D. and Badham, R. (1999) *Power, Politics and Organizational Change: Winning the Turf Game*. London: Sage.

Buchanan D.A., Boddy, D. and McCalman, J. (1988) 'Getting in, getting on, getting out, getting back: the art of the possible', in A. Bryman (ed.) *Doing Research in Organisations*. London: Routledge.

Bulmer, M. (1988) 'Some reflections upon research in organization', in A. Bryman (ed.), *Doing Research in Organizations*. London: Routledge.

Burgess, R.G. (1982) *Field Research: A Source Book and Field Manual*. London: Allen and Unwin, (2nd edn, 1991, Routledge).

[illegible] . (1983) 'Natural learning and managerial [illegible] study in the field setting', *Journal of* [illegible] 87–9.

[illegible] 6) 'The nature, use and acquisition of mana- [illegible] s', *Personnel Review*, 15(4): 19–29.

[illegible] unnymen', in J. Hassard and M. Parker (eds), [illegible] *tions*. London: Sage.

[illegible]) *Sociological Paradigms and Organisational* [illegible] .

Buzan, T. (1977) *How to Make the Most of your Mind*, London: Colt Books.

Calder, A. and Sheridan, D. (eds) (1984) *Speak for Yourself: a Mass-Observation Anthology 1937–49*. London: Jonathan Cape.

Campbell, D.T. and Fiske, D.W. (1959) 'Convergent and discriminant validation by the multitrait-multimethod matrix', *Psychological Bulletin*, 56: 81–105.

Campbell, D.T. and Stanley, J.C. (1963) 'Experimental and quasi-experimental designs for research', in N.L. Gage (ed.), *Handbook of Research on Teaching*. Chicago: Rand McNally.

Casey, D. (1985) 'When is a team not a team', *Personnel Management*, January: 26–29.

Castells, M. (2000) *The Rise of the Network Society* (2nd edn). Oxford: Blackwell.

Cattell, R.B. and Warburton, F.W. (1967) *Objective Personality and Motivation Tests*. London: University of Illinois Press.

Charmaz, K. (1983) 'The grounded theory method: an explication and interpretation', in R. Emerson (ed.), *Contemporary Field Research*. Boston: Little, Brown.

Clarke, I. and MacKaness, W. (2001) 'Management intuition: an interpretative account of structure and content using cognitive maps', *Journal of Management Studies*, 38(2).

Coffey, A., Holbrook, B and Atkinson, P. (1996) 'Qualitative data analysis: technologies and representations', *Sociological Research Online*, 1(1). http://www.socresonline.org.uk/socresonline/1/14.html

Cohen, A. (1986) *Two Dimensional Man: An Essay on the Anthropology of Power and Symbolism*. London: Routledge and Kegan Paul.

Collins, H.M. (1983) 'An empirical relativist programme in the sociology of scientific knowledge', in K.D Knorr-Cetina and M. Mulkay (eds), *Science Observed: Perspectives on the Social Study of Science*. London: Sage.

Comte, A. (1853) *The Positive Philosophy of Auguste Comte* (trans. H. Martineau). London: Trubner and Co.

Converse, J.M. and Previer, S. (1986) *Survey Questions: Handcrafting the Standardised Questionnaire,* Quantitative Applications in the Social Science No 63, Beverly Hills: Sage.

Cook, S.D.N. and Brown, J.S. (1999) 'Bridging epistemologies: the generative dance between organizational knowledge and organizational knowing', *Organization Science*, 10(4): 381–400.

Cook, T.D. and Campbell, D.T. (1979) *Quasi-Experimentation: Design and Analysis Issues for Field Settings*. Chicago: Rand McNally.

Cooper, R. (1992) 'Formal organization as representation', in M. Reed and M. Hughes, *Rethinking Organization*. London: Sage.

Cooper, R. and Burrell, G. (1988) 'Modernism, postmodernism and organizational analysis: an introduction', *Organization Studies*, 9(1): 91–112.

Critchley, B. and Casey, D. (1984) 'Second thoughts on team building', *Management Education and Development*, 15(2): 163–75.

Curran, J. and Downing, S. (1989) 'The State and small business owners: an empirical assessment of consultation strategies'. Paper presented at the 12th National Small Firms Policy and Research Conference, Barbican, London.

Currie, R.M. (1959) *Work Study*. London: Pitman.

Cyert, R.H. and March, J.G. (1963) *A Behavioral History of the Firm*. Englewood-Cliffs NJ: Prentice-Hall (2nd edn, 1992, Oxford: Blackwell).

Czarniawska, B. (1998) *A Narrative Approach to Organization Studies*. London: Sage.

Dalton, M. (1959) *Men Who Manage: Fusion of Feeling and Theory in Administration*. New York: Wiley.

Dalton, M. (1964) 'Preconceptions and methods in *Men Who Manage*', in P. Hammond (ed.) *Sociologists at Work*. New York: Basic Books.

Dare, G.A. and Bakewell, K.G.B. (1983) *The Manager's Guide to Getting Answers*. London: Library Association.

Davila, C. (1989) 'Grounding management education in local research: A Latin American experience', in J. Davies, M. Easterby-Smith, S. Mann and M. Tanton (eds), *The Challenge to Western Management Development: International Alternatives*. London: Routledge.

De Bono, E. (1971) *Practical Thinking*. London: Jonathan Cape.

Deem, R. and Brehony, K. (1997) 'Research students' access to research cultures: an unequal benefit?' Paper presented at Society for Research in Higher Education Conference, University of Warwick.

Denzin, N.K. (1971) 'The logic of naturalistic inquiry', *Social Forces*, 50: 166–82.

Ditton, J. (1977) *Part-time Crime*. London: Macmillan.

Douglas, J.D. (ed.) (1976) *Investigative Social Research*. Beverly Hills: Sage.

Easterby-Smith, M. (1980) 'How to use repertory grids in HRD', *Journal of European Industrial Training Monograph*, 4(2): 1–32.

Easterby-Smith, M. (1994/1986) *Evaluation of Management Education, Training and Development*. Aldershot: Gower.

Easterby-Smith, M. (1997) 'Disciplines of organizational learning: contributions and critiques', *Human Relations*, 51(9): 1085–116.

Easterby-Smith, M. and Ashton, D. (1975) 'Using repertory grid technique to evaluate management training', *Personnel Review*, 4(4): 15–21.

Easterby-Smith, M. and Malina, D. (1999) 'Cross-cultural collaborative research: toward reflexivity', *Academy of Management Journal*, 42(1): 76–86.

Easterby-Smith, M., Thorpe, R. and Holman, D. (1996) 'Using repertory grids in management research', *Journal of European Industrial Training*, 20(3): 1–30.

Easterby-Smith, M. and Wu Xia (2000) 'Learning within international organizations: the role of power, culture and social identity'. Paper for Academy of Management Conference, Toronto, August.

Eden, C. (1988a) 'Cognitive mapping as a visionary tool: strategy embedded in issue management'. Alfred-Houle Seminar, Faculte des Sciences de l'Administration, Univesite Lavel, Quebec, March.

Eden, C. (1988b) 'Strategic decision support through computer-based analysis and presentation of cognitive maps'. Alfred-Houle Seminar, Faculte des Sciences de l'Administration, Universite Laval, Quebec, March.

Eden, C (1990) 'Strategic thinking with computers', *Long Range Planning*, 23(6): 35–43.

Eden, C. and Jones, S. (1984) 'Using repertory grid for problem construction', *Journal of Operational Research Society*, 35(9): 779–90.

Eden, C. and Radford, J. (eds) (1990) *Tackling Strategic Problems: The Role of Group Decision Support*. London: Sage.

Eden, C., Jones, S. and Sims, D. (1979) *Thinking in Organisations*. London: Macmillan.

Eden, C., Jones, S. and Sims, D. (1983) *Messing About in Problems*. Oxford: Pergamon.

Eisenhardt, K.M. (1989) 'Building theories from case study research', *Academy of Management Review*, 14(4): 532–550.

Elbow, P. (1981) *Writing with Power.* Oxford: Oxford University Press.

ESRC (2001) *Postgraduate Training Guidelines*, 3rd edn. Swindon: ESRC.

Evered, R. (1981) 'Management education for the year 2000', in C.L. Cooper (ed.), *Developing Managers for the 1980's.* London: Macmillan.

Evers, F.T. and Rush, J.C. (1996) 'The bases of competence: skill development during the transition from university to work', *Management Learning,* 27(3): 275–300.

Eysenck, H.J. and Eysenck, S.B.G. (1973) *Eysenck Personality Inventory.* London: University of London Press.

Fairclough, N. (1995) *Critical Discourse Analysis: The Critical Study of Language.* London: Sage.

Fairclough, N. and Hardy, G. (1997) 'Management learning as discourse', in J. Burgoyne and M. Reynolds (eds), *Management Learning: Integrating Perspectives in Theory and Practice.* London: Sage.

Fairhurst, E. (1983) 'Organisational rules and the accomplishment of nursing work on geriatric wards', *Journal of Management Studies, Special Issue,* 20(3), July: 315–32.

Fineman, S. and Mangham, I. (eds) (1983) 'Qualitative approaches to organizations', *Journal of Management Studies, Special Issue,* 20(3), July: 295–300.

Fayol, H. (1916/50), *Administration Industrielle et Generale.* Paris: Dunod.

Fielding, N.G. (1987) 'The qualitative analysis'. ESRC Seminar, University of Surrey, September.

Fielding, N.G. and Fielding, J.L. (1986) *Linking Data.* Beverly Hills: Sage.

Finch, J. (1986) *Research and Policy: The Uses of Qualitative Methods in Social and Educational Research.* London: Falmer Press.

Flanagan, J.C. (1954) 'The critical incident technique', *Psychological Bulletin,* 1: 327–58.

Freeman, D. (1996) 'Fooled in paradise', *The Times Higher*, 27 December: 19.

French, W.L. and Bell, C.H. Jr (1978) *Organisation Development: Behavioral Science Interventions for Organisational Improvement* (3rd edn, 1984). Englewood Cliffs, NJ: Prentice-Hall.

Gash, S. (2000) *Effective Literature Searching.* Aldershot: Gower.

Geertz, C. (1973) *The Interpretation of Cultures.* New York: Basic Books.

Glaser, B.G. (1978) *Theoretical Sensitivity.* Mill Valley, CA: Sociological Press.

Glaser, B.G. (1992) *Basics of Grounded Theory Analysis: Emergence versus Forcing.* Mill Valley, CA: Sociological Press.

Glaser, B.G. (1998) *Doing Grounded Theory: Issues and Discussions.* Mill Valley, CA: Sociology Press.

Glaser, B.B.G. and Strauss, A.L. (1967) *The Discovery of Grounded Theory: Strategies for Qualitative Research.* New York: Aldine.

Golden-Biddle, K. and Locke, K.D. (1997) *Composing Qualitative Research.* Thousand Oaks: Sage.

Gordon, R.A. and Howell, J.E. (1959) *Higher Education for Business.* New York: Columbia University Press.

Green, P.E. and Tull, D.S. (1978) *Research for Marketing Decisions.* Englewood Cliffs: Prentice-Hall.

Guba, E.G. and Lincoln, Y.S. (1989) *Fourth Generation Evaluation*. London: Sage.

Gubrium, J.F. and Silverman, D. (eds) (1989) *The Politics of Field Research*. London: Sage.

Gummesson, E. (1988) *Qualitative Research in Management* (revised edn, 1991, Newbury Park: Sage). Bromley: Chartwell-Bratt.

Habermas, J. (1970) 'Knowledge and interest', in D, Emmett and A. Macintyre (eds), *Sociological Theory and Philosophical Analysis*. London: Macmillan.

Hakin, C. (1987) *Research Design: Strategies and Choices in the Design of Social Research*. London: Allen and Unwin.

Hales, C.P. (1986) 'What do managers do? A critical review of the evidence', *Journal of Management Studies*, 23(1): 88–115.

Hall, C.S. (1954) *Primer of Freudian Psychology*. London: Mentor.

Hamel, J. with Dufour, S. and Fortin, D. (1993) *Case Study Methods*. Newbury Park, CA: Sage.

Hammer, M. and Champy, J. (1993) *Reengineering the Corporation: A Manifesto for Business Revolution*. Cambridge, Mass: Ballinger.

Hammersley, M. and Atkinson, P. (1983) *Ethnography: Principles in Practice*. London: Tavistock. (2nd edition 1995).

Handy, C. (1978) *Understanding Organisations*. Harmondsworth: Penguin.

Handy, C. (1984) *The Future of Work*. Oxford: Blackwell.

Handy, C. (1989) *The Age of Unreason*. London: Business Books.

Handy, C. (1996) *Beyond Certainty: The Changing Worlds of Organizations*. London: Arrow Books.

Handy, C. Gordon, C., Gow, I. and Randlesome, C. (1988) *Making Managers*. London: Pitman.

Hardy, C. (1996) 'Understanding power: bringing about strategic change', *British Journal of Management*, 7 (Special Issue): S3–S16.

Hassard, J. and Parker, M. (eds) (1993) *Postmodernism and Organizations*. London: Sage.

Hayes, R. H. and Abernethy, W. J. (1980) 'Managing our way to economic decline', *Harvard Business Review*, 58: 67–77.

Hedges, A. (1985) 'Group interviewing', in R. Walker (ed.), *Applied Qualitative Research*. Aldershot: Gower.

Heron, J. (1996) *Co-operative Inquiry: Research into the Human Condition*. London: Sage.

Herzberg, F. (1987) 'One more time: how do you motivate employees?' *Harvard Business Review*, 65(5).

Herzberg, F., Mausner, B. and Snyderman, B.B. (1959) *The Motivation to Work*. New York: Wiley.

Hickson, D.J. (1988) 'Ruminations on munificence and scarcity in research', in A. Bryman (ed.), *Doing Research in Organizations*. London: Routledge.

Hofstede, G. (abridged edn, 1984 [1980]) *Culture's Consequences: International Differences in Work-Related Values*. Beverly Hills: Sage.

Hofstede, G. (1983) *Culture and Management Development*. Geneva: ILO.

Hofstede, G. (1991) *Cultures and Organizations: Software of the Mind*. London: HarperCollins Business.

Hoinville, G. and Jowell, R. (1978) *Survey Research Practice*. London: Heinemann.

Homan, M.G. (1979) 'Action research: the solution or the problem?', in C.L. Cooper (edn.), *Behavioral Problems in Organisations*. Englewood Cliffs, NJ: Prentice-Hall.

Holsti, O. (1969) *Content Analysis for the Social Sciences and Humanities*. London: Addison Wesley.

Honey, P. and Mumford, A. (1982) *The Manual of Learning Styles*, Peter Honey, Ardingley House, 10 Linden Avenue, Maidenhead, SC6 6HB.

Howard, K. and Sharp, J.A. (1983) *The Management of a Student Research Project*. Aldershot: Gower.

Huczynski, A.A. (1996) *Management Gurus: What Makes Them and How to Become One*. London: International Thomson Business Press.

Huff, A.S. (1999) *Writing for Scholarly Publication*. London: Sage.

Huff, A. (2000) 'Changes in organizational knowledge production', *Academy of Management Review*, 25(2): 288–93.

Huff, D. (1973) *How to Lie with Statistics*. Harmondsworth: Penguin.

Husserl, E. (1946) 'Phenomenology' in *Encyclopaedia Britannica*, 14th edn, Vol 17: 699–702.

Hussey, J. and Hussey, R. (1997) *Business Research: A Practical Guide for Undergraduate and Postgraduate Students*. Basingstoke: Macmillan.

Hyder, S. and Sims, D. (1979) 'Hypothesis, analysis and paralysis: issues in the organisation of contract research', *Management Education Development*, 10: 100–11.

Irwin, A. (1994) 'Science's social standing', *The Times Higher*, 30 September: 17–19.

Jenkins, M. and Johnson, G. (1997) 'Linking managerial cognition and organizational performance: a preliminary investigation using causal maps', *British Journal of Management*, 8, Special Issue; S77–90.

Jobber, D. and Horgan, I. (1987) 'Market research education: perspectives from practitioners', *Journal of Marketing Management*, 3(1): 39–49.

Jones, S. (1985) 'The analysis of depth interviews', in R. Walker, *Applied Qualitaitve Research*. Aldershot: Gower.

Jones, S. (1987) 'Choosing action research: a rationale', in I.L. Mangham (ed.), *Organisation Analysis and Development*. Chichester: Wiley.

Junkers, B.H. (1960) *Fieldwork: An Introduction to the Social Sciences*. Chicago University Press; Cambridge University Press.

Keat, R. (1981) *The Politics of Social Theory*. Oxford: Blackwell.

Kelly, G.A. (1955) *The Psychology of Personal Constructs*. New York: Norton.

Kidder, L.H. and Judd, C.M. (1986) *Research Methods in Social Relations*. London: H.R.W. Intermation. (6th edition 1991) London: Harecourt Brace Janovich.

Kirk, J. and Miller, M.L. (1986) *Reliability and Validity in Qualitative Research*. Beverly Hills: Sage.

Knorr-Cetina, K.D. (1983) 'The ethnographic study of scientific work: towards a constructivist interpretation of science', In K.D. Knorr-Cetina

and M. Mulkay (eds), *Science Observed: Perspectives on the Social Study of Science*. London: Sage.
Koestler, A. (1964) *The Act of Creation*. London: Hutchinson.
Kolb, D.A. (1984) *Organisational Psychology: An Experimental Approach to Organisational Behaviour.* Englewood Cliffs, NJ: Prentice-Hall.
Kolb, D.A. (1986) *Experiential Learning*. Englewood Cliffs, NJ: Prentice-Hall.
Kolb, D.A. and Fry, R. (1975) 'Towards an applied theory of experiential learning', in C.L. Cooper (ed.), *Theories of Group Processes*. London: Wiley.
Körösi, G., Mátyás, L. and Székély, I (1992) *Practical Econometrics*. Avebury.
Kotter, J. (1982) *The General Managers*. Glencoe, Ills: Free Press.
Kuhn, T.S. (1962) *The Structure of Scientific Revolution*. Chicago: University of Chicago Press.
Kvanli, A., Guynes, C.S. and Pavur, R.J. (1996) *Introduction to Business Statistics* 4th edn. St Paul, MN: West Publishing Company.
Latour, B. and Woolgar, S. (1979) *Laboratory Life: The Social Construction of Scientific Facts*. Beverly Hills: Sage.
Lavrakas, P.K. (1987) *Telephone Survey Methods*. Sage Applied Social Research Methods Series, Newbury Park, CA: Sage.
Law, J. (1994) *Organizing Modernity.* Oxford: Blackwell.
Lawrence, P. (1986) *Invitation to Management*. Oxford: Blackwell.
Legge, K. (1984) *Evaluating Planned Organisational Change*. London: Academic Press.
Lincoln, Y.S. and Guba, G. (1986) *Naturalistic Inquiry.* London: Sage.
Livingston, J.S. (1971) 'The myth of the well-educated manager', *Harvard Business Review,* 49: 79–89.
Locke, K. (1997) 'Re-writing the discovery of Grounded Theory after 25 years?', *Journal of Management Inquiry*, 5: 239–45.
Locke, K. (2001) *Grounded Theory in Management Research*. London: Sage.
Lofland, J. (1971) *Analysing Social Settings: A Guide to Qualitative Observation and Analysis*. Belmont, CA: Wadsworth.
Lofland, J. (1974) 'Styles of reporting qualitative field research', *American Sociologist,* 9 (August) 101–11.
Lowe, A. and Nilsson, T. (1989) *The Ideologies of Scottish Lawyers*. Centre for Professional and Legal Studies, University of Strathclyde.
Lu, Y. and Heard, R. (1995) 'Socialised economic action: a comparison of strategic investment decision-making in China and Britain', *Organization Studies,* 16: 395–424.
Lyles, M.A. and Salk, J.E. (1996) 'Knowledge acquisition from foreign parents in international joint ventures: an empirical examination in the Hungarian context', *Journal of International Business Studies*, Special Issue, 27: 877–903.
McClelland, D.A. (1961) *The Achieving Society.* Princetown: Van Nostrand.
McClelland, D.A. (1965) 'Achievement and enterprise', *Journal of Personal Social Psychology,* 1: 389–92.
McCormack, B. and Hill, E. (1997) *Conducting a Survey: The SPSS Workbook*. London: International Thompson.

Macfarlane, G. (1985) *Alexander Fleming: The Man and the Myth*. Oxford: Oxford University Press.

Mackinlay, T. (1986) 'The development of a personal strategy of management'. Master of Science Degree, Manchester Polytechnic, Department of Management.

Mangham, I.L (1986) 'In search of competence', *Journal of General Management*, 12(2), 5–12.

Margerison, C. and Lewis, C. (1986) 'Management educators and their clients', in J. Beck and C. Cox (eds), *Advances in Management Education*. Chichester: Wiley. pp. 277–82.

Maruyama, M. (1981) 'Endogenous research: rationale', In P. Reason and J. Rowan (eds), *Human Inquiry: A Source Book of New Paradigm Research*. Chichester: Wiley.

Mason, J. (1996) *Qualitative Researching*. London: Sage

Maxwell, A.E. (1970) *Basic Statistics in Behavioural Research*. Harmondsworth: Penguin.

Mayo, E. (1949) *The Social Problems of an Industrial Civilisation*. London: Routledge and Kegan Paul.

Mendes de Almeida (1980) 'A review of group discussion methodology', *European Research*, 8(3): 114–20.

Miles, N.B. and Huberman, A.M. (1984) *Qualitative Data Analysis: A Sourcebook of New Methods*. London: Sage (2nd edn, 1994).

Mill, C.W. (1959) *The Sociological Imagination*. Oxford: Oxford University Press.

Mills, C.W. (1972) 'Language Logic and Culture', in A. Cashadan and E. Crugoen (eds), *Language and Education*. London: Routledge and Kegan Paul.

Mintzberg, H. (1973) *The Nature of Managerial Work*. London: Harper and Row.

Mintzberg, H. (1978) 'Mintzberg's final paradigm', *Administrative Science Quarterly*, 23(4): 635–6.

Moingeon, B. and Edmondson, A. (1997) *Organizational Learning and Competitive Advantage*. London: Sage.

Morgan, G. (1979) 'Response to Mintzberg's', *Administrative Science Quarterly*, 24(1): 137–9.

Morgan, G. (1986) *Images of Organization*. Beverly Hills: Sage. (New edition 1997).

Morgan, G. and Smircich, L. (1980) 'The case for qualitative research', *Academy of Management Review*, 5: 491–500.

Moser, C.A. and Kalton, G. (1971) *Survey Methods in Social Investigation*, 2nd edn. London: Heinemann (new edn, 1993, Aldershot: Dartmouth).

Mullins, C.J. (1977) *A Guide to Writing and Publishing*. Chichester: Wiley.

Murray, H. (1938) *Explorations in Personality, a Clinical and Experimental Study of 50 Men of College Age*. New York: Oxford University Press.

Nichols, G. (1980) 'A study of the National Coal Board's productivity bonus scheme'. Master of Science Thesis, Strathclyde Business School, Glasgow.

Nisbet, J.D. and Entwistle, N.J. (1984) 'Writing the report', in J. Bell, T. Bush, A. Fox, J. Goodey and S. Goulding (eds), *Conducting*

Small-Scale Investigations in Educational Management. London: Harper and Row.

Nonaka, I. (1988) 'Toward middle-up-down management: accelerating information creation', *Sloan Management Review*, Spring: 9–18.

Nonaka, I. and Takeuchi, H. (1995) *The Knowledge-Creating Company: How Japanese Companies Create the Dynamics of Innovation*. Oxford: Oxford University Press.

Nor, S.M. (2000) 'Privatisation and changes in organization: a case study of a Malaysian privatised utility'. PhD Thesis, Lancaster University.

Norusis, M. (1986) *The SPSS Guide to Data Analysis*, Chicago: SPSS Inc. (SPSS7.5 Guide, 1997.)

Oppenheim, A.N. (1966) *Questionnaire Design and Attitude Measurement*. London: Heinemann.

Patchen, M. (1965) *Some Questionnaire Measures of Employee Motivation and Morale*. Ann Arbor, Michigan: ISR.

Patton, M.Q. (1980) *Qualitative Evaluation Methods*. London: Sage.

Pears, D. (1971) *Wittgenstein*. London: Fontana.

Pedler, M. (Ed.) (1998) *Action Learning in Practice*, 3rd edn. Farnborough: Gower.

Pesaran, M. and Pesaran, B. (1997) *Working with Microfit 4.0: Interactive Econometric Analysis*. Oxford: Oxford University Press.

Peters, T.J. and Waterman, R.H. (1982) *In Search of Excellence: Lessons from America's Best Run Companies*. New York: Harper and Row.

Pettigrew, A.M. (1983) 'On studying organisational cultures', in J. Van Maanan (ed.), *Qualitative Methodology*. London: Sage.

Pettigrew, A.M. (1985) *The Awakening Giant: Continuity and Change in Imperial Chemical Industries*. Oxford: Blackwell.

Pettigrew, A.M. (1985) 'Contextualist research: a natural way to link theory and practice', in E.E. Lawler (ed.), *Doing Research that is Useful in Theory and Practice*. San Francisco: Jossey Bass.

Pfaffenberger, B. (1988) *Micro-computer Applications for Qualitative Research*. London: Sage.

Phillips, E.M. (1984) 'Learning to do research', *Graduate Management Research*, 2(1): 6–18.

Phillips, E.M. and Pugh, D.S. (1987/1994) *How to Get a PhD: A Handbook for Students and Their Supervisors*. Buckingham: Open University Press.

Platt, J. (1976) *Realities of Social Research: An Empirical Study of British Sociologists*. Brighton: Sussex University Press.

Popper, K. (1959) *The Logic of Scientific Discovery*. London: Hutchinson.

Porter, L.W. and McKibbin, L.E. (1988) *Management Education and Development: Drift or Thurst into the 21st Century?* New York: McGraw-Hill.

Prahalad, C.K. and Hamel, G. (1990) 'The core competence of the corporation', *Harvard Business Review*, 68(3): 79–91.

Prince, G.M. (1970) *The Practice of Creativity: A Manual for Group Problem Solving*. London: Harper and Row.

Pugh, D.S. (1983) 'Studying organisational structure and process', in G. Morgan (ed.), *Beyond Method*. Beverly Hills: Sage.
Pugh, D.S. (1984) 'What is research?', in A. Chapman (ed.), *What Has Management Research Got to Do with Managers?* London: ATM Focus Paper.
Pugh, D.S. (1988) 'The Aston research programme', in A. Bryman (ed.), *Doing Research in Organisations*. London: Routledge.
Pugh, D.S. and Hickson, D.J. (1976) *Organisation Structure in its Context: The Aston Programme*. Farnborough: Saxon House.
Punch, M. (1986) *The Politics and Ethics of Fieldwork*. Beverly Hills: Sage.
Putnam, H. (1987) *The Many Faces of Realism*. La Salle: Open Court.
Pye, A. (1995) 'Strategy through dialogue and doing: a game of "Mornington Crescent"?', *Management Learning*, 26(4): 445–62.
Rappoport, R.N. (1970) 'Three dilemmas in action research', *Human Relations*, 23(4): 499–513.
Reason, P. (1988) *Human Inquiry in Action*. London: Sage.
Reason, P. (1994) *Participation in Human Inquiry*. London: Sage.
Reason, P. and Bradley, M. (eds) (2000) *Handbook of Action Research: Participative Inquiry in Action*. London: Sage.
Reason, P. and Rowan, J. (1981) *Human Inquiry: A Sourcebook of New Paradigm Research*. London: Wiley.
Revans, R.W. (1971) *Developing Effective Managers*. New York: Appleton Century Crofts.
Revans, R.W. (1980) *Action Learning: New Technology for Management*. London: Blond and Briggs.
Rickards, T. (1988) *Problem Solving Through Creativity at Work*. Aldershot: Gower.
Roethlisberger, F. J. and Dickson, W. J. (1939) *Management and the Worker*. Cambridge, MA: Harvard University Press.
Rogers, C.R. (1967) *On Becoming a Person: A Therapist's View of Psychotherapy*. London: Constable.
Roy, D. (1952) 'Quota restriction and goldbricking in a machine shop', *American Journal of Sociology*, 57: 427–42.
Roy, D. (1970) 'The study of Southern labour union organising campaigns', in R. Haberstein (ed.), *Pathway to Data*. New York: Aldine.
Ruggles, R. (1998) 'The state of the notion: knowledge management in practice', *California Management Review*, 40(3): 80–9.
Ryan, B., Joiner, B.L. and Ryan, T.A. (1985) *Student Handbook*. Boston: Duxbury Press.
Ryave, A.L. and Schenkein, J.N. (1974) 'Notes on the art of walking', in R. Turner (ed.), *Ethnomethodology: Selected Readings*. Harmondsworth: Penguin.
Said, E. (1978) *Orientalism*. London: Routledge and Kegan Paul.
Sapsford, R. and Jupp, V. (1996) *Data Collection and Analysis*. London: Sage.
Sayer, A. (2000) *Realism and Social Science*. London: Sage.
Scarbrough, H. and Swan, J. (1999) 'Knowledge management and the management fashion perspective'. Proceedings of British Academy of Management Conference, Manchester, Vol II: 920–37.

Schrudt, P. (1987) *Micro Computer Methods for Social Scientists*. London: Sage.

Seale, C. (2000) 'Using computers to analyse qualitative data', in D. Silverman, *Doing Qualitative Research: A Practical Handbook*. London: Sage.

Selvin, H.C. and Stuart, A. (1966) 'Data-dredging procedures in survey analysis', *American Statistician*, 20: 20–3.

Shotter, J. (1993) *Conversational Realities: Constructing Life Through Language*. London: Sage.

Siegal, S. (1956) *Non-parametric Statistics for the Behavioral Science*. New York: McGraw-Hill.

Silver, M. (1991) *Competent to Manage*. London: Routledge.

Silverman, D. (1970) *The Theory of Organisations: A Sociological Framework*. London: Heinemann.

Silverman, D. (1993) *Interpreting Qualitative Data: Methods for Analysing Talk, Text and Interaction*. London: Sage.

Silverman, D. (2000) *Doing Qualitative Research: A Practical Handbook*. London: Sage.

Simon, H.A. (1959) *Administrative Behaviour*, 2nd edn. London: Macmillan.

Sims, D. (1993) 'Coping with misinformation', *Management Decision*, 3: 18–21.

Slater, D. (1989) 'Corridors of power', in J.F. Gubrium and D. Silverman (eds), *The Politics of Field Research*. London: Sage.

Smith, H.W. (1975) *Strategies of Social Research: The Methodological Imagination*. London: Prentice-Hall.

Snell, R.S. (1993) *Developing Skills for Ethical Management*. London: Chapman and Hall.

Spender, D. (1980) *Man Made Language*. London: Routledge and Kegan Paul.

Spender, J.C. (1989) *Industry Recipes: The Nature and Sources of Managerial Judgement*. Oxford: Basil Blackwell.

Stake, R. (1995) *The Art of Case Study Research*. Thousand Oaks: Sage.

Steers, R.M., Bischoff, S.J. and Higgins, L.H. (1992) 'Cross-cultural management research: the fish and the fisherman', *Journal of Management Inquiry*, 1(4): 321–30.

Steinbeck, J. (1970) *Journal of a Novel: The East of Eden Letters*. London: Pan Books.

Stewart, R. (1967) *Managers and their Jobs*. Maidenhead: McGraw-Hill.

Stewart, R. (1982) *Choices for the Manager: A Guide to Managerial Work and Behaviour*. London: McGraw-Hill.

Stewart, V. and Stewart, A. (1981) *Business Applications of Repertory Grid*. Maidenhead: McGraw-Hill.

Strauss, A.L. (1987) *Qualitative Analysis for Social Scientists*. Cambridge: Cambridge University Press.

Strauss, A.L. and Corbin, J. (1990) *Basics of Qualitative Research: Grounded Theory Procedures and Techniques*. Thousand Oaks: Sage.

Strauss, A.L. and Corbin, J. (1998) *Basics of Qualitative Research: Techniques and Procedures for Developing Grounded Theory*, 2nd edn. Thousand Oaks: Sage.

Sudman, S. (1976) *Applied Sampling*. London: Academic Press.
Susman, G.I. and Evered, R.D. (1978) 'An assessment of the scientific merits of action research', *Administrative Science Quarterly*, 23: 582–603.
Taylor, F.W. (1947) *Scientific Management*. London: Harper and Row.
Taylor, S.J. and Bogdan, R. (1984) *Introduction to Qualitative Research Methods*. New York: Wiley-Interscience.
Teagarden, M.B., von Glinow, M.A., Bowen, D.E., Frayne, C.A., Nason, S., Huo, Y.P., Milliman, J., Arias, M.E., Butler, M.C., Geringer, J.M., Kim, N-M., Scullion, H., Lowe, K.B. and Drost, E.A. (1995) 'Toward a theory of comparative management research: an ideographic case study of the best international human resources management project', *Academy of Management Journal*, 38: 1261–87.
Thomas, A.B. (1989) 'One-minute management: a sign of the times?' *Management Education and Development*, 20(1): 23–38.
Thomas, B.E. (1988) 'Planning for performance: the management of change in general medical services'. Master of Science Degree Dissertation, Manchester Polytechnic.
Thomas, W.I. and Thomas, D.S. (1928) *The Child in America: Behavioural Problems and Progress*. New York: Knopf.
Thompson, D. (ed.) (1996) *The Pocket Oxford Dictionary*. Oxford: Oxford University Press.
Thorpe, R. (1980) 'The relationship between payment systems, productivity and the organisation of work'. Master of Science Thesis, Strathclyde Business School.
Todd, D.J. (1979) 'Mixing qualitative and quantitative methods: triangulation in action', *Administrative Science Quarterly*, 24: 602–11.
Tranfield, D. and Starkey, K. (1998) 'The nature, social organization and promotion of management research: towards policy', *British Journal of Management*, 9: 341–53.
Tsang, E.W.K. (1997) 'Learning from joint venturing experience: the case of foreign direct investment by Singapore companies in China', PhD Thesis, University of Cambridge.
Tsang, E.W.K. (1999) 'Internationalisation as a learning process: Singapore MNCs in China', *Academy of Management Executive*, 13(1): 91–101.
Tuck, M. (1976) *How Do We Choose?* London: Methuen.
Turner, B.A. (1981) 'Quality and quantity', *Elsevier Scientific Publishing*, 15: 225–47.
Turner, B.A. (1983) 'The use of grounded theory for the qualitative analysis of organisational behaviour', *Journal of Management Studies*, 20(3): 333–48.
Turner, B.A. (1987) 'Communications between supervisor and postgraduate about theory', ESRC Conference, University of Norwich, December.
Turner, B.A. (1988) 'Connoisseurship in the study of organisational cultures', in A. Bryman (ed.) *Doing Research in Organisations*. London: Sage.
Van Maanen, J. (1983) *Qualitative Methodology*. London: Sage.
Vidich, A.J. (1954) 'Participant observation and the collection and interpretation of data', *American Journal of Sociology*, 60: 354–60.

Von Bertalanffy, L. (1962) 'General Systems Theory – a critical review'; *General Systems* VII: 1–20.
Walker, R. (1985) *Applied Qualitative Research.* Aldershot: Gower.
Walton, M. (1989) *The Deming Management Method.* London: Mercury Books.
Watson, T.J. (1994) *In Search of Management: Culture, Chaos and Control in Managerial Work*, London: Routledge.
Watzlawick, P. (ed.) (1984) *The Invented Reality.* London: Norton.
Weick, K. (1995) *Sensemaking in Organizations.* London: Sage.
Whitley, R., Thomas, A. and Marceau, J. (1981) *Masters of Business?* London: Tavistock.
Yin, R.K. (1993) *Applications of Case Study Research.* Newbury Park, CA: Sage.
Yin, R.K. (1994) *Case Study Research: Design and Methods,* 2nd edn. Thousand Oaks: Sage.

Index